MW01595834

HUNTING AND GATHERING

An Urban Youth Survival Guide

Danny Quintana

Beckham Publications Group, Inc.
Silver Spring

Published in the United States by
Beckham Publications Group, Inc.
ISBN: 0-931761-77-8
10 9 8 7 6 5 4 3 2 1

TABLE OF CONTENTS

FOREWORD

Hunting and Gathering is advice to young Native Americans and youth everywhere on and off reservations about how to survive and prosper financially and emotionally in today's complex and competitive world. This advice is based on my adventures in law and in life. From multi-million dollar drug cases to international con artists, to national environmental projects, I have enjoyed my career. Those experiences as the Skull Valley Band of Goshutes' Tribal Attorney, owner of a small law firm, Danny Quintana & Associates, businessman, father, ex-husband and boyfriend are the basis for the observations reflected in this small book. Hopefully others will learn from my experiences and my clients' life lessons. Enjoy many of the same victories. Avoid the terrible decisions made by many people my firm has represented over the last 19 years from all parts of the world.

Ultimately, there is no substitute for life's many interesting and at times, outrageous lessons. However, the evil of society I've witnessed does not have to be experienced to be understood. The challenges of the modern world require courage. The same courage of the brave warriors of the Indian nations in the last two centuries enabled what remains of Native American nations and all of us to survive. Today's warriors, Indian and non-Indian, must reach within and use the courage of our ancestors to overcome not only the alcoholism, crime, drugs and domestic violence on and off the reservations, but also the desperation of the city streets and prisons.

I dedicate this book to my dear friend Richard Bear who taught me patience. His good humor and tremendous wisdom, knowledge of the environment, and understanding of his culture will be sorely missed. I traveled around the world with Richard, Lawrence and Leon Bear, and my former secretary, (White Bear) Beverly Slack. We have worked on some very interesting projects. We have known unbelievable success and hard-fought losses. They tolerated my poor sense of humor and embodied the spirit of teamwork. I will treasure the moments of working and laughing with them forever.

Moderation, the noblest gift of Heaven.
Euripides. 484-406 B. C.

1

ONCE, THREE LIFETIMES AGO

The more we can kill this year, the less will have to be killed in the next war, for the more I see of these Indians the more convinced I am that they all have to be killed or be maintained as a species of paupers. Their attempts at civilization are simply ridiculous.

General William T. Sherman, September 23, 1868

Once, three lifetimes ago, in the area of this very small planet we now call Utah, preceding Brigham Young and the massive migration of Mormons, for over one thousand years, a small group of people, the Goshutes, controlled the land mass from what is now Brigham City, Utah in the north to Delta, Utah in the south. From the Salt Lake valley in the east, to Ely, Nevada in the west, Utah valley and Heber valley were on some days held by the Goshutes. On other days, these areas were Ute territory. The Goshutes were a prosperous nation.

The Goshutes and their Shoshone relatives in Idaho and Nevada were once fluent in a Shoshone-based Athrobaskin language. The fierce Comanches of the plains are their cousins. The Utes controlled what is now Colorado and a small part of Eastern Utah. The Paiutes controlled what we presently call Southern Utah and Nevada. The formidable Dine, (Navajos) held present-day Northern Arizona and Western New Mexico. Their cousins, the battle-hardened Apaches, held all of Southern Arizona, most of New Mexico, and a good chunk of old Mexico. Various Pueblo tribes of Northern and Central New Mexico, who lived in apartment-like buildings, with help of the Comanches, fought off the Apaches. Then came the Spanish invaders. Spain was soon followed by other, much larger and better-armed European tribes into the Southwest.

For at least a millennium, the Goshutes made quality use of their territory. So did most North American hunter-gather bands. People had plenty to eat and were healthy, provided they had no major physical accidents or were killed or injured in war. The Goshutes survived in strong family unites. The men hunted big and little game. Like most hunter-gather cultures, the women and children provided the majority of the protein by gathering a large number of plants. In addition to wild rice, onions and pine nuts that were plentiful, tribal elders ate nutritious grasshoppers and fat, juicy ground squirrels. Members understood the complex food chain, and they did not violate the contract with nature. They also understood weather patterns and the food cycles. Although food was abundant, enemies were real and powerful.

Winters were viciously cold and like today, three months too long. Small villages with shelters were constructed of sagebrush covered by animal hides. Following the game, and avoiding the brutally cold winter weather, the warriors took their homes with them. The winter camping ground for the Goshutes was near the small town of Grantsville, Utah. The shelters were modest, but efficient.

This lifestyle worked extraordinarily well for a long, long time—certainly longer than the United States and the State of Utah have existed. The Goshutes, like numerous other tribes, had wondrous songs, imaginative stories, laughter, and healthy young people. Walking ensured strong hearts, and the high protein diet ensured long, healthy lives. Some men would walk 40 miles across the desert from present day Skull Valley, Utah to the Deer Creek Mountains in Nevada in one day. The Elders knew every watering hole in Utah's West Desert and were careful with all food sources. Their medicine men used not only herbal medicines from many different plants, but also holistic treatments that included spiritual and personal counseling. Warriors, out of necessity and good sense, took very great care of their war tools. They knew about the numbers and the health of animals in their territory. The forests and range areas were carefully utilized with controlled burns to ensure proper game habitat.

Like other North American tribes, Goshutes had a complex religion that included sweat ceremonies. These ancient religious rituals were held next to what is now the Jordan River in Salt Lake County, Utah. The ritual involved heating rocks in a fire pit next to a structure shaped like a woman's womb. The fire would heat the rocks. When they were placed in the sweat lodge and water was poured over them, they would cleanse the entire body. Four rounds of ceremony would take place for the four directions of the wind. The sweat lodge ceremony leaves an individual with a feeling of complete and total body relaxation unlike anything you will ever experience. After the ceremony they would bathe in the cool river water. The ancient religion brought inner peace and harmony with the universe. This sweat ceremony was common to all North American tribes in one form or another. Some tribes would not allow men and women to sweat together. Many tribes had the sweat lodge opening facing the East for the sunrise. A few had the opening facing the West for the sunset. Some tribes had dry sweats with hot rocks but no water. Other tribes would pour the cool water on the rocks that created a steam that goes right into the bones of an individual.

Once, three lifetimes ago, the skies over what is now Salt Lake City were clear and beautiful with giant condors, diverse hawks, and large, strong golden and bald eagles flying overhead.

Since there were no cars or factories, the air was pristine clean. Unlike today, where we can see what we breath, visibility was clear year round. The streams, like the present Jordan River, were full of healthy, clean, very large fish. Today, the Jordan River is full of tires, oil, concrete blocks, and industrial and human wastes. The canyons of the Wasatch Front had streams with beavers, ponds filled with trout and meadows with small herds of deer, elk and even moose. Black bears and even grizzlies controlled certain territories, while wolves and mountain lions competed for wild game. The many types of abundant wildlife were well fed and disease free, not having yet been exposed to European livestock. The Salt Lake valley aquifer and water table was not yet damaged by mill tailings from the world's largest copper pit. Unlike today, there were not thousands of subdivisions with look-alike homes and lazy children worshipping in front of televisions.

So much of human existence has changed in such a very short time. What and who we are today is a result of the combined hard work, courage, and intelligence of warriors and others who saved Native Americans from extinction. Survival came to pass by overcoming brutal, almost impossible, military odds and unbelievable hardships. In the last two centuries, all of the Indians in what is now the Western United States would have been completely killed off had their warriors not fought with such bravery against impossible numbers, armed only with poor, hand-made weapons. Without their incredible courage, most North and South American tribes would have perished completely.

This early example of ethnic cleansing in the United States took many paths. Many tribes in the Eastern United States no longer exist as a result. The European invaders used biological weapons. Smallpox, a successful use of germ warfare, was their most effective killer. Millions were murdered with this weapon that was deliberately spread among powerful Eastern tribes to destroy them and take their land. In fact, the fight in the Eastern seaboard and later in the Western United States was over one valuable asset: land.

The racial terrorism was gratuitously brutal. In addition to the many massacres of women and children, others who were not Indian were sometimes slaughtered. The Mountain Meadow Massacre in Southern Utah left dead over 157 peaceful California-bound white settlers. The murders, committed by Mormon extremists, were blamed on Utah's Paiute Indians. The children who would be too young to remember, were given to Mormon families to raise as their own. Those considered old enough to tell others were savagely murdered.

Most notably in Colorado was the Sand Creek massacre. Over 400 Indian women, children and old men were living peacefully with an American flag flying over their village. They were ruthlessly slaughtered by religious extremists among others. The warriors were away from camp hunting while their loved ones were slaughtered in cold blood behind their backs.

In 1863, Northern Utah was the site of the Bear River massacre where more than 250 people were murdered near the Bear River. Indian women and children were killed because they were not considered human, much less citizens. Their private parts were cut from their bodies and kept as souvenirs. Finally, before the century ended, there was Wounded Knee, where in excess of 190 men, women and children were killed as a result of over reaction and arrogance.

Since Indians were not citizens, they were routinely killed for sport without fear of legal retribution from the American authorities. They had no legal rights to respect and received no sympathy from the United States Courts. In each major case in the 19th Century, the white litigants prevailed over non-citizen Indians. The Indians did not have attorneys or people in Congress to represent them or fight their battles. There was not yet a World Court to hold political trials on crimes against humanity for genocide.

The great tribal nations, in what is now the United States, like so many other warrior societies in other parts of the world throughout history, lost at war, despite 500 years of heroic resistance. The biological weapons of smallpox and measles, repeating rifles and sheer numbers of over 1,000 soldiers to one warrior ensured their defeat and demise. The invasion was truly overwhelming and unprecedented in human history. A military defeat like those suffered by the Japanese, Germans, French, Spaniards, Italians, Greeks, Chinese, Russians, Vietnamese, Egyptians, Argentines and too many other nations is nothing compared to the loss of religion, language, identity and self-worth experienced by the Indian tribes.

Once, three life times ago, in the days of the Goshutes, each person really and truly mattered. Every life was very important to the small families and the tribe. There was no alienation and loneliness from being a replaceable cog in an assembly line at a manufacturing plant or fast food restaurant for minimal wages. The tribal members did not die from drunk driving. Goshutes and other tribal members did not go to prison and waste their youth behind bars in Draper or Gunnison, Utah for being constantly intoxicated or stoned on drugs. There were no under-employed individuals flipping hamburgers or completely unemployed citizens on state compensation. They did not have all of today's modern ailments associated with alcohol. Above all, once upon a time, Native Americans were a proud, healthy and spiritual people. The various members of numberless proud tribes walked the earth with courage and connection to their own lands. They were not the defeated and desperate drunks begging for change or food on the streets of Salt Lake and other cities.

Once three lifetimes ago, the Goshutes and hundreds of other tribes lived successfully, enjoyed good health and were happy. For at least one millennium, the Goshutes enjoyed peace with the natural earth environment and held political control of their territory. Their people were physically big and very, very strong. Goshutes, like all ancient warriors, had incredible courage, and were expert marksmen with spears, bows and arrows. Their hunting and fighting skills were outstanding. They respected their women, their elders and their children. The old were not dumped and forgotten in urine-smelling nursing homes or left to die quietly without bothering their relatives. The youth were not left to their own devices to be raised by friends, video games and television programs. The people ate well and nothing was wasted. The deer, antelope, elk and rabbit hides were tanned and used for clothes and shelter. Their intestines were used for thread and bow string. All members enjoyed a delicious pine nut soup. Wild strawberries and raspberries were there to be enjoyed with meals of rabbit and grasshoppers. They played games of chance and gambled before there were casinos.

A walk through the woods, the open range or desert, in search of meat meant knowing exactly where to go and how to get there. They had to be aware of body odors, the direction of the wind, the droppings of the deer and antelope. And they hunted in small, well-organized groups with each person doing his part; it was a great team that successfully fed their families.

Everything about the natural environment was known to these talented and disciplined Goshute hunters. There was no question in a young Goshute warrior's mind that rattlesnakes, mountain lions, wolves and bears were dangerous or that winter frost could kill you. Precautions were taken to ensure survival. Goshute warriors knew that if they ran into other enemy tribes, they would likely have to kill or be killed. So they were always armed.

Countless medicinal plants and roots were available near watering holes and riverbanks. The now rare and valuable reed baskets, woven by elderly Goshute tribal women, were used to store dried meat and plants in winter and for times of shortage. The Goshute Tribe had well over two thousand members. According to tribal sources, membership numbered as high as twenty thousand. This is substantially more people than the mere 124 in the Skull Valley Band of Goshutes today. They once had their own creationist myths about Coyote and how man came into being and even the origin of the universe. Some believed that man is evil.

Once, the Goshutes and hundreds of other Tribes were a people with land, language, traditions, and culture. They held the area where approximately two million Mormons and others now call home. There was not the "improvements to the land" which have been brought about by modern technology. Certainly there were not the more than one million cars that zip along congested routes in Salt Lake Valley and all along the Wasatch mountains. Like today, life was hard; but certainly worth living. Each sunrise offered a new exciting challenge and adventure.

It has happened throughout history in various parts of this wonderful planet: the Goshutes' land was invaded. Some were hunted for sport killings. Others died from the diseases introduced. Eventually, there was open warfare. Being outnumbered by over 1,000:1, not having repeating rifles, canons and horses, reluctantly, the great Chief Tabby surrendered. He ended the small, yet brutal Goshute War with the United States government. In 1863 the Goshutes signed a "peace and friendship treaty" at gun point. In exchange for not killing Pony Express riders and attacking stagecoaches, the U.S. government and various hired bounty hunters would not hunt Goshutes into extinction.

The courage of Chief Tabby and this treaty saved the tribe from total annihilation. Then the Goshute tribe was divided into two bands. The Skull Valley Band of Goshutes is the treaty tribe. The Confederated

Goshutes who live on the Nevada border are an Indian Reorganization Act tribe. The combined territory of both bands is only a small thumbnail sketch of their former territory. Their previous Mormon attorneys settled their land claims for approximately $.05 cents on the dollar and earned a great deal of money for themselves in legal fees. What is left today is 18,000 acres for the Skull Valley Goshutes next to a top-secret military facility that once tested nerve gas, biological and radiological weapons.

Throughout human history, in every part of the world, losing a war means not only military defeat and humiliation, but also occupation of your homeland, rape of your women, murder of your children, loss of your language, and destruction of your entire traditional, yet successful, thousand-year way of life. Like the numerous other peoples, the Goshutes suffered a total and complete military defeat.

Yet, there is no reason for the reader to feel guilty about immoral acts and intolerance committed three lifetimes ago. We are not responsible for the sins of our ancestors. We can only feel guilty if we learn nothing from them. Guilt is the worst of all human emotions. It builds resentment. Resentment leads to aggression. And aggression leads to more guilt. This world has more than enough resentment and intolerance. Countless other people in many parts of the world, throughout all of history, have experienced the same military defeat and destruction of their traditional ways of life.

This is the normal historical human experience we call change. Not progress, but just political change. Gone into history are the Summerians, the Assyrians, the Aztecs, the Incas, the Alani, the Goths, the Vandels, the Franks, the Huns and the Romans. Change comes, and it is not always good.

With the Decline and Fall of the Roman Empire, all of Europe fell into a lawless abyss that lasted for more than fifteen hundred years. The fall of Rome destroyed law and Western civilization. Military defeat and political change certainly did not mean progress. It meant death, terror, lawlessness, disease and destruction. Like the fall of Rome, the destruction of the great Indian nations of this continent meant millions of deaths from diseases, loss of language, depression, terror, and lawlessness. The conquered were far worse off as a result of the invasion of their lands and the loss of political control over their territories. The game herds were almost completely destroyed. Condors, wolves, grizzlies and other wild animals almost completely disappeared. Disease killed almost every member of the conquered Goshutes, Shoshones, Utes and other tribes. Life became a living hell with the introduction of alcohol and the new foods that result in obesity and diabetes. The mental depression that has lasted several generations is only now being overcome.

The old days of great health, a clean environment and abundant natural food sources are almost completely gone. Like Europe two thousand years later, life for all tribes is finally improving, and people are finally regaining their confidence and spirituality. The horrible wounds of the loss of the war and invasion of their homelands are starting to heal. In the 1950's, the Skull Valley Goshutes were down to 38 members. Finally, after over one century of military defeat, this small tribe and all tribes are beginning to increase their numbers. Like Europe after the fall of the Roman Empire, one thousand years later, eventually law and civilization returned. Indian country two hundred years after the invasion and holocaust, is finally starting to recover.

The dust has long since settled on the battlefields of the West. The American flag flies over the land. A new era has begun. This new era can be full of adventure if you dare to become a participant in the game of life. Or if you just want to be a spectator, this new age can also be very entertaining.

This new era has better medical care. For those of us who have been in need of having rotted teeth pulled because of the tremendous amount of sugar in our diet, it is nice to be able to visit a dentist. When we have gallstones, it is very convenient to have a simple gall bladder removal. Giving birth in a hospital rather than in the woods means more modern women are capable of surviving the pains of childbirth. Being able to see properly today means having eyeglasses and contacts available at an affordable cost. If you did suffer a major disability, the old days of "once upon a time" would have really sucked. You died. Today, there is wheel chair tennis, skiing, scuba diving and work.

The traditional songs are terrific. But so are sounds of a great Beethoven symphony and Rolling Stones rock and roll. Today, there is saxophone jazz, new age, and country and western music. All of it is available at your fingertips with modern stereo systems.

Once there was no jet travel because there were no jets. There was no scuba diving because there was no scuba gear. For that matter, there was no Internet, no computers, no big screen televisions, no pick up trucks, no socks, no books, no contact lenses, no food from various parts of the world, no deep sea fishing, and no hot tubs or swimming pools. There were no dishwashers, no microwaves, no refrigerators, no sports cars and no guitars. There was no piano, no chess sets from Mexico and Asia. No Homer Simpson, no football, no Robin Williams, no butter toffee peanuts and no videos. There were no pretty pictures of the sunset in Sweden. There were no cruise ships and no seafood restaurants. There was no U.S. Code online. There was no Comedy Club in Washington, DC or Midvale, Utah.

Yes, three lifetimes ago, like today, life could be very hard—and then you died. And when we die, whether it was two hundred years ago in the cold of winter in what is now Tooele Valley or forty eight lifetimes ago in Egypt, or today at home in an intermediate care nursing home in Salt Lake Valley, we are very dead. Yet three lifetimes ago worked extraordinarily well for those who were healthy. Three lifetimes ago, Native Americans were mentally and physically strong. To a certain extent, the same can be true for all of us today. But proper choices must be made in order to survive.

In 1924, after all of the Indian land that was thought to be valuable was taken, their people slaughtered and militarily defeated, the first inhabitants of this part of the planet were awarded the lofty political title of "American Citizens." By this point in our brief history, there was simply no reason not to make Indians American citizens. Having failed in the attempt at total genocide, we would be too impolite to kill the survivors. Remember that the U.S. had just finished fighting World War I and given women the right to vote. Finishing the genocide would have simply been bad manners.

Citizenship meant simply that now Indians were a small part of this vast American Empire. Pax Romana lasted for over 1,500 years. How long Pax Americana will last remains to be seen. Once, three lifetimes ago, the Goshutes and other tribes had their own nations. That time is gone. Today, Indians are part of the most powerful nation in the history of the world. Today, Indians are part of Pax Americana.

But what exactly does this mean for young Native Americans and others who want to survive in the new millennium?

2

NATIVE AMERICA TODAY

Like the Goshutes, all tribes nationally are witnessing a mass migration of tribal members to the unheavenly cities of America. They search for employment and a better way of life. Approximately 65 percent of Native Americans now live in cities. Hundreds of millions of humans all over the planet have moved, or are moving to cities to sell their labor, in this post hunter-gatherer world. This endeavor, that modern society calls work—or jobs—gives people small amounts of money that enable them to eat and survive. Throughout many reservations in America, there are no or very, very few new jobs. With the exception of tribal or Bureau of Indian Affairs jobs, employment opportunities on reservations are as rare as the California condor. So the majority of Goshutes live where they can sell their labor, in the neighboring urban centers in Tooele Valley and Salt Lake Valley. A few stragglers live in Nevada, Idaho, the Uintah Basin and some have gone as far as California and North Dakota. The same is true for other all tribes.

This current state of Native Americans is the reflection of what our grandfathers and others have experienced. Most Native Americans and other immigrants are the poorest of the poor in America's urban centers and in America. On average, Native Americans earn one-third the wage of "regular" Americans. It will take time to adjust to the transition from traditional reservation life to urban Indian America. Native America today is hope, coupled with desperation and drunks, and surrounded by individuals with courage. However, unlike Europeans, Asians and South and Central Americans, Native Americans did not ask to become Americans. Their citizenship was handed to them at the end of a gun. Those who have made the transition to the urban centers face new challenges. Language is one of the most critical challenges. But let's examine some salient aspects of their existence before discussing the language issue.

The Goshutes numbers have decreased from over 2,000 (again, some internal tribal estimates are as high as 20,000) to the current 124 members of the Skull Valley Band. This band, for such a small tribe, is a micro-reflection of Native America today. In the 19th century, the Goshutes went from a territory approximately one third of Utah, with stable families living in villages and a reasonable population size that co-existed with the environment, to near extinction.

Very few tribal members live on their reservation in Skull Valley, Utah. This is the situation with most tribes. Even fewer are fluent in Goshute; with good reason. There are exactly five jobs on the Skull Valley Goshute Reservation. One is at the Tekoi Rocket Test Facility as a part-time security guard, three are at the Pony Express Station, and one is at the Skull Valley Goshutes' own Tribal Store. These four positions keep them just over the point of being broke.

The Skull Valley Goshutes own the only rocket test facility on an Indian reservation in the United States. The 18,000 acres Skull Valley Goshute Reservation, like many other reservations nationally, was a dumping ground for the Defense Department. Similarly, other reservations were taken and used for bombing ranges during World War II.

The Tekoi Rocket Test Facility was moved from Salt Lake Valley to Skull Valley when neighbors in Magna, Utah complained air pollution and rocket engine test firings were blowing out their windows and cracking the foundations of their fine suburban homes. This rocket testing facility was built in Skull Valley in 1975 and has been there every since. The strategic sector of the nuclear arms race and the cold war ended, and so have the majority of the tests of military rockets.

Goshute tribal members hold on to their legal claim of political sovereignty. Like most reservations nationally, the belief in nationhood is still alive with this small group of stubborn people who refuse to migrate to America's unheavenly cities. Many tribal members have expressed an interest in moving back home to the Res. But there is no work.

The three security guard shifts available to tribal members were barely adequate for the six remaining reservation families while the jobs existed. The last remaining job is at the Pony Express Station, the Skull Valley Goshute's tribal store offering lonely riders gasoline or diesel and possibly a soda. The pretty log cabin structure was built over Bureau of Indian Affairs' objections, and adequately serves the tribal members and the tourist traffic of Skull Valley.

The frontiers of Goshute territory were simply beautiful examples of nature's splendor. Mountains rise from the desert displaying incredible sunsets with wildlife at every turn. Goshute country, like everywhere else at that time on this small planet, was simply paradise on earth. With few people and an abundance of natural wildlife and plants, life was a never-ending experience of adventure, freedom and near perfect health. Some of the scenery now remaining offers incredible displays of nature's finest works. While political boundaries constantly change over millennium, nature's heavenly works remain for man and creatures to enjoy.

But language is one of the first problems that needs to be addressed, not only to understand the current situation of Native Americans, but also to understand how current youth must survive.

Exactly seven tribal members, all over 50, still speak Goshute. The tribe has applied for a language grant four times to preserve its native tongue and culture, but has been turned down each time. The Administration for Native Americans gave money back to Congress and turned down the grant applications of Goshutes and many other small tribes. This administrative agency that is mandated to help the Indian community decided that the seven tribal members who speak Goshute are not few enough to consider this language "endangered" despite the fact that the tribe is loosing almost two of these native speakers each year. This failure to fund the language preservation of small tribes is deliberate. Washington's hope is that the loss of language will result in the loss of Indian nationalism. The loss of nationalism will result in a disbanding of the reservation system followed by the complete loss of property rights and what remains of Indian country.

The original Native American languages are a national treasure. However, the federal government is ignoring the necessity of preserving some very important knowledge. Once these languages and traditions die with the tribal elders, the knowledge will be lost forever. And with this final loss of language will come the fight to protect the sovereignty of reservations. The traditional and complex Native American cultures are no match for the power of the electronic Valium, otherwise known as television.

Looking throughout history, we see that the loss of indigenous languages is normal. This phenomenon has happened to other cultural groups in Europe and other parts of the world as they were conquered and urbanized. The French spoken today in France, Quebec and other parts of the French language world, is not the same language that was spoken at the time of the French Revolution. And it is much different from the language of the Middle Ages and before the fall of the Roman Empire. Obviously, the English spoken today is not what was common at the time of the prolific writer Shakespeare. Language evolves naturally with time and exposure to other cultures. We cannot even guess what language will be spoken 500 years from now.

Preservation of ancient Indian languages is of particular importance because of the special meaning that can be lost in translation and the inherent knowledge contained within those words. Indian languages, which are often visual as well as spoken, are integral to tribal history and cultural identity. Traditional dances and storytelling are used to pass knowledge from one generation to the next in an otherwise unwritten tongue.

Some Native American elders in the US and Canada still understand the language of nature. As Tom Goldtooth, an extraordinarily bright Indian activist once told me, "We need to preserve the language so we can still talk with the animals and plants." He meant it. He believed that communication with other species was clearly possible and routinely occurred before the invasion in pre-European America. Several Native Americans have told me the same thing. Even people who are not Indian and yet who have lots of animals and plants, believe such communication is possible. Animal communication is a mystery which can be solved with enough study and the realization that the two-legged ones, four-legged ones, the winged creatures, and those who swim the waters are all important parts of God's creation. This is not an exclusive Native American or indigenous people ideal. Communication with nature is an inherent part of the life experience.

Tribes with financial resources need to implement language programs on their own, and not wait for the government. If they wait, it could prove fatal to their language and cultural preservation. One tribe in the Northwest, the Quinauls, took video cameras and recorded all of the old people. They did not sit on their hands and wait for the legislators in Washington. They have implemented a full language preservation program. Children are taught the native language by tribal elders, and the bridge between generations is maintained and respected. The Quinauls have a fish cannery that sells some of the best smoked salmon in the country. They also carefully harvest their limited lumber resources.

One Plains Indian tribe that wants to remain anonymous has developed a private Internet language site that is only accessible to their members. The many and far-flung tribal members who live on and off the reservation are given a password and have free access to this site. With that password, they can access this private site and re-learn their fading language skills.

Nationally, the tribes that work to preserve their culture enjoy the most success. Preservation of culture develops self-esteem of tribal members and prepares them for the difficult world outside the confines of their extended family groups and reservations. Knowing and being proud of who you are contributes a great deal to the inner confidence of both children and adults. The language skills of many tribal members nationally, on and off reservations, are marginal. The sad reality is that most young Native Americans are not fluent in their native tongue. And tragically, they are also not fluent in English either.

One of my best friends, Lenny Foster, is the recipient of the City of Phoenix's Martin Luther King, Jr. Peace Prize for his religious activities on behalf of Native American inmates both locally and nationally. We often discuss the effects of the loss of language on our respective Indian and Hispanic communities. The logical processing skills for individuals who are not fluent in either language are sometimes lacking. This is similar to the experience of other communities. For example, within the Mexican community north of the border, it is common for most of the young people under thirty to no longer speak Spanish. However, their poor master of English is a setback in other areas. Education is difficult for them, and their labor is less marketable. Many Mexican immigrants are completely fluent in Spanish, but often cannot read the back of soup cans in English.

We cheat our youth by denying them access to language. Thought patterns, the ability to relate to others, and good manners, all center around language. Words are the most powerful weapons known to man. With mere words, Hitler caused young men to march into the snow fields of Russia and die. Words from the late great President Kennedy inspired men to go to the moon in ten years. Words ended the Vietnam War and dissolved the Soviet Union. We need to teach our children to communicate properly in American English because it is the written language of business and government worldwide. Since we Americans in effect now rule the world, it is a good idea. Language skills will give tribes and non-tribal members economic opportunities on an international scale. We cannot sell our products abroad if we cannot write a mere shipping invoice.

What prevents us from being bilingual? Laziness. It takes a concerted effort to be completely fluent in another language. In Europe, it is common to speak three languages—usually English, French and German. English and Spanish are the exception. There is no reason young Native Americans cannot speak Lakota and American English, Goshute and American English, Navajo and American English, Apache and American English, Shoshone and American English. At a minimum, Native American youth must learn American English and be proficient with it.

By insisting that people learn more than one language, I am certainly not endorsing the hate-filled politicians who introduce "English Only" legislation into various communities. These attempts at race legislation are a subtle cover to hide religious and racial hatred for non-white cultural groups. Living with the constant racism of people in Utah, I believe firmly that hate legislation only fuels the divisions among us. This is not rocket science. I am not asking young people to study applied physics or upper division calculus. I am asking them simply to study language to enable simple communication. Understanding of the language will avoid many problems. It is like finding work and communicating with people from completely different cultures.

Racism today is not as vicious as it was when I was growing up in the 1960s. People in modern urban society realize that being a racist is incredibly bad manners. Notwithstanding, Native Americans, Mexicans and other Third World types like myself are merely facing the same problems other cultural groups have encountered when they migrated to the unheavenly city. If all of the Native Americans and other non-white individuals were suddenly to become "white and delightsome" overnight, their social and economic standing would not improve by one dollar. The reason is that our thoughts are what govern our ability to earn money, and to consume energy and entertainment conspicuously. We think in language. Whether that language is Navajo, Spanish, German or Apache, the logic is what is important.

As migration to urban centers continues throughout Native America and all over the Third World, the transition to an urban environment occurs. And like other cultural groups throughout the world, Skull Valley Goshutes engage in the same endeavors and have the exact same personalities and behaviors as everyone else. Today, Goshute tribal members are employed in a variety of trades. Lane Thom is a published author and part-time forest ranger. Tad Bear is an inventor and speaks five languages. Others operate heavy equipment. Three members have black belts in karate. One is so pretty she should have been a model. And like everywhere else, some choose not to be employed and live on welfare. Others are on social security disability. A select few are incarcerated for crimes committed under the influence of alcohol or drugs. On a purely individual basis, there is simply no difference between the Goshutes and any other group of people anywhere else on earth. This is because, as humans, we have genetically developed personalities.

However, a disproportionate number of Goshute tribal members are alcoholics. The cause for this may be genetic, a surplus of unearned disposable income, or even the frustration of helplessly witnessing the United States Department of Defense poison Goshute land. In any event, my point is that each individual must take the responsibility for curbing self-destructive behaviors in his own life.

Crimes on reservations as a result of alcohol, whether against people and property, are a constant and sometimes humorous problem. Some members shoot at the water tower while intoxicated. One individual, an exceptionally bright lady when sober, ran over the tribal cemetery fence while intoxicated; a disrespectful act she never would have contemplated or committed if sober. The message here is that each of us is identified by the totality of our deeds, good and bad. Each of us has the power to be held by our familiars in the highest esteem and to be respected by strangers. And, each of us has the power to turn down that one last drink that brands us with the reputation of being "that wonderful lady, who, by the way, ran over the cemetery fence." Your reputation, like a house of cards, can be a compilation of a thousand good deeds and carefully considered acts that can be utterly destroyed and overshadowed in an instant of careless self-indulgence.

Nearly all crime experienced in Skull Valley is minor compared to what has occurred on other reservations. But most crimes in Indian Country, on and off the reservations, involve alcohol. Domestic violence, incredible child abuse, fetal alcohol syndrome, auto accidents and loss of employment, are all alcohol-related. The violence on reservations results in Federal prison time for the members. Like the rest of America, domestic violence is a frequent danger. In one case, the women and children were severely beaten, allegedly, with a tire iron. Drunken rage child abuse in some tribes is so horrific that the children never recover. The mental scars never heal and physical beatings often leave permanent damage to life and limb.

A tribal elder from a Canadian First Nation predicted that even as bad as times are for Native Americans, they will get worse. Talking about the increase in sexual abuse related directly to alcoholism, he was prophetic. In one of my cases, (not in Skull Valley) tribal children were placed back into a home where they had been sexually abused by drunken relatives. After the relatives applied political pressure on the tribal government, these damaged children were returned to the abusers by the tribal court. The children were again abused. After five years of litigation, the tribal regulations were changed and the problem was corrected, but too late for those children. When children are involved, we must all fight to protect them, whether the fights are in or out of Indian Country. Children are a gift from God that there will be a tomorrow.

Then we have the pregnant drunks within the Native American community. Fetal alcohol syndrome destroys babies forever. Rodney Grant, the star of *Dances With Wolves*, works to reduce this unnecessary crime on the unborn. He chairs a national non-profit organization committed to preventing this pre-natal evil that harms us all. The social cost of pregnant drunks is staggering. We taxpayers will pay over two million dollars per child over the course of their violent and or institutionalized lives.

Sometimes, through sheer good fortune, these damaged children find loving homes. One adopted fetal alcohol syndrome child is being raised by a friend of mine, a Navajo rug weaver. This child (half Navajo and Sioux) is partially blind and permanently brain damaged as a result of his biological mother's prenatal alcohol use. He had no say in her drinking. He will never be able to fully enjoy God's creations or contribute to the wealth of our society. He will be on taxpayer entitlements and dependent on the kindness of others until he dies prematurely.

Another case involved an Arapaho mother who completely destroyed her child while under the influence of alcohol. Drunk throughout her pregnancy, she produced a child with a very low IQ and little capacity to survive outside an institutional setting. When she moved from her reservation to Salt Lake City and continued to neglect her baby, the State of Utah's Division of Child and Family Services took her child from her. The state placed him in institutional care. After failing to comply with the plan calling for abstention of alcohol and her taxpayer-appointed social worker's plan for reunification and remain off alcohol, the mother finally lost her child. The tribe tried to have the child placed on her reservation. After much litigation, the juvenile court refused, and given the lack of cooperation of the mother, the tribe did not appeal.

In another case, the mother of two young children was brutally murdered by vicious drunks. Perhaps because she was Indian, the State of Utah has given up on the investigation and the killers have never been found. The widower is in constant litigation with relatives over who will have possession of the children. The winner of the custody battle receives both federal and tribal benefits that may or may not be spent in the best interests of the children. This young man has tried desperately to remain off alcohol and raise his two small children. But, without financial resources, no driver license because he lost it while driving under the influence, no vehicle, and limited employment skills, he has a difficult path out of poverty. Again, alcohol is his biggest barrier to success and the quiet enjoyment of his children.

Alcohol continues to impede the transition to urban life. Individuals come to the city and walk the streets looking for work until they give up. Bad luck catches up with them. A case I am still investigating involves the unsolved murder of a Navajo tribal member, Harry Bennelly, who ran into a knife, not a job, on Salt Lake's ever more dangerous streets. He was just looking for work. No effort has been made by Salt Lake's finest to identify the killer. After his death, Salt Lake City police made little effort to locate the family on the reservation. In the Navajo culture, you are required to bury the body in four days. He was cremated and over a year later the ashes were finally returned to the relatives. The killer or killers were probably under the influence of alcohol.

One young Goshute tribal member lost a portion of his mental capacity when he crashed his motorcycle into a hillside while intoxicated at a college party. Prior to the crash, he was a smart student and great athlete. Several years later, he was killed while wandering on a highway at night. Another member was killed while intoxicated by overcorrecting his vehicle on a curve near the reservation. Then there are the many individuals who die of liver and other health problems associated with alcohol use.

One Indian friend has been in and out of prison for parole violations involving crimes committed while under the influence of alcohol or drugs, the entire time I have been representing the tribe. He should get used to prison because I don't believe he will ever quit drugs and alcohol. I am always relieved when he returns to prison. At least there I know he will be fed, housed, provided with limited medical care, and is almost safe. You can never feel safe and secure in prison. There are too many sociopaths who will kill you for a pack of cigarettes or five dollars. Many tribal members nationally are quite young when they are injured and killed.

Some Goshute members are marginally employed because they cannot hold down a job due to constant alcohol consumption. Chairman Leon calls them Paycheck Indians. As soon as they have a job, the first paycheck is a call for a drunken weekend. Of course, come Monday when the money is gone, and all that remains is a hangover... the job disappears. Many people in my Mexican community have the exact same problem.

It is amazing how individual responsibility related to alcoholism is refused. This lack of acceptance of individual responsibility is visible in every community. It is always easier to blame others than to accept the logical consequences of one's own alcohol and drug-induced behaviors.

Transference of blame must be a human trait common to all of God's many children. Somehow, prison was the result of bad lawyering, certainly not due to crimes committed with the assistance of such socially irresponsible individuals as Budweiser, Adolph Coors, Johnny Walker, Jim Beam, Jack Daniels, Miller or that Mexican fellow, Jose Cuervo. For good or evil, our rewards are the fruits of our labor. Some recognize the folly in the misuse of alcohol; regrettably, others do not.

The Skull Valley Goshutes' Tribal Chairman, Leon D. Bear, is like the old leaders. He has courage. He cannot be snowed under with an excuse or conned with a story. He has heard just about every story possible from white businessmen who tried to defraud his tribe. He has also heard promises from the federal government that has excuses but rarely solutions. Alcohol is not a subject he considers polite for conversation. He just plain and simply will not tolerate the laziness and stupidity of drunks. Of course, this attitude makes some tribal members very angry. In every decision Leon and the tribal council have made over the ten years that I was involved with, whether it is a new tax program on multinational corporations, building a tribal store, investigating illegally buried sheep killed by nerve gas, working with local law enforcement agencies, or doing business deals with large utility companies, according to constantly drunk critics of the Tribal Council, these decisions were "wrong."

Chairman Leon knows that leadership requires patience with fools, brains against the stupid, and courage in the face of danger. He expects tribal members to work, and he holds down two jobs to show that it can be done. Despite no help and, at times betrayal from the federal government, political opposition from the State of Utah, and constant fighting from tribal members, he is committed to lifting his people out of poverty and preserving the sovereignty of his once mighty and powerful tribe.

Contrast the real leadership of Leon D. and other leaders with some of the inept former administrators of the Bureau of Indian Affairs. A previous assistant secretary for the bureau and her political appointees were getting drunk at the 25th anniversary of NARF (Native American Rights Fund) in Boulder, Colorado. My departed friend, Richard Bear and I made a special trip to meet with her to have some property transferred to the tribe which was at that time available due to cutbacks in defense spending and base closures nationally. The Tooele Army Depot was on the aboriginal territory of the Goshutes. They were entitled to have some of their land returned.

Richard and I briefly attended the anniversary party. He watched the Assistant Secretary for the Bureau of Indian Affairs and her staff drinking heavily, looked at me, at the wine bottles, at all of the people drinking, and said, "Those boys are gonna find trouble." Richard never said much. He was always extra careful with words. Each word counted. While the Assistant Secretary was getting liquored up, the Bureau of Indian Affairs budget was taking a beating in Washington, DC.

In Washington, if you are not there to protect your agency's budget, plan on the many 'hungry pigs' and 'beltway bandits' to feed at your trough. Nor was it amusing watching various tribal leaders falling down drunk at President Clinton's Inaugurations. Drunks cannot lead thirsty horses to water. No wonder that under leadership demonstrated by the Assistant Secretary, the BIA central office in Washington, DC. was a complete disaster. Her budget was cut by over $200,000,000 while she was busy getting drunk in Boulder.

Fortunately, she was replaced by Kevin Gover, an extraordinary and competent individual who has his hands full. In addition to being a successful attorney prior to venturing into government, he has a knowledge of technology that is important in the information age. He is well read and understands hardball Washington politics. He met with national tribal leaders soon after his appointment and solicited their views on various political issues from the controversial to the mundane. His office created an Internet site that enables tribes with computers to have immediate access to information and assistance. This simple change in leadership has produced great results. However, the Native American community cannot and should not rely on the BIA or anyone else to insure their success. It is folly to rely on government for one's success.

How to survive without the government? Support groups and nonprofit organizations sometimes rise to fill this need. The Indian Walk In Center in Salt Lake City, Utah is an example. This United Way agency has audited financial statements, and a mission to assist Indians and other urban poor. They offer a hand-up, not a hand-out. The center is managed by a tough, hard working, charming Arapaho lady, Gail Russell. She and her overworked, underpaid staff assist over 17,000 individuals annually with emergency food boxes, domestic violence counseling, alcohol treatment, senior programs, large pow wows, Thanksgiving dinners, Christmas dinners, art shows, neighborhood fairs, and a host of other activities. Their workers make at least $2.00 less per hour working at the center then if they worked for other nonprofit groups. They stay because they know the importance of their work and how much their services are needed. They assist all in need. Mexican migrants, poor whites, and members from over 45 tribes from over 26 states find help in the run-down, worn out edifice. Their philosophy is simple. "If you need help, we will help you."

The other two Salt Lake Indian non-profits agencies, the Indian Alcohol Recovery Center and the Indian Health Clinic, died bankrupt. Mismanagement of financial resources leads to the same consequences for us all, bankruptcy and failure. This is true of all nations, corporations and individuals whether we are the corrupt Mexican government constantly borrowing money to stay afloat, the Congo whose former dictator stashed international relief funds in Switzerland, the former Soviet Union which finally collapsed under its own mismanagement, Pan Am which went from the largest airline in the world to financial ruin, New York City, which without federal assistance would still be in bankruptcy, or the Indian Alcohol and Recovery Center and the Indian Health Clinic.

Money is a precious tool. Presently, the Salt Lake Indian Walk In Center desperately needs either remodeling or a new site. The current spot is a worn out 1940s building that doubles as a gym. The sickly green and orange carpet is torn and smells of twenty plus years of overuse. The broken chairs and worn out stairways need to be refinished. The hardwood floor and old windows need to be replaced. New computers with Internet access are a must. The Salt Lake Indian community depends on this place for cultural events and coordination of activities. The hope is to raise enough money from various fundraising activities to remodel this worn out but not broken antique.

Of course, Federal funding is out of the question. The shoestring budget of approximately $300,000 barely covers overhead and none of the employees has health or dental insurance. What the center lacks in funding is made up in activity. The place has a pulse of community love.

Annually, the Indian Walk In Center holds Native American art sales. Native American artists from the Intermountain area sell their artwork to the white and non-white liberal community. The proceeds from this event go to the artists and to the Indian Walk In Center. Most of the artwork is exquisite, including colorful Navajo rugs with their own story woven by traditional rug weavers. Some of the Elders who weave these rugs are over ninety years old and live in the most humble circumstances. Many rug weavers are helped by a friend of mine, Linda Myers, who helped create the Adopt a Native Elder. Her non-profit agency has assisted many Navajo tribal Elders who do not have electricity and running water.

You can also find incredible pottery from various Southwestern tribes. These include Junior Whiterock's original pieces with hand-carved paintings and colored sands from throughout the West. There is also a variety of silver and bead jewelry. Each piece of jewelry takes many hours of labor to produce. The knowledge is handed down from generation to generation and family to family. The various tribal artists sometimes work at nine-to-five jobs in addition to the supplemental income from their tremendous artwork. The hide paintings are breathtaking. After the deer hides are carefully tanned, natural colors are used to paint pictures of winter village scenes, wolves, bears, warriors, and other natural settings. The events also feature music and great food. The people in Salt Lake and Park City love to attend and support the artists. Hopefully, this annual event will continue into our children's future. Many communities throughout the Southwest hold various tribal art sales, either at galleries, fairs or in the open markets as those in Santa Fe.

Sale of artwork is only one small part of life that can be improved by nonprofit organizations in the Native American community today. Native Americans, quite like the Irish, the Italians, the Greeks, the Mexicans and others, are finally migrating to the cities of America and Canada in record numbers. With no jobs on the reservations and no hope of future employment, people have to eat. Life on America's many and diverse reservations is very hard. Many young people give up hope and commit suicide.

The suicide rate for Native Americans is a subject that is not discussed and is avoided: "If we ignore it, the problem will go away," seems to be the attitude. The suicides of Indian youth are especially hard on the already small tribes of the Southwest. Interestingly enough, suicide in Indian Country occurs most often with a sudden influx of money.

Anger and despair directed inwardly leads to suicide and outward to homicide. Many die at the hands of their own members from drunken frustration murders. Some of the crimes are absolutely vicious. A friend of mine and one of the nation's best trial attorneys, Jerome Mooney, litigated a case where some young Indian men on the Ute Reservation beat another tribal member to death with tire irons until the skull completely collapsed. A complex legal debate then ensued on whether or not the individual died on the reservation or on state land and which law, federal or state, applied. In another violence case, bodies of Navajo tribal policemen were burned with gasoline in southern Utah after being murdered by angry, drunk youths. Hidden within these acts are the larger issues of hopelessness, alcoholism, low self-esteem, and loss of culture. Not even the U.S. Supreme Court can assist these problems. And oddly enough, increased revenues in tribal coffers may intensify some of these social problems. But clearly, money is not the problem, only the symptom.

The need for tribal revenue creates all types of economic pursuits.

Indian gaming is not the giant money machine the press and dishonest politicians make it out to be. Gross revenues of tribal casinos in the year 2000 exceeded $6 billion annually. However, the economic picture for the majority of tribes is the equivalent of life in a Third World country. The majority of tribes do not have any gaming facilities to generate revenue. The logistics to set up the enterprises are not always there. My friend, Uintah and Ouray Superintendent David Allison, and I agree completely that gaming is greatly overrated. And if the revenue is not carefully used, it is going to be the modern day smallpox of tribes.

Many members of gaming tribes have a problem with compulsive gamblers who spend their meager resources trying desperately to hit the jackpot that will assure them of the materialistic American dream. Local residents also succumb and become gambling addicts. In New Mexico, Pueblo tribes have many casinos, and personal bankruptcies in that state are up in part as a result of Indian gaming. Gambling addiction is common near all casinos in the nation.

Gambling revenue is used by some tribes to provide much needed government services, like health care and elderly programs. But gaming is a double-edged sword, a necessary evil. It might benefit tribes. It's too soon to tell. Not enough time has passed to assess fully the benefits and possible dangers.

Since the federal government does not meet its true responsibility toward Native Americans, revenue from tribal business enterprises is used by some tribes to help members directly; the infamous, so-called "tribal dividends." The problem is that members insist on obtaining dividends from gaming and other enterprises. This can completely destroy what exists of a work ethic. For a few irresponsible members, instead of being mere drunks, with this new wealth they now can afford cocaine. The $6 billion generated from Indian gaming is approximately three times the total federal budget for the constantly under-funded BIA.

Of the 556 federally recognized tribes, fewer than 130 have gaming as a business enterprise. Only a handful of tribes are associated with gaming business because most live far away from major population centers. The Utes live over 240 miles and the Ibapah Confederated Goshutes live over 200 miles from Salt Lake City, Utah. Wendover, Nevada is closer and has full casino operations complete with hotels and alcohol. The Skull Valley Goshutes live over 85 miles from Salt Lake City, Utah. The Utah tribes are too far from the populated Wasatch Front to benefit from gaming. Even if they wanted to take advantage of the slot machines and gaming tables, federal law gives deference to states on gaming issues. If a state prohibits all forms of gaming, like Utah and Hawaii, then the tribes cannot turn to casinos to attract desperately needed revenue from larger communities. They are forced to compete in other markets.

Tribes are involved in gaming, manufacturing, lumber, land leases, and other ventures. Tribes are the only governments in America that absolutely depend on the revenue from their business ventures to run their tribal operations. The reason is that tribal tax bases are so incredibly small and their members are so poor, that they must turn to the market place to survive. This is why tribes are involved in construction, hotels, skiing, and a host of other business ventures. Some of the business ventures make money. Other ventures are mere rips-off from sophisticated con men. Some tribes have astute business managers. Others spend the money faster than they make it.

I must emphasize that they are like all cultures that go through urban transition. The Native American community nationally, and in Utah where I am most familiar, has few college graduates and even fewer professionals. There are only a handful of Indian attorneys nationally. But this lapse is rapidly changing.

One act of Congress by hateful politicians can cause more damage to the Indian community than thousands of volunteers and many decades can ever repair. The battles previously lost in Indian Country are now fought in Congress and before the courts. Whether it is the boarding schools' attempts to make Indians "white and delightsome"—which resulted in destruction of tribal pride and tradition and ruined the lives of tens of thousands of individuals—or congressional acts that attempted to terminate tribes and confiscate lands, decisions in Washington have had a long-term impact on Indian Country. Today's tribal attorneys and tribal leaders are the modern warriors of the Native American community.

I have tried to illustrate key features of the current state of Native Americans. These warriors are almost overwhelmed by loss of language, fetal alcohol syndrome, welfare, prison, loss of culture, blue-collar work, blue-collar crime, unemployment, poor salaries, and overcrowded living conditions. A few hard-working people manage to survive the racism of the educational system, the alcoholic parents and relatives, loss of language and religion, and have children who are healthy.

The television serves as the altar of the new religion. Toyotas, Nintendos and blatant consumerism are now equated with happiness. The traditions of sharing, using only what is needed, not wasting anything, being in good health, and making your own clothes and tools is gone...forever! Now, there are overcrowded apartments, mobile homes, and in a few cases, suburbia. In urban America, Native Americans, like everyone else in this powerful country, are now americans with a small "a." Some are happy. Most inter-marry with the majority culture. Many dye their hair or put on green contacts to give the appearance of their "whiteness" and denial of their strong heritage.

Like their Mexican cousins, Native Americans are one of the very last groups in America to urbanize. So they are experiencing the painful realities of what a city really is going to offer. There is the incredible entertainment and the absolute loneliness of being one in a sea of a million other humans, not one in two thousand. Native Americans are now facing the same prejudices and fears and successes of previous waves of immigrants who lived in squalid poverty, suffered from horrible blue-collar crimes, and the hopelessness of alcoholism.

How interesting it is to see the historical similarities of the Irish after the horrible potato famine in the 1840s with their migration to urban centers in America and Canada. The Italians and Jews who migrated to the great cities of the Northeast like New York and Boston and the Midwest—especially Chicago—at the turn of the century faced the same barriers of language and poor education. The poor black farm workers from the Southern United States migrated to the cities of the Northeast with the additional barrier of skin color. The Mexicans made their move after the Mexican Revolution in 1910 and again from the rural agricultural communities of Northern New Mexico and Southern Colorado after Hitler and fascism was defeated. All ethnic groups who migrated to the city faced a hostile reception from those already living there. New and different people mean more competitors for scarce jobs, affordable homes, and precious education. This competition translates to prejudice from angry, poorly paid and poorly educated workers who are already trying to eke out a meager living.

Because the human animal is so similar biologically, it only stands to reason that the experiences of Native Americans will be similar to what others in a different time and part of the world have experienced. Many white Americans were previously unwanted Europeans. The invaders came from the rural agricultural areas of Italy, Ireland, France, England, Germany, China, Japan and elsewhere in the last century. Some left the crowded poverty of Europe's filthy cities in search of a better life in land that was without question Indian Country. Sooner or later, all cultural groups from all parts of the world migrate to the evil, unforgiving and unheavenly city.

3

THE URBAN ENVIRONMENT AND IMMIGRANTS

"There is no work in our country"

Illegal Mexican Immigrant client

All cultures have a difficult transition from the hunter-gatherer, nomadic small agricultural communities to modern urban life. Writers like Jared Diamond, in *Guns, Germs and Steel* have described this difficulty vividly. This historical migration has been ongoing for the last one million years and will continue until we are no longer on this planet. In the last and very brief 6,000 years of recorded history, several cultures have had a head start at urban living. Some Italians, Greeks and Jews have been an urban people for at least 4,000 years. Gibbon's classic work, *The Decline and Fall of the Roman Empire* reveals the incredible, horrifying, hilarious and at times glorious experiences of the once united Europe. Lewis Mumford's *The City in History* lays out the formation of cities throughout the world. According to Mumford, humanity is like a car traveling at full speed with no lights on and no sense of direction.

Until recently, cities have not been the healthiest of environments. When the Roman Empire fell apart, as a result mostly to incredible mismanagement by emperors who placed their own hedonistic interests above the interests of the empire, European civilization descended into a horrible dark age that lasted longer than fifteen hundred years. After the fall of the Empire, the various European tribes lived in filthy cities long before their invasion of this continent. Some of these cities were so poorly maintained that disease spread like wildfire.

In the Middle Ages, bodies would finally be removed from English doorways in London when the stench became overwhelming. Until a few centuries ago, Paris urbanites lived on the edge of starvation. In some of Europe's cities, people defecated in one part of the river and others drank the same water downstream. Rats spread disease and garbage fed flies and larvae. The European city of the century of Karl Marx was an unforgiving place of crime, poverty, loneliness and disease. Unlike the Paris and London of today, which are finally modern, relatively clean, and in places breathtakingly beautiful, the pre-invasion cities of the Middle Ages were horrible places to live. If you did not get robbed by gangs of hungry youths, you might die from the plague or some other public health menace like cholera, dysentery, and other common diseases that exist in all filthy places.

Human life, in the last one hundred years, has obviously undergone the biggest change in all of its very brief history. There are 6,000 years of "recorded" history, and we have only been here a mere speck on the geologic timeline. New cities have popped up like mushrooms after a spring rain. So the cultural groups that won the race to the city have also won two very important intangible prizes, property and power. The new kids on the block, that is, the Indians, migrant Mexicans, Africans, Haitians and others, have what is left over. Let me emphasize again that this process is completely normal. The Irish, Jews, French, English, Russian and German peasants who were late arrivals to urban America started life in the dangerous blue-collar industries of the late 1800s.

In fact, hoping that discrimination against them would lessen, some of the later arrivals objected to further immigration from the home country. They were different from their immigrant cousins in the backward country of rural Europe. They could speak English in complete sentences, and were not embarrassed to be seen in public places. Their names sometimes changed from Greenberg to Green or Quintana to Quinn, from Martinez to Martin and on and on. Their "fitting in" made sense. The last thing some immigrants wanted was more people from the homeland. This shame of culture and ethnic pride was a barrier for acceptance. They were not dark Mexicans; they were of white "Spanish" stock. They were not completely black, they were "part Indian."

Since property and power are intellectual concepts, our thinking and ability to communicate is what make us financially and emotionally successful. Our skin color or ethnic background is not the determining factor. Rather, it is knowing how to lead emotionally and financially successful lives in an urban environment. That is the true difficulty for all of us. You cannot destroy a way of life that has been the same for thousands of years and then expect the survivors to adjust immediately to financial prosperity. This is especially true when some of the conquered did not have financial words or concepts as part of their everyday vocabulary. Unless our youth and others take the time to understand the concepts of money and power, we subject ourselves to a life of drudgery and financial poverty.

This urban transition does not have to be so painful. There are ways to accelerate this historical process. One small step is affirmative action. Despite the unpopularity of this program as "reverse discrimination," there have been encouraging results, opening doors that had been historically closed by an old boy network. There is now a small professional class among communities of color. The sting of urbanization is lessened. If you are not in college, you should learn the habits of success of the people who have won in urban environments.

The transition to an urban environment also does not mean that you must lose all of your cultural traditions. Native Americans and immigrants from Third World countries must hold on to the belief of their ancestors that the materialism and consumerism myths are unimportant. The shift from interaction with living beings, plants and animals to the plastic materialism of toys and technology are still no substitute for good physical health and above all, family love. Property and power do not matter if you are so unhappy that you fill your body with alcohol and drugs to mask the pain of a sad, lonely, unwanted life. Urban environments of downtown Salt Lake, Chicago, Washington, DC, Tokyo, Paris, Barcelona or any other large metropolitan area cannot possibly compare with the splendor of nature.

In many parts of our small planet, the natural environment is gone forever, like the carrier pigeon and the wild condor. Poorly managed cities are full of one form of life—human. There is no diversity of elk herds, buffalo, deer, rabbits, antelope, fish, game hawks and wild plants. But there are lots and lots of people. And with millions of people come problems of blue-collar crime and pollution.

The stench and environmental problems of the urban areas on planet earth are sometimes horrific. If you want to see the future of America, visit cities in Europe and Japan. There is no wildlife. Europe and Japan have destroyed their natural ecosystems and wildlife at almost every turn. Every inch of the export island, Japan, Inc., is used for some human activity. There are no great herds of wild animals. There are huge herds of people. As far as you can see there is an ocean of people, and more people and more millions and millions of people. In an area slightly larger than Salt Lake County, Tokyo and the surrounding suburbs is the second largest economy on earth. The urban future is gray, with tall concrete and glass buildings of neon lights, schools of people swimming on crowded streets between cars, cabs and light rail. Everywhere there are neon lights of different bright colors that bring life to the night sky. Canon, Coca Cola, Sony and others shine brightly in the heart of Tokyo. The streets in Japan are safe.

Within the inner cities of America are Indians from various tribes and immigrants from various parts of the world who have given up. They walk the streets totally lost and often intoxicated. Their clothes smell of body odor, urine and alcohol, like the Irish and Italians of the 19th century. They sleep under bridges, in parks and at the homeless shelters with the mentally ill and illegal Mexicans who could not find work in the land of promise and hope. Some hang together in gangs waiting for the kindness of strangers. Others get hit by vehicles and die or are brutally murdered and forgotten. The migration to the cities is not always filled with the cornucopia of suburban "success." With so many people, there are not always the jobs and housing to supply adequately this never ending demand. With so many people chasing the urban environment for jobs and homes, inevitably some are left behind. America has over three million homeless.

The urban environments of spaceship earth are all very similar. The main reason for the similarities of our urban areas is that humans are all very similar. And therefore, the economic, political and emotional problems are similar. From behavior to personalities, there is little difference. Some city governments are incredibly corrupt and poorly managed. Others are well run and efficient. All who govern face similar challenges in managing our ever-expanding populations. The world now has over six billion people. Managing the behavior of the masses of humanity is always the political question. The solutions vary only with the complexity of the environments and situations.

All cities are governed by similar financial principles. The tax revenue coming in has to be greater than the amount of money going out for public services. This financial principle applies to both Salt Lake City and Chicago. The logistical problems of services are similar for all cities. Municipal garbage is the same problem in Tokyo, Japan as in Tooele, Utah. The difference is amount. Mass transit is the same problem in Seattle, Washington as in Salt Lake City, Utah. Summer youth programs are a governance dilemma for Los Angeles, California and for Provo, Utah. Traffic is a nightmare for commuters in Washington, DC and Sandy, Utah. Clean parks and safe streets are concerns in Mexico City, Mexico and Ogden, Utah. Blue-collar crime is a governance concern in Venice Beach, California and in Vernal, Utah. Unhealthy behaviors like illegal drug use are cause for alarm in Park City, Utah and Paris, France.

Employment and economics are political problems in Wendover, Utah and London, England. Education of youth is a concern in Stockholm, Sweden and Moab, Utah. The staggering cost of day care is a family problem in Atlanta, Georgia and St. George, Utah. Management of jail space is important in San Francisco, California and West Valley City, Utah. Cooperation with other governments is important in San Diego, California and Murray, Utah. Air pollution is a health issue in Chicago, Illinois and in Bountiful, Utah. Water quality is a very real problem worldwide. The import of foods to market is the same logistics problem in New York City and Brigham City, Utah. The bottom line is that living and surviving in an urban environment is the same problem for everyone else who has migrated to the city everywhere on Earth.

Most American cities are less than one hundred and fifty years old. In Europe and Japan there are bridges and castles that are older than this country. The result is that they, Europeans and Japanese, have a very long historical experience in a city environment.

The old world cities are now fantastic. From bullet trains in Tokyo, to one-thousand-year-old castles in Barcelona, to museums in Paris, to churches in London, much of what these cities have to offer is worth the travel and expense. Similarly, Native Americans and other immigrants have a great deal to offer the planet's ever expanding cities. The art is world class. Our indigenous knowledge of nature is not yet completely lost because the appreciation of the many living things on the planet still exists. However, Native Americans, indigenous people worldwide and all of us must first learn how to hunt and gather in cities. This knowledge will come in time. But we have to be patient. And patience, as the Honorable Richard Bear taught me, is hard. Let's look at hunting in the dangerous city.

4

SUCCE$$FUL HUNTING IN THE CITY

MONEY, (mun'e), n., pl. Moneys, monies, adj. _n 1..gold, sliver, or other metal in pieces of convenient form stamped by public authority and issued as a medium of exchange and measure of value. 2. See Paper money 3. Any circulating medium of exchange, including coins, paper money. And demand deposits. 4. Any article or substance used as a medium of exchange, measure of wealth, or means of payment as checks on demand deposit, wampum, etc. 5. a particular form or denomination of currency. *Webster's Encyclopedic Unabridged Dictionary of the English Language.*

Wealth is a very good thing, but it's good mostly because it allows one to follow one's passion and promote change.

Michael Milken

In the pre-invasion days, Native Americans and indigenous people throughout the world were very successful hunters. In fact, they were so successful that their simple way of life lasted at least ten thousand years. The various hunter-gather tribes knew exactly what they were doing. They had excellent values and fed their families. By incorporating the hunting and gathering skills of the past, we can achieve the same kind of success today. Instead of hunting and gathering near riverbanks and foot-hills in organized groups or alone for big game or ground squirrels, you now are hunting for a new kind of game in a relatively new environment, the city.

How do you hunt in a city? The game is no longer covered by hides that become clothes and meat that fills your belly with protein. The hunt now is for money. What is money? What do you do with it? How does it work? Where do you find it? How can you obtain this money?

Obviously very few people, not just Native Americans, understand this hunt for this new game because almost all of today's' warriors and the rest of society do not have any money. The sad reality about today is that most people most of the time in most parts of the world are very, very poor. My poor clients never talk about sex and money. Consequently, their children are always pregnant and they are always broke. Money is not some great mystery. Like chemistry, physics, biology, geography or history, if you study the subject and have reasonable intelligence, you will master this fascinating subject.

Most of us do not speak Lakota or Navajo or Japanese. This does not mean we are stupid. It just means we have not studied these languages. We can only know and understand that which we have taken the time to study. Most people have not studied the language of money and therefore do not understand these concepts. When I was a mere babe-in-the-woods at the age of 19 and still believed that Communism was the way of the future, I did not know a portfolio from a balance sheet. I had no idea of the difference between return on investment and interest payments. I had read so much socialist literature that I was convinced that nationalization of the oil companies, national health insurance, public housing, and a whole host of public projects were in the best interests of all. My views have since been refined and moderated by time and experience.

My love affair with Communism ended when I formed my own business, paid taxes and dealt with the Social Security Administration. I learned that government workers are usually people who, unable to work in the private sector, must have employment somewhere. If all else fails, the government will hire you. And, even if you are totally incompetent, you cannot be fired. My idealism did not change. It just became practical. The only thing I knew about money was I did not have very much and my family did not have any.

To give you some idea on how the public lacks knowledge of financial matters, realize that approximately three percent of the 100 million US households own almost half of the nation's entire wealth. These people understand what money is, how it works, how to accumulate it, how to spend it, and how not to lose it. These millionaires, whose identities would surprise you, are not any smarter, taller, better looking, or even healthier then you. They are people who have saved a portion of their income over their entire lives and just know how to properly live *below their means* and accumulate financial wealth. They do not flaunt their money. They do not drive fancy cars or live in expensive homes. By just looking at them, you would never guess they are millionaires. In fact, if they have fancy cars and jewelry and big homes, they probably do not have any real wealth. Just real expensive debts. We call it big hat, no cattle.

An excellent guide on the subject is *The Millionaire Next Door: The Surprising Secrets of America's Wealthy*, by Thomas J. Stanley and William D. Danko. They describe seven common traits that millionaires have.

Money is a very important weapon or tool. Our ancestors clearly knew the importance of being very careful with the limited number of arrows and spears in their possession. Since these important hunting tools were very difficult to produce, they were almost never wasted on stupid shots. Arrows did not magically grow on trees, they could not be obtained easily, and there was not an endless supply. They were hand crafted with hours upon hours of careful detailed work to make certain they were perfect.

Our money is the modern equivalent of hunting and fighting arrows. Money is very difficult to make and even easier to lose. I have seen workers and professionals spend their entire year's wages and misappropriate client's funds at casinos in Reno and Las Vegas, Nevada. I spent money on black jack that would have been better spent on groceries. When I felt the pain of being broke for a couple of weeks after a few hours of fun, I stopped finding humor in gambling.

In a few hours of misguided adventures, compulsive gamblers have lost everything, including their freedom. And some attorneys have even lost their right to practice law. If you shoot your arrows at rocks and trees, don't count on having them available for game and to defend yourself in times of combat. With money, it is exactly the same logic.

If you waste your money on alcohol, gambling, television, non-essential plastic items often known as toys, and the huge amount of environmentally harmful and useless junk which invariably ends up in our too plentiful national and local landfills, don't expect to have money available when you really need it—to buy decent shelter, nutritious food, and reasonable transportation.

Money, like arrows, can be used to obtain food, protect you from enemies, and help you achieve success. They are only tools—not the ultimate pursuit. Money and weapons are means to an end. We do not hoard arrows just for the sake of having them. The same is true with money. Acquiring it is a way of life, whether the end is success in battle or in hunting. Just as our ancestors knew how to use their weapons to feed and protect their families, you too must know how to use money if you want to survive in the unheavenly city. Remember always the words attributed to Jesus Christ, "The lust for money is the root of all evil." So be careful not to make it the end all and be all of human existence. They are just numbers and nothing more. Want to see a million dollars? Here it is: $1,000,000.00. Amazed? You should be. Here it is again: $2,000,000.00. Wow, incredible, you say! And here is $3,000,000.00. Are you impressed?

First, you must understand that money is used as a tool for exchange. It makes the exchange of labor and services in this society easier. Unlike one hundred and fifty years ago, when possessions were like rocks that weighed you down while you were hunting and gathering in the ocean of life, ownership today is very different. Paper has very little weight. Your balance sheet may weigh less than one pound, yet it gives you the power to travel worldwide, to provide you with incredible opportunities, and to feed you with exotic foods. Money is sometimes made out of paper. You exchange some money with the cashier at Wendy's or some other food establishment, and they give you a meal. You exchange money with the landlord and he trades you a place to sleep and shower. You exchange money with the car salesman, and he trades you a vehicle. You exchange an employer your time and he or she trades you money.

The important question you need to ask yourself is not so much how to get this tool that makes people commit murder and lie through their teeth to obtain more and more out of insatiable lust. Making money is not usually your problem, just as making arrows was not the problem faced by your great grandfathers. The real help you and most members of society need is in learning how to use your money; that is, how to shoot your money arrows, knock down game and keep it. Your great grandfathers knew how to make arrows. You can and you have made some money. Your ancestors also understood the importance of hunting properly and fighting to survive. They did not waste anything and did such a good job that you are alive reading this book. It is now your turn to hunt properly and fight to help your children survive. Yes, the stakes are just as high. The prize this time is about the survival of the planet earth.

If it is a medium of exchange, you need to understand what it is you have to sell. Complex math is not required to grasp this concept. If you can add and subtract on an eighth grade level, you can succeed financially, and even become a millionaire in the information age.

The formula is quite simple. Revenue (R) minus Expenses (E) equals

Profit (P).

R-E=P.

And profit, if properly invested with compound interest, will make you financially wealthy. The only other requirements are time, continuous investment of profit, compound interest, and discipline.

The Time Requirement: There is no quick way to become rich. Only the careful use of time and resources will protect you from harm. Live a rich life very slowly. As humans, all we have is time. We come from darkness into light for 60 to 80 years, then we return to the spirit world. In a market economy, selling your time, even through a minimum wage job, will feed you. But unless you team up with other warriors and split rent costs, you will not be able to find adequate shelter and transportation. All of these are possible without an expensive college education.

Let's look at the actual expenses of survival in Salt Lake City, Utah. The average cost in the heavenly city of Zion for a run-down, two-bedroom duplex in a dangerous part of town with drug dealers nearby who will shoot at you, is $650 per month. A car payment averages $100 for something barely above safety inspection. Food will cost approximately $300 on a no-frills white rice diet with a few vegetables. If you actually want lights and heat plan, on spending another $100. Add car insurance of $50 and gas and car maintenance of $100, and now you know what you will need to survive. The total money arrows you will need for one month just to survive in some rat hole on a Spartan diet is $1,300. At $6.50 per hour working 40 hours per week, you will net after taxes a whopping $832 per month. Now you are $468 short of satisfying your basic needs. It's hard to pull yourself up by your bootstraps when you don't have boots. Welcome to the city. If you don't learn the importance of using money as a tool while you are young, plan on financial poverty. Because that is exactly what you will have the rest of your natural life.

Modern urban life is outwardly different from the traditional society of your great, great grandfathers. In the old days, if everyone worked, then everyone ate—easy to accomplish since there was an abundance of natural, healthy food. The Goshutes and other tribes did not have welfare. The earth was their welfare. Chief Tabby did not have a sense of humor about lazy warriors. If you wanted to be on his team, Team Goshute, you got up before the sunrise and went to bed with the owls. The deer and elk did not care if you were tired. Enemy warriors hoped you wasted all your arrows on beer and wine. There was hunting and gathering, and eating and sleeping. Tribal spiritual leaders told communal stories around the campfire. How can we eat and live today without losing our freedom? We carefully use our limited money arrows.

If you and two other warriors share the costs of the apartment and utilities, then your costs will decrease by $500 per month. My Mexican clients do this all of the time. I once had a drug case in East Los Angeles. There were four families living together in a small two-bedroom home they rented for $1,200 per month. And they took turns sleeping and eating. This was all they could afford. Selling their labor at minimum wage gave them a place to sleep that was slightly better then under a bridge. Down the street from my house, at least five Mexican families live in a single home. Cars are parked on blocks, and a toilet is by the front door.

So if you team up like cockroaches, you will just barely break even. Now what? If you work 15 hours per week overtime you will have an additional $123.75 to save and lift yourself out of financial poverty. That means you must work 55 hours per week for the right and privilege of living in an overcrowded apartment, in a dangerous neighborhood, using a car you hope does not break down on the way back to the 'Res' or to work, and a diet of rice and bread. What a wonderful life. This, beats the hell out of hunting and gathering in the 19th century? This life is what cities have to offer?

Yes, it is very difficult to pull yourself out of financial poverty. If it were not difficult, everyone would be rich. Well, quit wasting time complaining. Warriors, there have been others in many parts of the world, throughout history who have faced tougher times. Suck it up, work hard, and above all be very patient. When hunting, good things come to those who wait. Patience, patience, patience. Yes, I know you want to kill something or at least your boss or landlord. But wait. Some of my clients lived in refugee camps for four years waiting to come to America and leave Iraq forever. Others walked many miles from Mexico illegally to get the right to clean American toilets, pick fruit, get paid under the table in dangerous construction jobs, and cook in hot kitchens.

If a very courageous modern Indian warrior named George Roybal could do six months straight of lock down 23 hours per day in a small, stinky Utah prison cell so other inmates could practice their religion in Utah's prisons, you can work 55 hours per week at $6.50 per hour. The main reason you can do this is that many Americans are too lazy and dishonest to work minimum wage jobs as janitors, cooks and laborers. They would rather receive welfare, worker's compensation or social security disability, or just be so constantly stoned and end up in jail. Some people believe that a broken finger qualifies you for some kind of state aid or federal entitlement program. Millions of people in America are on some type of entitlement program. But do you really want others to carry you?

You will always be able to find a minimum wage job in America. And you will really have to try or lie to be unemployed in this current economic cycle. If you could not find minimum wage jobs in America, millions of Mexicans, Haitians and others would not be dying to try to cross our borders to work here. Until you own your own business and are selling products, you will need to sell your labor. Without an education, the only thing you have to sell is your time and your honesty. Employers are always interested in employees who are honest and willing to come to work early, sober and ready to help them make money.

It is hard to find good employees that are not stoned or drunk and willing to show up to work on time. This is why cheap illegal Mexican labor is in such high demand. These workers still come to this country to work, and they do a great job. My clients from Mexico are interested in helping their families in their homeland survive. Approximately four billion dollars annually is sent back to Mexico from their relatives in the U.S. Very few ever commit a blue-collar crime.

In the traditional days, you did not have a choice about being honest. If you came home without a deer, a rabbit, or a squirrel, you could not lie about it. Feeding your family meant being a good hunter and gatherer. Or you starved. Very few Indians starved because very few were lazy. Chief Tabby, Chief Joseph, Chief Red Cloud and the dozens of other terrific leaders would not put up with lazy, dishonest warriors who wanted to live with their mommies. They would throw them out of their tribes, and these lazy warriors would have to hunt and gather elsewhere. The lazy did not live long for various reasons that are too obvious to restate here. If you didn't hunt, you and your family did not eat. And the tribe as a whole was weakened by the presence of each nonproductive member.

Imagine following this advice for six months. The problem is no longer do you make enough money to pay your bills. Now, hypothetically you are possessed with extra money and ample places to rid yourself of these fine funds. Because you stuck out your first job at $6.50 per hour and now you are making $8.00 per hour, that equals $1,376 in gross wages and $1,032 after taxes. Now you only have to work 30 extra hours each month to break even. This is hard. The temptation is to quit and start drinking. It is boring to work for six months straight without a break and without any real support from family and friends. Even the most disciplined warriors will tire without adequate rest and recreation. Survival is now assured, but life is much more, a hell of a lot more, than just survival.

Whatever shall we do with ourselves when we are not cleaning toilets, making beds, delivering newspapers, pumping gasoline, flipping hamburgers, picking fruit and the numerous other tedious and dangerous blue-collar labor some white Americans are absolutely unwilling to undertake?

It is one thing to lose one's way of life that existed for thousands of years. It is quite another to ask a man to engage in very routine and seemingly unimportant work for a lifetime. Hell truly is repetition. Modern urban life can be very boring and difficult. Although it has been said that only boring people get bored, think about what life offers people who come to cities: mindless, dangerous blue-collar labor, sweat shop conditions in factories, poor wages, crowded housing, inadequate transportation, and tedious routine. For most workers, one day is as different from the next as one slice of white bread is from another. It's the same, just a different day. Nobody likes to be treated as if he is disposable and replaceable. Yet unlike the traditional days of the Goshute Nation and other pre-industrial urban cultures, if we sell our labor, we all are replaceable. We all want to be appreciated for our contributions to society, for our individuality, and for knowing that we are a part of something larger; that we belong and have a stake in our society. All of us want to be loved and generally appreciated. We would not be human if we didn't.

Once again, be patient. It is hard to stick it out, to want badly to just quit and do something else, anything but what you are doing. But don't quit. Here is why you should stick out these incredibly poor, disgusting and dangerous jobs. The relatively short time you spend as a janitor, dishwasher, fruit picker, newspaper boy, gas station attendant, or forklift driver will soon pass. Then you discover that five years have gone by and you are finished with college. Soon you are in your 40s and life is tolerable. In fact, it is down right enjoyable.

Many of us did not inherit wealth. Most worked the dirty, difficult and dangerous jobs other people did not want. We worked those jobs because people did not want them and they were the only jobs we could obtain. I remember the janitor job at the Tooele Army Depot in the summers of high school. My friend Joe Valerio and I would move sleeping government workers from their tables so we could sweep and mop under them. I took ditch-digging jobs in New Mexico for my neighbors. One woman paid me seventy-five cents for three hours of hard work. She had a smug look on her face as she gave me my three quarters. She actually thought she was doing me a favor. I worked as a migrant field worker in San Luis, Colorado for $5 a day. You appreciate not wasting food when you have to pick it up off the ground and put it in baskets, then on the back of trucks.

Then a graveyard gas station job at Lakepoint, Utah needed my attention. You cannot appreciate the true nature of work until you see the sunrise as you are pumping gas in the cold of winter. Even the warmth of the waitresses is not enough to keep you from exhaustion because you have not slept. Seeing the sunrise on a graveyard shift makes you appreciate your hard-earned wages. You are not as inclined to buy drugs with hard-earned money when the choice is food and rent or drugs and the streets.

The Albertson's Food Store bag boy position had my name on it briefly. I was fired for being rude to customers who did not like Mexicans with attitudes. I made the mistake of being rude to people because some customers without manners had been rude to me. I did not have to respond to the rude shoppers. I did not realize that we do not stoop to the level of other people's ill behavior with our own ill behavior. I was fired.

I stacked salt bags for Morton Salt and drove a forklift. I worked with individuals who had one skill, strong backs and the ability to show up to work on time. Some were bored to tears with their work. The plant that provided me with summer work is now shut down. I had the good fortune to work there while I was going to college. Most workers took this job because this heavy labor job fed them and their families. Some of the workers had great senses of humor and got along quit well. Others hated Indians, Mexicans and blacks. There were women working on my shift who were as strong as some of the men. They stacked salt bags with the best of the men and would kick your ass if you were rude to them.

I worked a few summers at Mag Corp in Rowley, Utah. This, the worst polluting plant in America, had a dangerous position smelting molten magnesium and stacking 50-pound ingots in 120-degree heat. You drive 60 miles from Tooele, Utah to work 12-hour shifts in dangerous working conditions for a company that seemed not to care if you lived or died. They treated their workers as expendable. The workers would get high on the way to work and drunk on the way back from work. The pay was good. If the company treated the workers with even the smallest amount of respect, the turnover would not have been so high. It was always a test of endurance to see who was going to quit next. The pollution was so bad that car paint would be eaten away by the brown smelly gases that were released straight into the atmosphere. There were no plants or animals anywhere near the facility. I could just imagine what was happening to the workers' lungs. I remember on one graveyard shift, a old man said, "Those politicians and rich people, they don't care about us little guys."

His wrinkled old face still is engraved in my memory. He was a hard-working individual who loved his family. All of these workers loved their families. They were not criminals; just blue-collar workers who wanted to make an honest living.

Bryant Junior High School in Salt Lake City, Utah had a position open as a counselor. Some of the parents would not understand that their children were failing every class. The parents did not get it. Their children were in danger of not learning enough to read a job application or the back of a soup can. I could not impress on these parents that their children were not going to be able to sell their labor to anyone at a price above minimum wage unless they learned how to read and write in English and had a basic understanding of math. I got this job right out of the hospital while I was still going to school.

Then there were the positions as law clerk for several solo practitioners and small firms. They taught me that law practice means long hours with a ton of research and very difficult people with very difficult problems. If others could do it, I could do it too. I learned what worked and what did not work. After law school, I formed my own firm, won a ton of cases and made some money. I made my first million by the time I was 30 years old. I thought the money would never end. I knew how to make it, and boy could I spend it!

I started reading my own headlines and believed I could do anything. After all, I was a good trial attorney. If I knew how to try cases, certainly I could manage apartments. I could buy speculative stocks. I knew everything, just ask me. Wrong. I got divorced. Then I ran into an international con artist. Then one of my best friends died of a heroin drug overdose and another died while drunk in a horrible car wreck. Suddenly, I was almost completely ruined financially and emotionally.

I finally learned to save what I made and kept enough to retire after having come so close to being on the street again. I kept custody of my wonderful son, my law firm, my home, and every debt we ever incurred. I formed my own law firm because I could not stand working for anyone.

This all took 24 years of hard, sometimes-backbreaking work. I know what it is like to stay up all night and see the sun come up because I have been at work on the graveyard shift. I know what it is like to sleep in a trailer on the job and wait to work another 12 hours of hell in a 120-degree refinery. I will never advise you to do something I have not tried myself. If I could do this work, you can do it. Hell, I'm nothing special. I just never ever quit. I fight until I win or I am defeated in battle. I succeeded financially because I was forced to learn about how money actually works and how to manage this nebulous entity. But money, like the arrow, is only a tool. One day you and I will die. Then money will not be a problem.

But you don't want to work at a menial job and be a janitor. There is no glamour in cleaning up after other people. You don't want to pick green beans. You don't want to dig ditches. You don't want to work in 120-degree heat in dangerous refineries or stack salt bags until your back hurts. Then don't. It is your life and you are free to do with it as you please. If you can survive and live happily by not working, more power to you. After all, there is homelessness, or worse yet, there is jail. Jail sucks, but at least you don't have to pay rent, and you get free meals. These are choices.

What will replace the menial jobs? You are no longer hunting deer, elk, rabbits, snakes, and the various other life forms that have protein and will feed you. In the old days, if it moved and you could kill it, you would eat it. Yes, this new life of not drinking, going to work, coming home and saving money is certainly not exciting. It is sometimes lonely holding to your values, not drinking and being careful with your money arrows. But in time, this patience is worth it one million fold. In every situation in life throughout history, the winners never quit and the quitters never win. But winning is not easy; if it were, everyone would be a winner. Most of the people in cities worldwide are poor.

Most people do not save their money. Consequently when they lose their jobs or situations occur that require immediate use of finances, a bad day or week or month becomes an intolerable life situation. Imagine two hundred years ago, you are in the foothills near a certain resting spot for mule deer. You have been walking all day; it is now sunset. You saw an interesting formation on a tree. Just for the fun of it you shot two of your arrows. Then you weren't paying attention when a rabbit was nearby and you missed an easy meal. Now you have one arrow left and you are tired. You did not use your tools properly and have only yourself to blame if you do not get any meat for your family. Suppose you did kill an old doe with one well-placed shot. On your way home an enemy war party is approaching. Now you are completely out of arrows.

This is the same thing that happens every day in cities where people face life's hard choices and are out of money. Arrows and money are hard to make and very easy to lose. So if you stick to your tiring, boring job, some better job will come along.

And in addition to discipline, you will also need to understand this English language. As mentioned earlier, it is not as difficult and exciting as killing and skinning an elk. I often get clients who have been in the United

States for many years, and they still do not speak enough English to carry on a conversation. They are making an already difficult life more difficult. One client was working as a maid and her husband died. Her already bad situation is now horrible. These non-English speaking clients are so easy to rip off. They are no match for a smooth-talking car dealer or vacuum salesman. Con men can almost see money. Foolish people will buy anything at any price and are unwilling to wait for the common sense of a reasonable price. Because so many of my clients do not speak English, they are stuck in their labor jobs until their backs break and they can no longer sell their labor.

Here are some rules of thumb. Get immediate employment: minimum wage jobs and sharing an apartment with obnoxious roommates are better than living under a bridge. Don't waste anything: buy only food at low cost, fuel for your run-down automobile, rent for your shelter and utilities. Learn constantly: the white-collar manager knows how to do the job of every blue-collar worker beneath him. In other words, make every arrow and opportunity count.

With every paycheck, save ten percent of your money, and very carefully invest it. This will save your life many times over. Stay six months at a minimum wage job while looking for other work in your spare time, or work two jobs. Better opportunities will come along. Like hunting in the wild, don't rush your shot. When you are hunting in the mountains, deserts or plains, wait until the deer, elk or buffalo are within arrow shot before you let one fly at their heart.

In the city, you have to wait for the right job while you are still working your difficult, boring, minimum wage job. Don't be too proud. It is like the warrior who will not eat grasshoppers and squirrels because he is waiting for an elk. It could be a long wait. And if the elk comes and you are too hungry to shoot straight, then what? A minimum wage job is certainly not as great as a high-paying job. Small game is not as tasty as elk meat. However, the high-paying job will not come to you because you are so special in this life that we all live for you. High pay will come because your knowledge and experience is valuable to someone else. The good high-paying job will come as a result of long hard work and patience. Believe it or not, others will not be responsible for your success.

The hunt for money is always difficult. It is meant to be difficult. Once all of your debts are paid, you will face even greater dangers. Make no mistake about it: the city can be every bit as dangerous as the old days of traditional life. Danger and fear come from a lack of knowledge. What we don't know will cause us to lose all of our hard-earned money.

Through ignorance and fear, we can also lose our lives or our freedoms.

5

THE DANGEROUS CITY

There were 23,000 homicides in the US in 1998.

U.S. Department of Justice

If there is one lesson that must be learned about the city, any city, it is this: beware of the human animal. It is in the nature of humans to be able to do harm to your body or steal your possessions. Certainly there are more people in a city than on the reservation; and therefore more people to do you harm. It is ever so important to watch and listen at least twice as much as you speak.

America's cities are dangerous territory. Each year there are tens of thousands of assaults, hundreds of thousands of rapes, and at least 23,000 murders. In Salt Lake County, with a population of approximately 1,000,000, there are at least 500 crimes committed each day. What makes a city so dangerous is the unknown and unpredictable behavior of thousands of people. Some are intoxicated, and many are mentally ill. Mix job frustration and life's emotional difficulties with alcohol and drugs, and you get tens of thousands of violent crimes. There are thousands of hideous acts of senseless bloodletting against others who usually know their attacker. In almost every case I have handled in over 19 years of law practice where physical violence was involved, the victim and attacker knew each other. Many were domestic fights that got out of hand when alcohol was involved. Others were enraged husbands and boyfriends fighting over women. Some were drug deals gone bad. A relatively small number consisted of totally unknown attackers and unlucky victims.

Some "straight-edgers," a white racist hate group, killed a young person outside my office for the simple reason that he was in the wrong place at the wrong time. A young lady was killed near my home in suburban West Valley City, Utah. There was no motive. She was just in the way of a bullet intended for someone else. There was no way on earth her parents deserved such horrific suffering inflicted by total strangers who just shot at her car by random.

My son's car was stolen right from my driveway. At night, we often hear the ambulance and police sirens. Shots ring out late at night on weekends in my neighborhood. Our cars are vandalized and our homes are burglarized. A client was shot in the knee by some crazed inmate who missed his target.

This city is the permanent home for many of you because it is probably the only place you have ever known or will know. However, most Indians on reservations still are fighting to protect the little bits of sovereignty that remains. At the end of the last century, our country was transformed from a primarily agricultural nation to an urban nation. Today, over 70 percent of the nation's people live in communities where populations are greater than 30,000 individuals. Today, the majority of Native Americans live in cities and have become or soon will become urbanized.

When I worked at the Utah State Prison after the *Roybal v. DeLand* sweatlodge case, my friend Lenny Foster and I estimated that over 90 percent of the Native American inmates were there on crimes committed under the influence of alcohol. Frustration leads to drinking. Drinking leads to violence, and violence leads to prison.

In our cities and in our prisons are individuals who commit, and inmates who are incarcerated on, child sex crimes. When you finally have children, watch them like a hawk. When Mormon child killer, Gary Bishop was alive, our son never left our sight. We knew where he was 24 hours a day. America's cities offer a very dangerous environment for our youth. When a person hurts a child, that person hurts all of us and destroys the future.

Today, urban society and righteous politicians have created the most massive corrections industry in the history of the world. But the corrections industry does not correct. Draper University, a.k.a. the Utah State Prison, does have its merits. It is an excellent crime school. The admissions requirements are very high and there is definitely a preference for minority students. The repeat drunk and drug offenders and the hardest of the hard are given one of these expensive ($71,000 to construct and $31,000 annually to maintain) crime beds. Once you pass the strict admissions requirements set by our judges, juries, prosecutors and defense attorneys, you will have the opportunity to learn Advanced Burglary; Rape 205; Aggravated Assault 350; Breaking and Entering 501; Basic Methamphetamine for your science requirement, and weight lifting or basket ball for exercise. Drugs are available upon demand, and if you are into homosexual sex, the opportunities are endless. If you meet the strict admissions requirements to Draper University, or any other state or federal prison institution of higher learning, tuition, room and board are free.

And when the board of pardons feels that this expensive educational institution (approximately $31,000 per student, per year, which is more than Harvard) has nothing more to offer you, they will let you loose on our wives, grandmothers, children, and honest, hard-working citizens. Tens of thousands of inmates receive their education in crime from older criminals with life tenure. Then they are released on our populace. We ruin most people by sending them to prison. People should not remain in prison unless they are a continuing danger to themselves and society.

Warriors, you do not ever want to become involved in this politically created industry. Once you are labeled a criminal, you will lose the opportunities to sell your labor and you will be stuck in the corrections quagmire forever.

Why are so many minorities involved in blue-collar crime? In every state of this ever great, ever expanding American empire, minorities make up a greater portion of the blue-collar crime element then whites. White-collar crime, like the owners of industry, is almost exclusively a white male domain. Approximately 65 percent of the 2,000,000 people incarcerated in the United States are young, non-white males. *There are more people behind bars per capita in the United States than in any country on earth.* And the overwhelming majority are non-white. The majority are in corrections for crimes committed under the influence of alcohol and or drugs. And at least 60 percent of the people behind bars are incarcerated initially for non-violent crimes.

I personally think we minorities are just not trying hard enough. I know our kids are smart enough to engage in bank embezzlement, securities fraud, check kiting schemes, antitrust and environmental crimes. These courses are typically not taught at Draper University and are usually reserved for the Ivy League federal prisons. I just know that if our kids had the opportunities to steal $600 million dollars like the Bonneville Pacific thieves, they too would engage in this behavior. As we get more minority college graduates, we too will have our share of white-collar criminals. I doubt however that the same ratio of minority prison population to general population will be seen in white-collar crime.

The closest minorities get to white-collar crime is the tremendously lucrative drug trade which, according to the United Nations, has gross revenue of over $400 billion dollars per year. Over 15,000,000 Americans consume illegal drugs, and over 1,000,000 non-violent people are behind bars on drug crimes. There are far too many black, Native Americans and Mexican males behind bars in the United States; and 60 percent of these for non-violent drug offenses. But that is to be expected. Our society's priorities are measured by the manner in which we allocate financial resources. We spend more money on prisons than on higher education.

There is a great temptation for minority children to do as the Russells, Forbes, Peabodys, and other rich white families, who in the early 1800s sold opium to China over the adamant protests of the Chinese government. But these rich white folks were not facing minimum mandatory sentencing guidelines of over ten years in prison for satisfying consumer demand. White Americans use drugs. Mexicans, Blacks and poor whites sell them. The Native American community has not yet given in completely to the lucrative drug trade. It is not worth the risk. More importantly, selling illegal drugs is just plain wrong. You do not sell substances to others that you know beforehand will harm them. You must behave better than that if you want to be successful; walk the more difficult path.

Let's face it, for millions of people in America life really sucks. This is why they self-medicate with illegal drugs and alcohol. They are spectators in the game of life because playing the game seems to be just too difficult. If warriors in Chief Tabby's day wanted to treat themselves to an herbal delight, he could not care less. The reason he did not care what people did to themselves was that he respected each member's absolute right to do as he pleased with his own body. Goshute land was a free nation where individual liberty actually meant something. Quite unlike America, the Goshute government was not so oppressive that every aspect of life of each tribal member was regulated into the ground. Chief Tabby saw the absolute wisdom of letting his people do stupid things and learning from their own hard lessons. If warriors were so stoned on drugs that they could not feed themselves, they did not have welfare, workers compensation, social security or Medicaid to carry their lazy, pitiful asses. If the warriors died from their own stupidity, the tribe and the gene pool was far better off. In other words, Chief Tabby did nothing about consensual crimes in his day because he knew the members of the tribe had the good sense to take care of their own behavior or would continue that behavior despite his disapproval.

Being in jail is a real drag. When I was sixteen and got busted in Ely, Nevada for underage drinking, my white Mormon stepmother Wyona responded to the Sheriff's call by saying, "I'm sorry I don't know anyone by that name." At the time I thought that was a real mean thing to do to a sixteen-year-old. It was tough love. I never went to jail as a prisoner again. Once was quite enough. So if you associate with people who crank out and are stoned, you had better hope like hell that you don't give them a ride anywhere. You will get in trouble. It is as smart as going into the forest after the medicine man has told you in advance that a snowstorm is coming and you need to stay in the village.

Blue-collar crime is very easy to prosecute. The pay is poor—on average less than $3,000 per robbery and less than $20,000 per drug deal. The time is long—six years for $3,000 and ten years for a $20,000 drug deal versus six months with an ankle bracelet for the $600 million theft in Bonneville Pacific. If you are not doing white-collar crime, plan on doing lots of time.

Yes, drugs are dangerous to warriors. Chief Tabby, nor any one else in this day of small hunting parties called corporations, would have you on his team if you were drugged out or drunk. The corrections industry is very dangerous. The criminal sentences are more dangerous then the drugs. You will lose your youth and your liberty. Stay away from it and you will likely save your life. But there are other even more dangerous behaviors you must understand.

The biggest danger in an urban environment comes from those closest to you. Be especially careful of who you choose for your mate. Those close to you can cause more harm than from any enemy you will encounter in the field of battle. If you cheat on your mate or if your mate is cheating on you, your entire house is completely insecure. You must have a secure castle to go out into the world and slay dragons! In an unstable home, you go to work with a gut that hurts. There is no sleep as all you can think of is the emotional pain you are enduring. Just understand that you cannot make people love you. *You* must love you. If you want a healthy home environment, be careful with those you keep in your home. If this means telling a drunk or stoned relative to leave… do it.

All you need is one divorce to ruin you financially for years. Divorces are among the most painful of all experiences. After the emotional pain is gone, the money has all gone to the lawyers. Some attorneys deliberately do divorces and bankruptcy. They delay the divorces and run up the costs. When their clients are broke, they file bankruptcy on their behalf, causing even more harm. Choose your mates carefully. A wrong choice can cost you years of financial ruin and untold emotional heartache.

How do you chose a good mate? Be a good mate. Be involved with someone who gives, not just takes. It is the tendency of some people who have a soft heart to attract people who constantly take and take and take. Their partners either leave them for someone else or they finally get tired of being used and get rid of their loser mates. In either event, after the emotional pain is healed, the financial cost is staggering. Successful people are usually in stable, long-term relationships. They don't mate shop at every bar and club or store, constantly looking for someone to make them happy. They love themselves and attract equals.

When we are young, it is very easy to mistake the allure of sex for love. My office has handled more than 275 divorces in 19 years. I think we saw just about every type of behavior imaginable. My favorite always is, "I love her, but I'm not in love with him." It takes two to make a good relationship, but only one to really screw things up. If you get involved with someone before you are age 25, there is a better than 90 percent chance you will split up. The same is true of cross-cultural and different religion relationships. Real love is a growth process that happens slowly after you are friends with a person.

Infatuation, which occurs because someone is physically attractive, ends very quickly when this pretty boy or girl becomes abusive. One pattern was very clear in 275 divorces: the more attractive the person, the more arrogance and the greater the likelihood of abuse. Some men and women have absolutely no respect for anyone other than the person in the mirror. A person can look real ugly when he is screaming at you or smacking you or running up bills, or being stoned out of his mind or drunk until they vomit. When a bad relationship ends, several months later, my clients will tell me they are so relieved to be out of the hell that was once part of their home.

Far too many relationships are bad. Ask yourself, how do people really treat each other when they are alone and the curtains and doors are closed. Some people are so cruel and horribly mean to each other, I am not surprised at the number of cases of domestic violence. I have seen women rip men off for tens of thousands of dollars and even put innocent men in prison. I have seen men break women's collar bones and jaws because they were so drunk that they thought their mate was an alien monster. The majority of people I have seen who have been physically, financially or emotionally injured have almost always suffered these injuries at the hands of their mate.

Be civil with each other both during your relationship and after it ends.

Have class when you go your separate ways. Recognize that sometimes you are just not compatible, and leave it at that. There is just no reason for being nasty and ugly with each other. Treat your mate or former mate with the manners and respect that you displayed when the relationship began. Relationships do end. Accept it and move on. If you lost your vehicle or house as a result of a bad relationship, start over. Don't look back at what you had. Cut your losses and move on. If you dwell on the loss, you are responsible for the pain, not your former mate. It is usually cheaper and far more profitable for people to quit fighting over what they had together and accept the fact that their relationship failed. Profit comes from living today and planning for tomorrow. It does not come from trying to change yesterday. Lost your car or your house? Buy another vehicle and find another place to live.

As you are careful choosing your mate or people in your home, watch your hunting partners. There is nothing worse then having to carry someone who will eat from your plate but won't carry his weight. Partners, if they are good partners, can be a blessing. In addition to the safety of numbers, a doctor usually needs a helper to assist in carrying the patient. In business or love, your partner can help you or break you. Only you can make you. I have had great partners over the years and I have had slackers. Some were so dishonest I eventually couldn't stand being in the same room with them. One partner got the ax after four months in business. I caught him lying and simply told him he was on his own. When hunting, good partners can help to clean the game and cut the meat after your successful shots. Other partners can claim all of the meat for their own and leave you with guts and gristle if you let them. Since money is food and shelter, if your partners are dishonest, plan on going hungry and not having a safe place to sleep.

Expect others to lie in money matters and be surprised when they tell you the truth. Listen to what they say and be surprised if they follow through. I give people one shot to perform. After I lose a small amount of money, they will never get work from me again. The successful people you will meet do what they say, and there are no surprises. Hunt with people who have as much to gain or lose as you do.

There are those who through some fault in their character are just not capable of seeing beyond today. There is no reason to save money for tomorrow, as tomorrow will take care of tomorrow. They are always reacting to events in life instead of making plans and successfully carrying them out. Without a road map, the bumps on the journey of life constantly cause them irritation. Partners who have nothing to lose never fear losing everything that includes violating the laws of the land. Jail is no concern. At least this place will provide a roof and free meals. People will only take advantage of us if we willingly let them.

If you are in the forest and walk toward a herd of elk, making noise and not being careful to hide yourself, plan on not eating elk. Don't be loud and proud. Don't ever flaunt your money. If you do, others will make it their quest to get your money. People who really have money do not let others know this simple fact of life. Quiet hunters are successful hunters.

The city is dangerous with people who want your game that you work so hard to capture. They want your money arrows that you work so hard to craft. They are either oblivious to what it takes to be a successful hunter, or are aiming at stealing the bounty of your labors from you rather than exerting the effort to achieve their own success. Once you have a small home, all of your lazy relatives and friends who are unwilling to pay the price of success will want to come and live with you. Every one of my friends who own homes has at one time or another put up one of her relatives or friends. At one time or another, this small house would better have been labeled the heartbreak hotel. In addition to my ex-drunk, drug-addicted brother-in-law (one year), ex mother-in-law (one year), friends from California (one month with large dogs), nephews (two years), there were several ex-girl friends who were entertaining but at times expensive to maintain (five years). All added their own memories to this fascinating home in the suburbs with its neighborhood gunfire and criminals on the prowl.

A small house is also helpful because, like a small cave, tepee or cabin, there just is not enough room for relatives and friends for pro-tracted stays. I remember coming home one time from a business trip and one of my doors was kicked in. There were beer cans from one end of the house to the other. Two of my worthless drug-using relatives were asleep on the couches and my previously clean home was completely trashed. Like freshly caught fish, friends and relatives bless you by leav-ing within three days. Of course, when their phone is disconnected they will stop to see you and make long distance calls while you are not home. It's okay, you have a good job and you can afford it. Despite a full economy, they are unemployed and are "just about to get hired." You can always borrow money…

Another big danger to avoid in the city is debt. With the exception of your home, *Never borrow money*. Bankers are such caring individuals. I place them right up there with insurance agents in terms of public service. They do not give a damn if you live or die. They will lend you money if they see a good way to take everything you have ever worked for should times become tough and you can't repay them. They earn interest on the money you borrow. You pay them interest and therefore never get ahead financially. Never borrow arrows if all you are doing is hunting for someone else.

I have had several cases involving minority clients whose vehicles were repossessed despite being current on their payments and having small children to support. When a banker turns you down for a loan, thank him. He sees something so wrong with the deal that he is not willing to share the risk with you. He is seeing a danger that you are blinded to.

There are other ways to borrow. These are known as hard money loans. Congressman Chris Cannon had so mismanaged his finances that he was forced to borrow one million dollars from a very tough individual named Tom Gallagher. Tom is my friend who lives in Florida. He does not have a social security number and uses enforcers to collect his money. In one of his loans, an individual did not pay him $70,000. Somehow this debtor had an accident in which his legs were broken. Congressman Chris Cannon repaid his one million dollar loan. And he paid it on time, high interest and all.

There are clearly two types of people in the world—those who earn interest and those who pay it. The more debt, the more of your future you lose. If you cannot pay for a car or truck with cash, ask yourself, do you really need it? What will happen if your company fires you or you hate your job so much that you quit? How will you make the payments? If you are buying a car on payments, you are required to have full coverage for your vehicle insurance.

This legal requirement that we have insurance has made that industry legalized gambling. You are betting over one hundred dollars per month that something is going to go wrong, that you are going to be involved in a major car wreck, get sick, have your house burn down ... and soon. In Vegas when you gamble, you are betting that something is going to go right ... you are going to win. In both cases you are out your money. Since you have to have insurance, you should keep your costs as low as possible. Shop around. Loans are made for a reason—to make money for someone else if you are foolish enough to borrow. Most people in the city owe so much debt that they are slaves to banks and finance companies. Some live at the level or above the level of their income in expensive homes with large utility bills. They drive cars with large car payments and large insurance payments. But they own virtually nothing. They are frauds, and their lives fall apart with the first economic storm or major health problem.

Be extremely careful of doctors and the entire medical profession. Unlike medicine men, many of today's doctors could not care less if you live or die. In one California city, the death rate went down after doctors had a strike. There are so many unnecessary surgeries and unnecessary prescriptions and missed diagnoses that you take your life in your hands when you visit a medical center. They just want your money so you can pay for their huge homes, fancy cars and high-priced vacations. The medical profession will take your money. But don't believe that this interesting profession can give you a blessing of good health that only God can bestow and you can properly maintain. It is not that difficult. Eat less and exercise more. Being in good shape is fun.

I do practice workers compensation law with Mexicans and Indians who constantly get hurt on the job. Many hurt their backs. We are now finding out that surgery, which makes doctors some very good money, does not necessarily make the person whole. If you hurt your back, lose weight and improve your stomach and leg muscles. Don't smoke. For some reason, smoking is very damaging to back injuries, as if the nicotine stimulates the nerve endings and causes more back pain.

What would happen if you realized that you, not your doctors, are responsible for your health? Having good health is a true blessing from God. Keeping your good health is your responsibility as a young adult. Preventing medical problems is your best bet at keeping your health costs down. If you don't eat right, smoke and fail to exercise, expect health problems even Dr. Koop cannot solve.

Since I am wheelchair bound, I do not have any health insurance. So I work out one hour each day, watch what I eat, and make sure that I don't get totally stressed out. There is no way I am going to give some insurance agent with six children $500 per month for a medical policy that has an exclusion that does not cover my neurological disease, transverse mylities, because it is in fact a pre-existing condition. Like one third of this country, I am uninsured.

Also, watch out for the lawyers. Law is the dumping ground of all major professions. People could not make it in engineering so they went into law. They could not make it in sociology or history or art or English or psychology, so they became attorneys. Most attorneys did not choose law as a first profession. Utah has two law schools and more than 9,000 attorneys from Ogden to Provo. Over half make less than $30,000 per year. In Southern California there are over 100,000 attorneys. In Chicago there are more attorneys than in all of Japan. Most attorneys can barely afford to pay attention, much less their bills. If you checked on the trust accounts of every attorney in America, you would find that the majority misused their clients' funds. These guys and gals are desperate. If they have a large paying client, the case will drag on until the client can no long afford the legal fees and finally agrees to settle.

If you are in the public eye, attorneys will sue you. You become a target. I had one very visible client who told me, "I don't have any idea why I am being sued." I explained to him, "You have money, don't you." Lawyers do not sue poor people. Prosecutors do that with our criminal drug laws. Every business that I know of or have invested in is being sued for something. Every company I own stock in is being sued, usually in frivolous class-action shareholder suits. Some firms specialize in doing nothing but filing class action suits. Try to put yourself in the position that you don't need an attorney. Litigation is for losers. The reason is, someone in litigation is always losing. The only good use of a lawyer is to prevent and protect yourself from litigation before the issue arises.

Likewise, if you stay away from the corrections industry you will not need a criminal lawyer. Make no mistake about it; if you are a minority, the police will sometimes beat the hell out of you. The police report will say, "It happened by accident" or "the suspect resisted." When you are pulled over by the police, raise your hands high into the air, do not make any sudden movements, do not argue with the police, listen carefully to what you are being instructed to do, and do it. Make it clear to the officer that you do not have a weapon and you are not a criminal. Look into the officer's eyes. Realize that even if you go to jail after this arrest, it is better than being shot dead by an overreaction from a young or inexperienced police officer. I have lost track of how many times I have been pulled over. I have had officers pull guns on me twice. Both times I did not over react. I am alive to tell you, do not make any sudden movements or give cause for alarm.

Understand that police officers have battle fatigue. They are so accustomed to dealing with drunks, drug addicts, and violent people, you could easily be mistaken for some criminal just because you are poor or your skin is dark. Have street smarts and patience. The police officers are human and are just as prone to making mistakes as you or anyone else. I have had clients who have had their teeth kicked in by Utah's finest. Then they were deported. I have had clients who had their homes raided and everyone was placed on the floor with police officers pointing guns at them in front of their children.

I know of one case where the police officers went into the wrong house on a drug bust. The homeowner mistook the police for burglars and pointed his gun at them. They killed him in front of his children. The family never filed suit. The case quietly died. I turned down a case where a young girl was shot through the head by a police officer after she pulled out a hairbrush. She was high on illegal drugs and had just committed a felony. I once had a case where the police mistook a Latin businessman for a gang member and beat the living hell out of him. A friend, Ed Havas, one of the nation's best personal injury attorneys, litigated a case where the police shot through the back window of a car and did permanent brain damage to a young Latin male who was stealing beer from a convenience store. Havas was not able to help that family. I just finished a case where the police dislocated the arm of a young man who would not follow instructions and leave when he was told to leave.

Respect those in authority as the warrior respects the grizzly bear. The bear harbors no specific animosity for the individual warrior, but because both hunt in the same range with divergent goals, there are bound to be confrontations. The police, like the claws of the bear, are not to be reasoned with, but merely respected for their ability to deliver brute and deadly force.

Your poor planning in life does not create some emergency for some sorry attorney or over-reacting Deputy Barney Fife. The best situation is to not need a criminal attorney or civil attorney as a result of civil fraud. By being careful with your money and your behavior, you will not put yourself in a situation where an officer or attorney is going to aim the law at you.

Unfortunately for the Indians, the laws of man rather than nature are the nemesis in urban survival. The two areas where the Indian, minority and poor white communities need the most help are law and medicine. Too many lawyers today could not give a damn about truth and justice. Their first concern is getting paid. Some deliberately use perjured testimony to win at any cost. They hide evidence that they know will clearly lose their cases. They instruct their clients to lie. They have no honor. Hopefully, these are the exceptions. Most attorneys try to do justice. The great ones have class.

Since money attracts accountants, most of you reading this book don't see an accountant until tax time. Get only the most basic insurance for your small house, for your paid-for used vehicle, for your health, and for your business. Life insurance is a joke. Unless you have children under ten stay completely away from it. Shop your insurance. Make them give you a better rate and force competition by shopping around. Some insurance companies price fix by having the same policies on those whom they will insure and whom they will turn down. When my son's car was stolen from my front yard, my own insurance company accused me of stealing his car. After three months and a full investigation where I threw the investigator out of my office for accusing me of theft, I drafted a complaint that was going to be filed in district court. They paid for the car. These are just dangers to your purse that I have been discussing in this chapter. There are other more lasting dangers.

In the city there are criminals who are killers. And the majority of them kill members of the minority communities. These are people in our society who are dangerous not only to themselves, but to those all around them. Having nothing to lose, they are, therefore, unafraid to lose everything. They are full of anger from abusive childhoods or other contributing situations. Alcohol incites their fury. Despite popular government propaganda, there are very few killings by people who are high on drugs. These killers are completely and totally lost—too high to carry out intentional harm or even care. They have seen killings and participated in them, but the actual cause of death is usually accidental rather than the result of a meticulously executed plan. They will kill you and not understand or care that it is wrong. Killers almost always know their victim. If you know someone that engages in reckless, dangerous behavior, stay away from him. America leads the industrial world in murders; there were more than 23,000 in 1998.

Some situations will create killers out of otherwise almost sane people. Involving yourself with someone else's mate will almost always ensure some violence. If you are a liar or cheat, expect a physical confrontation either from your mate whose feelings have just been devastated, or from her mate who is so angry that you had better hope that he doesn't have a gun handy. Leave any partner who cheats you. It is that simple.

Killing someone over a cheating mate is gross stupidity. And getting killed over a failed romance is just as tragic. You can replace your small home, your junk car and your just-over-broke job. You cannot replace your life or your freedom. People of color are the most frequent victims of blue-collar crime. This is true of Native Americans, Mexicans, African Americans, and poor whites. We get shot. We get killed. And we shoot each other; usually under the influence of alcohol or drugs. Give a killer a gun and alcohol, and you will have several dead relatives and friends.

One absolutely amazing discovery about the Utah State Prison is that so many people were in there for killing their girlfriends, wives, their lovers and other triangle participants. These deaths were totally unnecessary. If you are not in love with someone and if someone is not in love with you, don't ever invade that person's rights by doing harm. You are not God. It is someone's absolute right to be with or without you. This is also your right. Control your anger, walk away alive and free.

This is easy advice on a difficult path. The city is dangerous because people are crowded together from different families, cultures, backgrounds, and behaviors. These are the people who inhabit our cities. People kill people. Not storms, not earthquakes, not the summer heat or winter cold. People are the human animal that becomes intoxicated and violent. Be careful of the man who has nothing to lose, for if he loses everything he loses nothing. However, you are responsible for your own behavior. If you associate with angry alcoholics, expect violence. If you are lucky enough to have survived without a criminal record and still are holding down a job, have avoided drugs and alcohol, stay completely clear of the drug trade. Like the growl of the grizzly bear, our society has given you fair warning of its intolerance of drug use or trafficking. If you fall into this pit, you will never get out.

6

THE FAILED WAR ON DRUGS

Insanity is doing the same thing over and over again and expecting a different result.

Arron Nelson

The so-called war on drugs, by any objective measure, is a total and complete failure. Instead of preventing crime, the drug laws create crime. Although this is certainly not the same society that introduced and later repealed prohibition on alcohol, some analogies are appropriate. According to the US Census Data and the FBI Uniform Crime Reports (UCR) in 1933, the homicide rate peaked during prohibition at 9.7 per 100,000 people. Approximately 50 years later, the homicide rate peaked again at 10 per 100,000. Most of today's drug crimes are turf related. For example, in 1988 in New York City, 85 percent of crack-related crimes were caused primarily by territorial disputes between rival crack dealers.

The drug war is creating an entire new industry that is a danger to civil liberties, our freedom, and our pocket book. According to the FBI Uniform Crime Reports, in 1973, there were 328,670 arrests logged in for drug law violations. In 1996, that number rose to 1,506,200 arrests for drug law violations. Despite the propaganda promoted by politicians, the majority of people arrested are not major drug dealers. They are young kids just like you.

Alcohol is associated with more violent crime than any illegal drug, including crack, cocaine, and heroin. Twenty-one percent of violent felons in state prisons committed their crimes while under the influence of alcohol alone. Only three percent were high on crack or powder cocaine alone, and only one percent were using heroin alone.

The harsh drug laws inflict greater penalties for low-level mules and small-time drug dealers than most Nazi war criminals served at Nuremberg. This inequity has created the largest prison system in the world.

Crime and Prison

In June 1997, there were 1.7 million inmates nationally: 1.2 million in state and federal prisons and 1.5 million in local jails. Assuming recent incarceration rates remain unchanged, an estimated one of every 20 Americans (or 5 percent) can be expected to serve time in prison during their lifetime. For African-American men, the number is greater than one in four, or 28.5 percent. The real significance of this discrepancy in terms of societal cost is that a prison record all but bars any contribution to society by the ex-con. The longer sentences imposed by minimum mandatory guidelines only exacerbate the loss.

In the *Sourcebook of Criminal Justice Statistics*, the Bureau of Justice Statistics estimates the total costs of our judicial system for 1993. That year, the United States had 1,364,881 adult jail and prison inmates. Based on this information, our cost per inmate year was:

+ corrections spending alone: $23,406 per inmate;
+ corrections, judicial and legal costs: $39,201 per inmate;
+ corrections, judicial, legal and police costs: $71,465 per inmate, or more than twice the amount of money required to attend Harvard annually.

More than 80 percent of the increase in the federal prison population from 1985 to 1995 was connected to drug convictions. In 1993, nearly 17 percent of the total federal prison population were drug-offenders with no prior criminal history. Eighty-four percent of the increase in state and federal prison admissions since 1980 was accounted for by nonviolent offenders. In 1995, only 13 percent of all state prisoners were violent offenders.

In 1985, our incarceration rate was 313 per 100,000 of population. By the year 2000 it is 645 per 100,000, which is three to 10 times higher than rates of the other modern democratic societies. The largest single factor contributing to this imprisonment wave is an eight-fold rise in drug arrests. In 1980, when illicit drug use was peaking, there were about 50,000 men and women in prison for violating drug laws. In 1998, there were about 400,000. As of 1996, there were 5.5 million adults under some form of correctional supervision—prison, jail, probation or parole. This translates into one of every 35 adults. The overall U.S. incarceration rate is six times that of its nearest Western competitors. We have more people behind bars than any other democracy on earth. With less than 5 percent of the world's population, we have over 25 percent of the worlds' inmates. This is the true reflection of American society and life in the industrial age.

Incarceration is supported by politicians who want to be "tough on crime." This attitude has translated into passing more and harsher drug penalties. If one compares 1996 to 1984, the crime index is 13 points higher. This dramatic increase occurred during an era of mandatory minimum sentencing and the "three strikes you're out" philosophy. According to the Department of Justice, studies of recidivism report that "the amount of time inmates serve in prison does not increase or decrease the likelihood of recidivism, whether recidivism is measured as parole revocation, re-arrest, reconviction, or return to prison." Since the enactment of mandatory minimum sentencing for drug users, the Federal Bureau of Prisons budget has increased by 1,350 percent. Its budget has jumped from $220 million in 1986 to $3.19 billion in 1997. Prison is now an industry. Just like war.

The result of spending on our newest industry—the corrections industry—is less tax money is available for other public needs, like education. From 1984 to 1996, California built 21 new prisons, and only one new university. California's state government expenditures on prisons increased 30 percent from 1987 to 1995, while spending on higher education decreased by 18 percent.

Economics of the Drug Trade and Prison Industry

The fuel for the drug war is money. Because the government has intervened in the marketplace, illegal cocaine, heroin and methamphetamine are among the most lucrative commodities in human history. According to the United Nations, drug trafficking is a $400 billion per year industry, equaling eight percent of the world's trade. This is greater than the exports of the automobile industry, worldwide.

My law partner, Scott York, believes:

> *Americans buy 95 percent of all illicit drugs. The price of drugs is made artificially high by a U.S. drug policy cre-*

ated and perpetuated by U.S. politicians. In the United States, politicians can only achieve and maintain office with the sanction and support of big industry. Politicians are inherently beholden to the dictates of big industry. Big industry is only an extension of its source of funding. U.S. banks and insurance companies fund 85 percent of all big industry. Insurance companies and U.S. banks also fund 85 percent of the loans made by the International Monetary Fund and World Bank. Third World, drug-producing countries owe huge sums to the IMF, the World Bank and our own multi-national banks. If drug proceeds from American sales were not available to Third World governments, these nations would default on their loans to the IMF and World Bank. Drug cartels are in control of both drug proceeds and their governments, and the governments are powerless to impair drug production and distribution to the United States. Therefore, despite the overwhelming evidence of the futility and destructiveness of the war on drugs, the true powers that be—U.S. banks and insurance companies—will continue to put profit first and ignore the societal cost of the drug war. Meanwhile their puppet politicians continue to mouth the rhetorical 'tough on crime' chant. And the American voter is just gullible enough to buy it. If the politicians came right out and taxed us enough to pay off U.S. banks for Third World loans, we would scream to high heaven. But that is exactly what is happening; minorities and the poor are paying artificially inflated prices for the drugs that numb them, and then the middle class pays to cage them. At the end of the day, the rich count their money and keep the benefits of America for themselves.

His pessimism may not paint a rosy picture of our society, but it could just raise enough consciousness and discomfort to encourage other citizens to try to change the status quo.

It costs approximately $8.6 billion a year to keep drug law violators behind bars. Not including federal funds, states spent $28.9 billion on corrections in 1997 alone. By comparison, states only spent $14.0 billion on welfare to the poor. And since the people behind bars are parents, we taxpayers pay the increased costs of the inmates' offspring who end up on public assistance.

A 1998 report by the National Institute on Drug Abuse (NIDA) and the National Institute on Alcohol Abuse and Alcoholism (NIAAA) estimated the economic costs of alcohol abuse in the United States to be $148.02 billion in 1992, 80 percent of which were due to alcohol-related illness. This 80 percent figure includes health care expenditures, impaired productivity and premature death. By contrast, drug abuse cost a total of $97.66 billion in 1992, of which less than 40 percent ($38.71 billion) was drug-related death. This figure includes $4.16 billion in HIV/AIDS and Hepatitis treatment costs. Sixty percent of drug costs were applied to drug-related law enforcement, incarceration and crime. Only three percent of drug costs were for victims of drug-related crime.

According to the United Nations, illegal drugs create enormous profits. One kilogram of raw opium in Pakistan averages $90, but sells for $290,000 in the United States. The United Nations also states that profits in illegal drugs are so inflated, that three-quarters of all drug shipments would have to be intercepted to reduce seriously the profitability of the business. Current efforts only intercept 30 percent of cocaine shipments and less than 15 percent of heroin shipments.

Enormous sums of money fuel the industry we call the drug war. In 1969, $65 million was spent by the Nixon administration on this war; in 1982 the Reagan administration spent $1.65 billion; and in 1998 the Clinton administration raised this amount to over $17 billion. Several foreign countries involved in the international drug trade owe substantial amounts of money to the International Monetary Fund and American banks. For several drug-producing countries, illegal drugs are the largest sources of revenue. Recent estimates indicate that Colombia repatriates $7 billion in drug profits annually. This is nearly as high as the total legitimate exports for Colombia, which were $7.6 billion in 1993. Without the drug trade Colombia's economy would decrease by 50 percent. Their government does not have the power to cut their economy in half and cause further poverty in an already poor country.

Corruption at home and abroad is an inevitable result when so much money is involved. It is estimated that Colombian narcotics cartels spend $100 million on bribes to Colombian officials each year. In 1993, 98 percent of Bolivia's foreign exchange earnings from goods and services came from the cocoa market. In one of my many drug cases, the police stole over $2,000,000. In another, four kilos of high-grade cocaine had disappeared before the trial. In another, $1.2 million dollars in cash disappeared. At home and abroad, corruption is inevitable.

Despite the rhetoric about the threat of the illegal drug trade, the single largest cause of death in the United States today is lack of exercise.

Whether legal or illicit, we are a drugged society depending upon chemical help for pain, sleep, weight loss, skin care, and even sex.

Environmental Consequences of the War on Drugs

The war on drugs has very high ecological costs that could damage many future generations. In order to comply with United States' demands to stop cocoa production, Colombia uses aerial spraying to drop herbicides on illicit crops. Since these crops are the peasants' only source of income, they move into the Amazon rain forest and farm on steep hillsides. This constant push on peasants has led to the clearing of over 1.75 million acres of rain forest.

When sprayed, the herbicide Glyphosate can drift for a half mile. In Colombia, where the herbicide Glyphosate is sprayed from airplanes, children have lost hair and suffered diarrhea as a result of its application. In its attempts to control peasant production of illicit crops, the Colombian government dumps chemical herbicides on over 100,000 acres every year. Despite a record year of aerial cocoa fumigation, Colombia's Ruben Olarte, the chief anti-narcotics officer, labeled the program a failure, noting that cocoa production had increased from 111,000 acres in 1994 to over 195,000 acres by the start of 1998.

Colombia's forests account for 10 percent of the entire world's biodiversity, making it the second most bio-diverse country in the world in terms of species per land unit. Deforestation in Colombia induced by the drug war has led experts to theorize that Colombia could become another Somalia or Ethiopia within 50 years. It is a fast growing population that is larger than the food production can support because of poor agricultural soils or techniques.

Again, since it is illegal to manufacture cocaine, its producers must hide their facilities in the fragile rain forests of South America—making it impossible to dispose properly of chemical wastes created during drug processing. It is estimated that the unregulated manufacture of cocaine results in 10 million liters of sulfuric acid, 16 million liters of ethyl ether, eight million liters of acetone, and from 40 to 770 million liters of kerosene being poured directly into the ground in the Andean region that is mainly Colombia.

In Colombia alone, as a result of the unregulated manufacture of cocaine, it is estimated that more than 200,000 tons of chemical wastes are dumped into the ground and streams each year. Since the entire planet is ecologically connected, damage to the rain forest in Colombia or elsewhere damages us all.

Property Forfeitures

It is in the nature of governments to become oppressive. My Spanish ancestors had forfeiture laws down to a fine science. Long before the Nazis, the Spanish Inquisition would routinely accuse the unpopular elements in society (namely Jews) of not towing the party line. Today's drug war has established new laws which have never existed in the brief history of our republic. These laws run completely counter to the principles of due process. For example, the concept that one should be heard by a court of law before government acts or overreacts is being eroded by the war on drugs. Further, our forfeiture laws grant the right to government to take property on mere accusations. They are a direct attack on our Constitution. As in the days of the Nazis and the Spanish Inquisition, money is a key motive for forfeitures.

Federal forfeitures totaled approximately $730 million in 1994. During a 10-month national survey, it was discovered that 80 percent of people who had property forfeited were never charged with a crime. Innocent ownership is not a constitutional defense to forfeiture, and the U.S. Supreme Court has held, in *Bennis v. Michigan,* that property may be taken from an owner who had no knowledge of its illegal use.

Forfeiture can be used even when there is insufficient evidence to make a criminal case against the defendant. The government need only seize the assets, and it is then up to the owner to challenge the seizure in a costly and unpromising hearing. As a civil action against the property itself, few of the constitutional safeguards imposed on criminal prosecutions apply to forfeiture. There is no presumption of innocence, no right to an attorney, and no objection to hearsay.

The burden of proof is reversed: once the government establishes probable cause to believe the property is subject to forfeiture, the burden shifts to the property owner to prove by a preponderance of the evidence that the property does not belong to the government. There is no constitutional requirement that the property owner be prosecuted for the underlying criminal activity prior to action against the property. Forfeiture may occur even if the owner is acquitted of the crime.

Forfeiture laws have not simply enhanced the ability of law enforcement to do its job, but rather have changed the nature of the job itself. Both the crime prevention and due process goals of our criminal justice system are compromised when salaries, continued tenure, equipment, modernization, and budgets depend on how much money can be generated by forfeitures.

According to a 1998 article published in the *University of Chicago Law Review*, the ability of law enforcement agencies to benefit financially from forfeited assets, and the provision of large block grants from Congress to fight the drug trade "have distorted governmental policy making and law enforcement." The authors believe that "the law enforcement agenda that targets assets rather than crime (the 80 percent of seizures that are unaccompanied by any criminal prosecution, the plea bargains that favor drug kingpins and penalize the 'mules' without assets to trade, the reverse stings that target drug buyers rather than drug sellers, the overkill in agencies involved in even minor arrests, the massive shift in resources towards federal jurisdiction over local law enforcement) is largely the unplanned by-product of this economic incentive structure."

The Department of Justice has periodically adopted as their official policy the practice of forfeiture as a priority over the prosecution of violent and property crimes. For instance, in 1989, all U.S. Attorneys were directed "to increase forfeiture production" including "divert[ing] personnel from other activities or to seek assistance from other U.S. Attorney's offices, the Criminal Division, and the Executive Office for United States Attorneys."

Interdiction and Enforcement

Interdiction efforts intercept only 10 to 15 percent of the heroin and 30 percent of the cocaine. Since drug traffickers earn gross profit margins of up to 300 percent, at least 75 percent of international drug shipments would need to be intercepted to reduce substantially the profitability of drug trafficking.

Without destroying the Constitution, law enforcement is not capable of stopping the supply of drugs despite the increase in funding. Thirteen trucks of cocaine are enough to satisfy U.S. demand for one year. The United States has 88,633 miles of shoreline, 300 ports of entry, and more than 7,500 miles of border with Mexico and Canada. Stopping drugs at the borders is like trying to find a needle in a haystack.

Illegal drugs are an international business enterprise, and drug dealers use common market principles. One of the major problems with supply reduction efforts (source control, interdiction, and domestic enforcement) is that suppliers simply produce for the market what they would have produced anyway, plus enough extra to cover anticipated government seizures. Sometimes the busts are set up to allow the government to take their necessary public relations quota and appear to be doing something.

From 1985 to 1995, the federal drug control budget has increased almost five-fold, from about $2.7 billion to about $13.25 billion. Yet, in that same period, the percentage of 12th grade students that reported marijuana as "fairly easy" or "very easy" to obtain increased from 85.5 percent in 1985 to 89.6 percent in 1995.

Enforcement and attempts at interdiction are a complete disaster. All we have accomplished with this strategy is a greater prison population. To achieve a one percent reduction in U.S. cocaine consumption, the United States could spend an additional $34 million on drug treatment programs, or 20 times more, $783 million, on efforts to eradicate the supply at the source.

Getting Tough on Crime

It is amazing to watch political candidates constantly harp about how they are going to get tougher on the war on drugs—a war that they created and from which we suffer. Our drug laws are harsh beyond belief. But like every other aspect of the war on drugs, they have completely failed. Mandatory minimums have not actually reduced sentencing discretion. Control has merely been transferred from judges to prosecutors. If a prosecutor wants to cut you a deal, your client will receive less time. It's that simple.

This perversion of our legal system is new to our history. Prosecutors, not judges, have the discretion to decide whether to reduce a charge, whether to accept or deny a plea bargain, whether to reward or deny a defendant's "substantial assistance" or cooperation in the prosecution of someone else, and ultimately, to determine what the final sentence will be. In every case I have had in 19 years of practice, the corporate executive drug dealers never even entered the country. Like any top-level corporate executive, they leave the line work to low-paid, poorly educated, expendable employees who not surprisingly make up the bulk of our prison population. Fifty-five percent of all federal drug defendants are low-level offenders—the mules or street-dealers. Only 11 percent are classified as high-level dealers. According to the U.S. Sentencing Commission, only 5.5 percent of federal crack defendants are considered high-level crack dealers.

The result of this quagmire is more government spending on a failed policy, more people on public assistance, and greater costs for businessmen because of more dangerous streets and higher taxes. Since the enactment of mandatory minimum sentencing for drug users, the Federal Bureau of Prisons budget increased by more than 1,350 percent, or from $220 million in 1986 to about $3.19 billion in 1997.

The Military and the War on Drugs

Here are some historical footnotes that seem unimportant to our politicians and our courts. Yet, they help set the initial framework for the military and the war on drugs.

1878 — The Posse Comitatus Act makes it illegal for the military to act as police on U.S. territory or waters.

1981 — Posse Comitatus Act is amended to allow limited military involvement in policing.

1991 — Posse Comitatus Act is amended to allow counter-drug training of civilian police by the military.

1995 — Joint Task Force 6, under direction of the Secretary of Defense, is expanded to the entire continental United States. It has 700 troops, including 125 combat-ready troops on the U.S.-Mexican border.

May 1997 — Esequiel Hernandez becomes the first U.S. citizen shot and killed by JTF-6 troops.

The National Guard currently has more counter-narcotics officers than the DEA has special agents on duty. Each day it is involved in 1,300 counter-drug operations and has 4,000 troops on drug duty. Eighty-nine percent of police departments have paramilitary units, and 46 percent have been trained by active duty armed forces. The most common use of paramilitary units is serving drug-related search warrants (usually no-knock entries into private homes). Twenty percent of police departments use paramilitary units to patrol urban areas.

Everyone should be skeptical of using the world's most powerful military to attempt to stop the voluntary behaviors of 15,000,000 Americans. History has already suffered the experience of militaries directed at their own civilians. Even the most hardened question this shift in government policy.

In 1996, "Drug Czar" Retired General Barry McCaffrey said of the drug war, "It makes us all very uncomfortable to see uniformed military units getting heavily involved." Despite the similarities to uniformed Nazi SS troops on the streets of Germany policing (targeting) alleged deviant behaviors (being Jewish), not enough people in this country seem to realized that we have the power to vote our politicians out of office and end their reign of intolerance before our Constitution is completely undermined. But we had better do something fast; remember that you cannot vote once you are convicted of a felony.

Drugs, Race, and Prison

The disturbing evidence of the racist nature of the war on drugs is overwhelming. Between 1990 and 1996, the number of black men and women in federal prison for violent and property crimes decreased by 726. Despite these reductions in violent and property crime sentences, 12,852 black men and women were added to federal prisons for drug law violations over the same period.

My friends in the minority community have argued that the war on drugs is in reality a war on minorities. In 19 years of practice, the great majority of defendants I've seen in state and federal courts have been either non-white or poor whites. Only 11 percent of the nation's drug users are black; however blacks constitute almost 37 percent of those arrested for drug violations, over 42 percent of those in federal prisons for drug violations, and almost 60 percent of those in state prisons for drug felonies. Of course, the vast majority of drug abusers are white, but then again, no one is busting down doors for possession of Prozac.

This war on drugs has had a horrendous impact on minority communities. One in three black men between the ages of 20 and 29 years old is under correctional supervision or control. At current levels of incarceration, newborn black males in this country have a greater than one in four chance of going to prison during their lifetimes, while Latin-American males have a one in 6 chance, and white males have a one in 23 chance of serving time.

In 1986, before mandatory minimums for crack offenses became effective, the average federal drug offense sentence for blacks was 11 percent higher than for whites. Four years later, following the implementation of harsher drug sentencing laws, the average federal drug offense sentence was 49 percent higher for blacks.

Fifty-four percent of blacks convicted of drug offenses get sentenced to prison versus 34 percent of whites convicted of the same offenses. Forty-four percent of blacks get prison sentences for possession versus 29 percent of whites. Sixty percent of blacks are sentenced to prison for trafficking while 37 percent of whites are sentenced to prison for the same crime.

Despite similar or equal levels of illicit drug use during pregnancy, black women are 10 times more likely than white women to be reported to child welfare agencies for prenatal drug use. Across the board, the criminalization of drug addiction impedes access to healthcare. The Hispanic community has been disproportionately affected by HIV/AIDS. Although Hispanic persons only represent 12 percent of the U.S. population, they represent 17.8 percent of all AIDS cases. In 1995, the incarceration rate for white and Latin-American women combined was 68 per 100,000. For black women it was 456 per 100,000.

All major Western European nations' incarceration rates are about or below 100 per 100,000. In the United States, in 1995, the incarceration rate for African-American women was 456 per 100,000, and for African-American men 6,926 per 100,000. Since blacks and other minorities are disenfranchised by the war on drugs, the pressure on politicians lessens to change these horrible laws. Approximately 1.46 million black men out of a total voting population of 10.4 million have lost their right to vote because of felony convictions.

Treatment versus Criminalization

Addiction is first and foremost a medical problem, not a criminal problem. We need to change our drug laws and direct federal funding away from enforcement and toward a medical solution. Treatment is 10 times more cost effective than interdiction in reducing the use of cocaine in the United States. A recent study by the RAND Corporation found that every additional dollar invested in substance abuse treatment saves taxpayers $7.46 in societal costs. The same study found that additional domestic law enforcement efforts cost 15 times as much as treatment to achieve the same reduction in societal costs.

When analyzing options to reduce the societal costs of cocaine usage, we should consider the following relationships. For every additional $1.00 spent on enforcement versus treatment, the societal benefits can be listed accordingly:

1. source-country control- a LOSS of 85 cents;
2. interdiction- a LOSS of 68 cents;
3. enforcement- a LOSS of 48 cents

However, the treatment GAIN is $7.46! We include among the societal costs crime, violence, and loss of productivity. In 1992, the U.S. government spent only seven percent of its drug-control budget on treatment; the remaining 93 percent of its budget went to ineffective programs of source control, interdiction and law-enforcement.

The National Treatment Improvement Evaluation Study (NTIES) found that with treatment, drug selling decreased by 78 percent, shoplifting declined by almost 82 percent, and assaults declined by 78 percent. Furthermore, there was a 64 percent decrease in arrests for any crime, and the percentage of people who largely supported themselves through illegal activity dropped by nearly half—decreasing more than 48 percent.

In 1997 NTIES concluded, "Treatment appears to be cost effective, particularly when compared to incarceration, which is often the alternative. Treatment costs ranged from a low of $1,800 per client to a high of approximately $6,800 per client." By contrast, the average cost of incarceration in 1993 (the most recent year available) was $23,406 per inmate per year. Tuition at Harvard and Notre Dame was approximately $20,000.

A recent study by researchers at Substance Abuse Mental Health Services Administration has indicated that 48 percent of the need for drug treatment, not including alcohol abuse, is unmet in the United States. Treatment decreased welfare use by 10.7 percent and increased employment by 18.7 percent after one year, according to the 1996 National Treatment Improvement Evaluation Study.

According to the National Center on Addiction and Substance Abuse (NCASA), the cost of providing treatment for inmates, accompanied by education, job training and health care, would average about $6,500 per inmate. For each inmate that becomes a law-abiding, tax-paying citizen, the economic benefit is $68,800. Even if only one in 10 inmates became a law-abiding citizen after this investment, there would still be a net social gain of $3,800.

Politicians are glorified public employees. We, the taxpayers, are their employer. And, although they often forget, they are our servants who are elected to work for us. The war on drugs is a huge mistake. Like all employees, politicians make mistakes. Our national wart, Richard M. Nixon started this war. Every administration since has exacerbated his mistake and made it worse. Our politicians need a face-saving way out of this quagmire they created. The electorate is the only force that can demand accountability from our public employees. With mere votes and numbers, we can end the madness. If we do not end the war on drugs, all of us —not just the poor and unpopular in other countries and here at home—will become casualties.

Hundreds of thousands of people are wasting their lives in prison as a result of the failed policies associated with fighting this behavioral problem. Many organizations are trying to change government policy. For example, Families Against Minimum Mandatory sentences was formed to try to get Congress to realize what a huge mistake they have made. They lobby on behalf of the tens of thousands of prisoners who have no political voice in Washington.

The solution to the war on drugs is not that complex. But it is very difficult. It will require major changes in politics and policy. There will be classes of very powerful people who have a vested interest in the continuation of the drug war who will suffer financial harm if the war ends. There are several major changes to American society that must be implemented to stop this drug disease from spreading and sucking the guts out of our country.

To begin with, we need to work directly with the peasants of the Third World. The poor farmers of Colombia, Laos, Pakistan, Afghanistan and other countries produce the elementary products for heroin, and cocaine. Many poor countries rely on the money from the lucrative drug trade to feed their starving masses. Since developed countries refuse to pay a decent price for coffee, tea, nuts, and other commodities, the farmers and their children sell cocoa leaves to drug dealers. It is not that complex. Farmers sell products that give the highest market price. This is just simple market economics. Since American consumers buy 95 percent of the illegal drugs, our government can afford to step into the market place and pay a higher price for legal products directly from the farmers. This policy will stabilize countries by giving farmers a fair price for their goods.

As a consequence, struggling democracies in these countries will be less susceptible to bribes and the inherent corruption of politicians. Drug dealers buy elections in countries outside the United States. Until recently, the Mexican government was owned by the drug cartels. They paid market price and have got what they paid for. At every level, the Mexican government was one of the most corrupt governments on earth. In the early 1990s, the Salinas government was an arm of the drug trade. The money from the drug trade was used to pay back the debt Mexico owed American banks and financial institutions.

Secondly, we must forgive the debts of Third World countries and allow them to default on their loans to America's greedy banks. Much of the drug trade began when our government ran up interest rates in the early 1980s to kill inflation. In addition to the inherent harm inflicted on America's manufacturing sector, the American Federal Reserve Board-induced recession killed the economies of the Third World. Desperate, many of these governments turned to selling drugs as a means of paying foreign debt to our greedy banks. By allowing these countries to default on their debts to loans which were ill-advised at best and speculative in many instances, their resources can then be spent on economic development. America cannot be an island of prosperity in a sea of turmoil. As the empire that rules the world, we should understand that self-interest requires us to assist our colonies in economic development.

Thirdly, we must spend money on rehabilitation. Clearly, money spent on reducing the demand side of drugs will be the greatest market approach to success, combating the greatest danger to this country since Hitler. No matter how many people we incarcerate, the failed and ill-advised war on drugs will never succeed unless we reduce the demand side of the drug trade.

Finally, we need to teach children to seek happiness in manners that do not involve materialism, financial stress, and getting high on marijuana or other illegal drugs. Using drugs and alcohol leads us to a basic question. What is it about our society that is producing the massive consumption of illegal drugs? Is it the fact that people feel so unimportant and a cog on an assembly line? Are we raging against the machine that causes us to use drugs as a means out of this painful reality? Is human isolation the problem?

Until we address the causes of the behaviors instead of the symptoms, our war on drugs will continue to be a failed disaster. Over 15 million Americans use illegal drugs. Millions more abuse legal prescriptions. And then there are the millions who are weekend alcoholics. Clearly, our society produces very self-destructive behaviors from people who are unhappy with their lives.

This is a tall order for change. However, it is not impossible. We eliminated smallpox. We won World War II. We landed men on the moon. We ended the cold war. We developed the Internet. We can develop a society where individuals do not self-medicate to escape from their unhappy existence. We can conquer this problem. It just requires political leadership and public understanding.

As you can see, this country's longest war is not without cost. If you get involved in the drug trade, you will become a statistic. As warriors, we must watch out for dangerous situations. As businessmen, we always have to be conscious of how costs affect the bottom line. And as patriots, we must be ever vigilant against politicians armed with good intentions and our tax dollars.

7

GATHERING IN THE INFORMATION AGE

The best time to invest is when you have money.

Peter Lynch

If you follow this advice and stay away from the drug war and all it represents, you will have to learn to gather properly to protect yourself against times of hunger.

In 1986, I was at Club Med in Cancun, Mexico on a working vacation. I was rather full of myself, and a lady in her late forties was observing my obnoxious behavior. She asked me if I was saving any money. I replied smugly, "Oh hell no. I'll just make more next year."

She said, "You'll be sorry." She was right. If we don't gather food and save it for the times when hunting is difficult, plan on not eating on lean days. Chief Tabby was smart about gathering. He knew there would be days when game was scarce. He led his people through winters when food was scarce.

Today and throughout all of human history, very few people save large amounts money with any consistency. Even fewer invest. Since most people are in debt and are paying interest, their savings become irrelevant. A loan takes money away from you, and a careful investment might gain you some money. Most of the time, the two cannot really balance each other out. Debt bleeds you, and interest on your investments feeds you. The best thing to do is not bleed. Even if you do not have any money invested, not being in debt is its own blessing. There is the weight on your shoulders of knowing you owe. You owe, you owe, so off to work you go. Then you die, and it is irrelevant to anyone but your relatives whether or not your debts are paid.

Saving money is just not that difficult. It is like being in good physical shape; it requires discipline. It requires the ability to say no. Accumulating wealth happens a little bit at a time over a long period of time. After your bills are paid, you save just a little bit for tomorrow. For example, it costs you $25.00 for two days of groceries. Since you have already been fed and are presently not hungry, saving the $25.00 for future meals is smart. The problem with most people is they are not disciplined enough to wait for tomorrow's meal. Tomorrow will take care of tomorrow. Since they are always reacting to events, they never plan for success. With careful savings of money, you can retire. Whether or not you will live happily ever after is a completely different story. Figure out what your total costs are each day and save for those future costs. If you know you spend $50.00 per day to support your standard of living, figure that you will have to save this amount of money for one future day. In other words, the more money you have saved, the more certain you are to live the same lifestyle you have accomplished.

How much does it cost each day for you to pay every single one of your bills and feed yourself? Is that figure $50.00 per day, or $75.00, or $100.00? If you are extravagant like some of my foolish clients, your daily costs to support your high standard of consumption can be over $250.00 per day. How much exactly do you require each day to pay every bill you have? Once you know this, the next step is to figure out how much money you make each day and actually take home. If you are earning $9.00 per hour and your cost of living each day is $50.00, then you have some money left over; namely $4.00 per day after taxes. If you manage to save $4.00 per day for 20 working days per month for 12 months, you have $960.00 per year to invest carefully. What does this money become with compound interest at a very conservative 10 percent return on investment?

Year	Principal	Interest at 10%	Total
1	$960.00	$96.00	$1,056.00
2	$1,056.00	$201.60	$2,217.60

And so forth . . .

Over five years, which passes very quickly, that is $6,446.00. Over 10 years, this $4.00 per day quickly becomes over $15,299.94 with interest at 10 percent. This is enough money to feed you for almost six years at $7.00 per day. And if you save more than $960.00 per year the sum can soon reach the amount you will need to retire. For people who own a business and save over $10,000.00 per year, they can easily reach one million dollars. That is right, one million dollars.

You see, there is no great mystery about how to make and keep money. It just takes discipline, time and a willingness to live below your means. Anyone can do this. You do not have to be very smart. A fool with a calculator can make and keep one million dollars. I know some millionaires who I personally believe are right-wing-loony-tunes whose knowledge of history, ecology and other subjects is completely lacking. But their knowledge of hoarding money is astute.

What if we don't want to live in the same lifestyle we have now? What if we want to travel, eat expensive food, scuba dive and enjoy sunshine? The only way we can afford the lifestyle of the rich and famous is to own a business. It is not possible selling your mere labor to become mega-wealthy financially. If you are honest and work at a refinery making $15.00 per hour at 45 hours per week, 12 months per year over 25 years, the most you would earn is $877,500.00. However, the cost of being alive would mean that you would only be able to save $100,000. Even with a retirement from your employer of $150,000 and social security and your house mortgage being paid off, you would not be rich and famous. But you clearly would have enough money to take you and your wife to Mexico or Florida or Hawaii or Alaska or Europe once a year on a nice vacation. You would eat, but it would not be lobster every night by the beach while your maid is cleaning your condo. But so what? It is not what you have and how much, it is who you are that makes people love you.

Gathering over a long period of time is possible. It has been successfully accomplished by approximately three million Americans. It should be accomplished by more people of color. Native Americans and others just need to understand the money path that has been followed by countless other people throughout history. Old age does not have to mean eating dog food out of a can in a lonely, one-room studio. Being alcohol free and watching your diet can mean having good health and enjoying your grandchildren. Taking care of your money now can mean being able to enjoy the time you spend with your mate later. This goal is reachable. It does not require the courage of the astronauts who successfully made a lunar landing or the strength of a Hernando Cortes and the conquest of an Aztec empire. Financial success can be accomplished by average people everywhere in the United States, Western Europe and Japan. In other parts of the world, it is nearly impossible to pull oneself out of poverty. These countries need our help.

Do not expect the federal, state or tribal governments to assist you with your retirement or any part of your life. Chief Tabby was more than willing to help warriors hunt, gather and do battle to save his people. But he was not responsible for their retirement. We cannot expect others to be responsible for our care in our old age. The days of the old taking care of the young while they are children and the children taking care of the old when they are adults are gone. "Government" does not have the organizational skills or manpower to assist you with your old age and retirement. This support was attempted through social security programs in the U.S. and Communism in the Soviet Union. After 70 years, it proved to be a dismal failure in both places. You simply cannot get something for nothing.

There is no safety net other than your own smarts and prudent behavior. The same is true of your personal health. You have responsibility for your health, welfare and safety. Chief Tabby did not hold his warriors' hands while they went hunting or when they were on the warpath. It is not possible for your tribal leaders or any leader to baby-sit you and take care of your problems. The last thing you should ever expect is that the Social Security Administration will be properly funded when it is time for you to retire. The harsh reality of life is the majority of people die within three years of retirement. They no longer feel needed and a part of something much larger. Financial pressure leads to poor health from worrying, and poor exercise and eating habits mean an early death. This does not have to be your future. But it is the everyday reality for millions of people in America and throughout the world.

I have seen so many cases where people did not gather properly, so their family paid the price of their laziness. A young man over six feet tall came into my office for advice with his mother. He was in trouble with the law . . . again. And mommy dearest was there to hold his hand while he explained to me that he really did not mean to break that store window while he and his friends were intoxicated out of their minds. The police were picking on them, "because we're Indian, man." And that is discrimination and that is bad. He could not get a job because he did not have a car. He could not get a car because he did not have a job. So he would sit at home until his friends came over to pick him up in their borrowed car. I asked him what he would do 200 years ago. He became quite upset when I told him to quit sponging off his mother and to get a job. He would have starved 200 years ago.

"I can't go hunting, man. I don't have a horse."

Chief Tabby did not care if you had a horse or walked everywhere. It was not his responsibility to get you a damn horse. Since he walked everywhere, he would not expect you to do more than he would do himself. He was disciplined with his arrows and careful about gathering enough food for winter. This is why his family did not starve to death and his descendants are still leading this tiny tribe.

I have had many employees over the years who did not have a car and rode the bus to work. They paid the hard price of success by engaging in the behaviors that would make anyone successful. You cannot gather for later if you are so selfish and lazy that you won't take care of today. Excuses of "we are discriminated against" will just not work anymore. The white people who run this country and the industrial enterprises of planet earth are tired of hearing about all of the damn discrimination. The majority of white people want to see results. And surprisingly enough, the overwhelming majority of white people in America are not prejudiced. Most want to see you succeed financially and emotionally. Many executives I talk with would love to hire poor whites, blacks, Indians and Mexicans, if they are sober and ready to perform.

Gathering requires that you understand that everyone wants your money because this is the new food of the information age. It requires knowing that you can save your money carefully. Your $15.00 per hour feeds you today, and there is also money left over for tomorrow's meals and bills. This is not advanced math or physics. Eat today, save the extra for tomorrow so you can eat and have shelter then too.

None of this is possible with the consumption of alcohol. One six pack costs $5.00 and a pack of cigarettes costs $3.50. This is more than the cost of one meal. At $8.50 per day cost of alcohol and cigarette consumption, you will be broke all of your life. Go ahead and be broke. Nobody gives a damn if you don't. Everyone has problems and the daily stresses of life. Don't expect others to solve your financial problems and gather for you. This is not how life works. Over 200 years ago it was just not possible for tribal, state and the national governments to carry you any more than it is possible to carry you today. Most governments can barely govern, much less plan to protect your future.

Not only do individuals have to save for tomorrow's meals, but tribal governments must also save and carefully invest their members' money.

This problem or blessing of not having a large tax base forces tribal governments to be careful with their money. Of course, some still are not prudent with their finances and are just as broke or even poorer than their white neighbors.

Some tribes have money from oil and gas revenues. Other tribes have revenue from gaming. A few have money coming in from leases on land, timber sales, water share sales, or manufacturing. One tribe, the Skull Valley Band of Goshutes, is trying to take care of their future by building a storage facility for spent nuclear fuel—a tribal business venture that has caused worldwide uproar.

Whether you are managing a household or a business or a government, the concepts are the same. The most basic one is more money has to come in (revenue), than goes out (expenses). Anything left over is profit. R-E=P.

Obviously, this is a very simple formula. The Roman government had to budget their money and make sure they could pay the vast armies that brought peace to Europe for over one thousand years. The French government, under Napoleon, had to make sure enough money existed to pay for their navy, army and colonies. IBM has to make sure they make enough money from the sale of their products and services so that all expenses are covered, and a profit is shown to their investors. In your household, you must make more than you spend. If you do not save when you are ahead, and spend less then you make, plan on filing bankruptcy or sponging off someone else or worse yet, living on the street or with your mother.

Gathering in any age to prepare for times of shortage is just age-old, simple wisdom. Times change and one can either be prepared for changes or react to events. If we prepare carefully for change, we not only survive, but we are also prepared when times get better. By not wasting money on alcohol, drugs and senseless material items that eventually end up at the landfill, we can buy food when our employer has downsized. We can take trips to visit pesky relatives. We can make repairs on vehicles prior to their breaking down. We can do simple things like change tires and fan belts prior to getting flats and overheating.

Tribal governments who have carefully invested their tribal revenue and have a permanent trust fund can run their operations from the interest derived from their investments. Tribal governments can make a profit in their various business ventures. Once enough profit is generated and the money is carefully invested, the interest can be used for tribal elder programs, youth programs, reservation improvements, assistance with housing, tribal education, and language preservation.

Gathering the interest stream from money that has been carefully invested, and using this money for public good, is in everyone's best interest. The ideas are as endless as the imagination. From alcohol and drug prevention, tree planting to revive areas which have been over cut, and building fish hatcheries, to hiring law enforcement, and providing day camps for children with working parents. None of this is possible if the tribal government treasury is empty or if your family is broke.

In the information age, gathering means you are accumulating money. This is far different from accumulating material and consumer goods. Some individuals are so adept at gathering, or rather hoarding money, that the amount of their wealth is public discussion. Some tribes are worth over one billion dollars. Others are completely broke. Some individuals are worth over one billion dollars. Most individuals are three paychecks away from the homeless shelter. You do not have to be among the just over broke crowd and one step out of jail crowd. However, like anything else, success has a price. It is the high price of discipline. Most people are not willing to pay that price. It isn't because they can't. Numberless people have talent. Many quit before the race has begun. Others quit early in the race. Most quit before the finish line would have rewarded them with success.

Had they stuck it out over five years, saving $4.00 per day, not spending more then they made, and wasting money on junk, they would have been in good shape. A few made it the distance. It is like watching dry alcoholics. A few quit for life. Many lie to themselves everyday and tell others how they know they are stronger and know better. Then they drink or use illegal drugs. Since they cannot be honest with themselves, they are not honest with others. Only you are really going to give a damn if you save your money. Your family members and friends will love you. But they will not be there to bail you out when you really need their help financially. They can't. They don't have any money. They don't have any discipline to run the long race of saving a little bit over a long period of time. It is very easy to be poor. That is why 98 percent of the public pay interest and fewer than two percent earn interest. It takes tremendous self-control not be financially broke.

When you pull your bowstring back as you wait to take a shot at that fat buck eating by a stream, not paying attention to the lurking danger, you must have self-control. One false move and the buck is spooked. You will not eat tomorrow if you are not careful today. Tomorrow does not take care of tomorrow. At least you will not be eating deer meat. Hope the roots and berries are in season. Gathering is like that. The control and discipline to save enables you to survive until you take your next shot. Gathering habits are taught to us when we are knee high to a grasshopper.

If our parents were so drunk they could not stand up straight, much less sing us a bedtime story, we are going to have to learn to gather from others. This is not a fault of our character if we were never taught to be careful with money. It is like not knowing mechanics, electrical work, plumbing and the various other forms of specialized knowledge. Unless you have been taught, you cannot possibly know.

Many of my good friends who are Native American and Mexican American do not like to discuss money. It is considered impolite. Money is a dirty subject, a non-talked about secret, like sexual abuse of children in the Mormon community. Part of the reason money is not discussed is that people do not like to engage in conversation about areas they do not understand. Just as I do not like to talk about the sizes of tires because I am not interested in tire shops, Mexican and Indian people do not like to talk about money. Another reason is religious. Mexicans and Indians can be poor and go to heaven. White Protestants must prove their worth here on earth to get up to Heaven in the hereafter. Real poverty is the poor relationships we have with God, our families and friends. Real poverty is poor health and a bad attitude.

Gathering is a choice. So is attitude. After you have made the conscious decision to gather for tomorrow, learn to invest your savings. Once you have accepted that you are committed to saving for the rainy days that are a part of human financial life, you need to learn the best way to save. Learn that savings will earn you interest. You are investing in your future. The return of interest on your savings is what will enable you to survive well above poverty if, and only if, you are careful. This knowledge about how to invest your savings is most likely not in your present frame of reference or cultural experience. But like any skill, learning how to save and protect your own security and future is well within your capabilities if you are willing to exercise discipline and self-control. And money management is the one skill that you can use no matter what your station in life, education, profession, or talents. It is the only skill that can guarantee your survival and success.

8

WHY THERE IS POVERTY

Money doesn't talk, it swears.

Bob Dylan

I remember my youth in a small dusty village in northern New Mexico. My biological mother, Amelia, died at age 26 from complications of child-birth for who would have been her fifth child. My Grandmother Ramonsita and my Aunt Celsa took on the task of raising three more hungry children, adding to my two cousins who were already there. By every federal government social service indicator, we were financially poor.

Someone forgot to inform us young ones. We were so busy fishing in the crisp mountain springs and lakes, hunting in the wooden aspens and meadows, working on our small subsistence farm, socializing and yes, praying, that none of us knew we were poor. Our ignorance of this basic economic fact was furthered by the fact that our neighbors, friends and relatives were poor, too.

Economics was not a major concern for a six-year-old Mexican-American. We all had terrific health, friendly faces and lots of love. When I was growing up, there were no millionaires in Costilla, New Mexico. Like most agricultural communities, there was no market locally in which to sell your labor. Except for the few teaching jobs at the local dusty, adobe structure with the gravel playground we called an elementary school, most village residents of working age traveled fifty miles in each direction to find work.

The villagers grew a lot of their own food. Some of us supplemented our diet with government rations of horse meat, powdered eggs, and cheese.

Occasionally, we got additional protein from illegal game. Despite being well fed, healthy from 5:00 a.m. breakfasts and feeding the animals before the school bus arrived, plus all of the hard work of living on a subsistence farm, we were poor. We were happy and healthy, but poor.

There is a vast ocean of difference between the financial poverty inflicted on the residents of rural agricultural communities like Costilla, New Mexico by geography, history and birth, and the spiritual poverty that plagues America today. Being young, healthy and poor on our own twenty-acre subsistence farm are still some of the fondest memories this 43-year-old owner of a small law firm can recall.

My Spanish-speaking, Catholic grandmother never bought me fancy electronic toys or expensive new clothes. We didn't even have a television. At night, Grandma would tell us complex and interesting stories before prayer and much needed sleep. While blatant materialism and conspicuous consumption of energy—which define success—were lacking, we enjoyed wonderful meals, warm hugs and good humor. My grandmother was religious to the point of superstition. Yet, values were instilled in us from the time we were old enough to kneel down for Sunday mass and evening prayer.

In all of my many fond memories of youth and curiosity, I do not recall one discussion or fight over money. Thirty plus years later, none of my poor clients ever talk about sex or money. Like most poor people, they share two qualities: their kids are always pregnant, and they are always broke. Most poor, working class and allegedly middle-class people are three paychecks away from having their vehicles repossessed or losing their meager dwellings to foreclosure. Like the overwhelming majority of the American public, poor people pay interest on their money. The truth is, people own their health and their time—and very little else. So why is there poverty?

Financial poverty is caused in part by not understanding the language of money. Believing that materialism and the conspicuous consumption of energy will bring us happiness causes spiritual poverty. Despite the deaths of my biological parents and grandparents, my youth was filled with incredible memories.

There is no mystery to why we never argued about money. We didn't have any. And like the majority of people, we really didn't know what it was, its language and its many uses. The powerful words of portfolio, balance sheet, income statement, return on investment, break-even analysis, initial public offering, cash flow, secondary offering, or book value were ancient Greek to my family and the various residents of Costilla,

New Mexico.

The language of money is foreign to most people. A common complaint from political demagogues and leftists is wealth and power are concentrated in a few hands. Its true. Power and property are concepts that exist between the right and left ears. Like the languages of math, chemistry, history, psychology, physics or any other field of study, one must learn the concepts to be successful.

Over the course of my life I have known many individuals in all walks of life: terrific cooks, wonderful parents, great inventors, outstanding engineers, competent secretaries—and in every way normal. Yet the majority of the people I have met and known are, shall we be polite, financially challenged.

If you don't have wealth, math at an eighth grade level is sufficient education to accumulate it. Yes, even a thousand thousands ... a million dollars. While it certainly helps to have at least some money to make money, the essential requirement is knowledge. What is money, how does it work, how do you make it, and most importantly ... how do you keep it? I remember making my first million by the time I was thirty, and being divorced and losing it all at thirty-four. I had certainly learned to make money, but had no idea on how to keep it.

Many times my clients come in wanting a divorce and stressed to the point of ulcers. Their stress and anger are the symptoms. Their problems are caused by a misuse of money. Constantly worshipping in front of their entertainment altars at least six to ten hours per day, many people never unlock the key to unhappiness. They compare themselves to others. If they just buy more plastic junk that ends up in landfills, bigger homes that consume vast resources, recreational vehicles that spend the majority of the year parked as a monthly expense and on rare occasions enjoy a stress-filled get away to crowded campgrounds or crowded waterways, they will be happy. If they just take that trip to Disney World or some other amusement park to wait thirty minutes for a five-minute ride, they will be happy.

Like overeating and the subsequent health problems created as a consequence, Americans are terrible consumers. Buying what you don't need and seldom use, spending money you don't have, and constantly incurring debt creates not only spiritual poverty, but also incredible financial stress. It was not what my grandmother had, but who she was, that caused so many people to love her.

I have a few friends who are multi-millionaires. Others are poor to the point of hoping their paychecks are handed out early. Some friends and clients take out high interest loans on their vehicles and max out their credit cards. A handful earn interest on their numerous successful investments.

The main difference between my handful of rich friends and many poor ones is that the wealthy ones earn interest, and the rest pay interest. The millionaires are not any smarter, better looking, or even happier. The difference is that my wealthy friends understand the language of money. People who love them for who they are surround most of my poor friends and relatives and clients. The few wealthy ones often attract individuals who want them for what they have.

"Happiness," according to Albert Schweitzer, "is good health and a poor memory." I believe happiness is relative, dependent more on attitude, health and good company. In answer to the question of why there is poverty, the main cause is a lack of knowledge of money. Another misguided, well-intentioned federal or state or tribal income redistribution entitlement program, complete with horse meat, powdered eggs, cheese and government housing, is not the solution. What we need is a mandatory course on the basics of money as part of school curriculum.

The eighth grade formula for financial success is Revenue (R) minus Expenses (E) equals Profit (P).   R-E=P.

By avoiding debt and very carefully investing your profit, with compound interest and time, you will have a healthy portfolio, a positive cash flow, an adequate return on investment, and financial peace of mind. And having financial peace of mind requires a knowledge of environmental matters as well as finances. We have no choice but to study money environmental issues carefully. If we don't, we might end up turning America's rural areas into garbage dumps.

9

RESERVATIONS AS GARBAGE DUMPS

Like the miner's canary, the Indian marks the shifts from fresh air to poison gas in our political atmosphere; and our treatment of Indians, even more than our treatment of other minorities, reflects the rise and fall of our democratic faith.

Felix Cohen

Gaming and garbage are the new business deals for Indians and poor rural communities. Using reservations as garbage sites is the new deal of choice for hustlers. Several reservations nationally have been approached as the proposed dump sites for municipal solid waste, hazardous waste, municipal solid waste sludge, low-level radioactive waste, medium level radioactive waste, and high-level radioactive waste. Over the last decade, I have seen numerous deals brought to Indian Country. It is easy to come to the conclusion that the politically motivated charge of environmental racism has some basis in reality.

Why are tribes, rural communities, and Third World countries the beneficiaries of such generous and thoughtful white businessmen? Most of it has to do with the limited sovereignty currently enjoyed by tribes, the dollar value of rural areas, and the corruption that is possible with Third World governments. These garbage deals have far too many problems associated with them. The difficulties are with what types of waste, for how long, and what results will occur when these areas are used as dumpsites. Also, who are behind these "deals"? Remember, who you are in business with is as important as what type of market you are trying to conquer.

We should first ask what are the differences in these types of wastes? Since these waste streams never existed prior to the European invasion, it is important to look at each one and study them carefully. Municipal solid waste is the most common. It primarily consists of garbage from homes and businesses: glass, paper, metals, plastics, and packaging materials.

Over 90 percent of all municipal solid waste is packaging. This waste can be reduced though a variety of means. One reduction method is to change packaging laws. In this materialistic society, where consumerism is the religion, more dump sites will continually be necessary. How much municipal solid waste is there? We continue to produce so much munici- pal solid waste annually that if we line up all of the garbage trucks on earth back-to-back, they would reach half way to the moon. Our moun- tains of garbage will grow until we change our consumption habits. But we should expect the conspicuous consumption and materialism myths to continue to pollute the earth. And our municipal solid waste problem will continue to become larger and larger. Consider these numbers. Imagine that a typical middle-class child born in America will in his or her lifetime:

- Go through 12,000 paper grocery bags;
- Drive 700,000 miles, using more than 28,000 gallons of gasoline;
- Wear and discard 250 shirts and 115 pair of shoes;
- Use and discard 27,500 newspapers, 3,900 weekly news magazines and 225 pounds of phone directories;
- Purchase a dozen automobiles;
- Go through 28,627 aluminum beverage cans, weighing 1,022 pounds, of which 17,700 will be recycled;
- Consume enough electricity to burn 16,610 pounds of coal;
- Burn out 750 light bulbs;
- Account for the use of 69,250 pounds of steel and 47,000 pounds of cement;
- Eat 8,486 pounds of red meat;
- Eat 17,591 eggs, and
- Throw away 600 times his or her adult weight in garbage.

This means that each adult will leave a legacy of 90,000 pounds of trash for his children. What can be done to solve this horrible problem? Reach back to the roots of Native America and remember the values that worked. Recycling is a traditional concept followed by all Native Ameri- can people. Recycling all of your home's waste newsprint, cardboard, glass, and metal can reduce carbon dioxide emissions by 850 pounds a year. Each of us generates on average of 4.4 pounds of waste per day, per person. Enough energy is saved by recycling one aluminum can to run a TV set for three hours or to light one 100-watt bulb for 20 hours.

Americans throw away enough aluminum every three months to rebuild our entire commercial air fleet. Annually, enough energy is saved by recycling steel to supply Los Angeles with electricity for almost 10 years. Americans discard enough glass containers to fill the Empire State Building every week! You can make 20 cans out of recycled material with the same amount of energy it takes to make one new one. Five recycled plastic bottles make enough fiberfill to stuff a ski jacket. In this decade, it is projected that Americans will throw away over one million tons of aluminum cans and foil, more than 11 million tons of glass bottles and jars, over 4.5 million tons of office paper, and nearly 10 million tons of newspaper. Almost all of this material could be recycled. Incinerating 10,000 tons of waste creates one job, while landfilling the same amount creates six jobs, and recycling the same 10,000 tons creates 36 jobs.

American politicians talk recycling, yet they won't pass laws making it mandatory. How do we dispose of household and office waste? There are several methods. We can burn garbage. Incinerator deals are routinely presented to tribes and poor rural communities. What exactly is an incinerator?

An incinerator is a burn unit that very quickly allowed communities to solve waste problems partially. The machine has several complex moving parts and burns garbage and other toxic substances at very high temperatures. So there are many things that can break and need to be replaced. Incineration is one way to reduce volume and spread toxins into the air. This disposal method enables us to better share our waste with our neighbors. Many incinerators exist in rural communities throughout this country. After the burn, there is highly toxic ash that must be disposed of at a hazardous waste site. The federal rules on waste disposal have changed so that incinerators in cities are no longer common. Instead, these waste burn units move to poor, often non-white rural areas, where property values are lower.

These waste facilities also include higher toxic releases to the atmosphere from dioxin and furans. These atmospheric releases produce numerous health problems because the human body is not meant to breath fine particulate matter. Our nose hair follicles and lungs were not designed to process this material, and it goes directly into our bloodstream. This is why air pollution causes so many health diseases and respiratory problems. The waste also produces heavy metals, rock salt, and new organic compounds whose long-term toxic effects on humans are still unknown, but probably undesirable.

Toxic waste incinerators are not as common. However, since reservations are usually in rural areas, in land no one else wanted until now, tribes are routinely approached as sites for these highly toxic waste burners. Many toxic waste incinerators do not make money and shut down. Now there is not just toxic garbage stored on the site, there is also mechanical equipment and infrastructure. Tribes need to be extremely careful about not only whom they deal with on these waste issues, but also what will happen in the long term if an incinerator is placed on their lands. It is very easy to be stuck with over-priced and obsolete equipment that once was represented to be an incinerator.

Selling over-priced equipment to the Indians is one of the oldest scams around. If you buy one of these incinerator deals, what are you going to do with the equipment after the market changes and the deal has lost all of its value? Many of these equipment deals are fabricated by one company for the sole purpose of selling the junk to an unsuspecting community or tribe. When they go out of business, there are no replacement parts to fix your junk garbage machine.

Many inventors want to try their new incinerator inventions on the Indians. This is a common desire. In 19 years, I have seen every bad business deal imaginable at one time or another smell it's way to Indian country. One could not make it in California, one could not get bank financing, and one incinerator deal I saw had new technology; a single producer, no track record of prior operation and wanted one million dollars to set up on a reservation. Thanks but no thanks.

The people who are interested in selling waste-burning equipment to Indians are usually approaching these communities in hopes of making a quick buck. If these deals are such a bargain, why are they being offered to the Indians? The white community has rarely approached Indians about anything positive. The reason deals are usually offered to tribes is they are usually cons and scams. And when in doubt, whether you are Indian or not … DON'T. The general rule of thumb in business is that if they cannot obtain bank financing, it is a bad deal. Probably a very, very bad deal! If a bank won't lend them money, why should you or your tribe?

The other and most common alternative for disposal of garbage is burial of municipal and hazardous waste—the landfill. We have mountains and mountains of city waste. In Florida, one of the highest points in the state is the dump next to the freeway between Miami and Orlando.

Of course, Florida is as flat as a pancake. But this extra large mound of waste continues to increase in height annually. Other communities export their garbage to rural county dumps or unsuspecting communities in a Third World country. The new federal rules require extensive liners for municipal dumps. These liners protect the ground water from contamination and are 50 years overdue. But they are a start.

Sending city garbage to our country's Indians is an ugly, cynical, racist idea. There are various problems with making reservations municipal solid waste and hazardous waste dumps for cities. Among these are having the sufficient land base and technology to dispose safely of the waste. The land base is a big problem. Most reservations are quite small. Indian country is a mere speck of the former traditional lands. Less than two percent of America remains in Indian hands. Municipal solid waste dumps require distance from populated centers. The smell is close to that of a dead human body. Papers, dirty diapers, flies, rats and plastics fall off the dump trucks on their journey to the dump. The road to the Salt Lake County Land Fill is littered with garbage that constantly flies off the trucks. The areas near the landfill are littered from garbage that becomes airborne. Rats, seagulls, flies and disease have a safe, warm home.

The transportation costs of hauling waste to rural locations are onerous on any business. You need expensive and reliable garbage trucks. Then there are the handling costs. Truck drivers hauling smelly garbage do not come cheap. Then there is the potential liability for hazardous waste being dumped in garbage cans and ending up at the landfill instead of the proper disposal site. By the time garbage arrives at a rural location, the cost of getting it there has removed most of the potential profit. What makes any tribe think they will get paid over a long period of time if they build a municipal solid waste dump? What if the people who start the contracts and build the dump leave the deal after a couple of years and stick the tribes with the garbage and the liability?

East Carbon, Utah receives a whopping 50 cents per ton for the garbage they receive from all over the United States, Mexico and Canada. The haulers, the handlers, and all others make money. The average tipping fee for the rest of Utah to take waste is $35.00 per ton. One tribe now has been approached as the potential site for a new municipal solid waste dump for Salt Lake County, Utah. This is a very bad idea which should be immediately killed.

Some con artists simply plan on going into bankruptcy from the beginning, and pull the plug once the deal is completed. Then you get stuck with the equipment, the garbage, the liability, the loss of your money, and all the legal problems which follow. Numerous communities have been hustled by con artists on garbage deals. In one Utah community, the cost of garbage incineration is so high that the residents pay $60 per ton to rid themselves of their waste. Reservations were not approached because of the high costs of transportation and the complexity of the project.

Reservations and waste industries in Utah provide an accurate reflection of the state of waste disposal problems in all areas of residential life and industry in America. The Tooele Chemical Agent Disposal Facility in Rush Valley, Utah is the site of a nerve gas incinerator. This incinerator is in the process of destroying approximately 42 percent of the nation's stockpile of chemical weapons. These weapons are among the deadliest substances humans have ever produced. This incinerator process is one of the safest methods of disposal currently known. The billion dollar plant is destroying some of the most toxic and dangerous materials known to man. Among the chemicals are nerve agents VX, GB, Sarin, Tabon and numerous others. Six other incinerators have been planned and might be built nationally over the next twenty years.

Other methods of disposal of these horrible weapons create their own problems. The chemicals are still hazardous, and now have to be disposed of at a special hazardous waste dump. However, incineration is not without risks. Again, there will be toxic releases in minute quantities into the atmosphere. Over time these will accumulate. We invented these weapons, and now we are sorry that we did.

One of my clients, the Skull Valley Goshutes, after carefully reviewing the disposal alternatives of chemical weapons, chose not to file suit to block this incinerator. I have turned down other cases that still ended up in federal court. Suing one's neighbors is not wise, and harms community relations—especially when their jobs will be lost by your lawsuit and the litigation has a very questionable scientific basis. Always remember, "Thou shall not bear false witness against thy neighbor."

Tooele County, Utah is also the home for a hazardous waste dump at Grassy Mountain on the road to Wendover, Nevada. This hazardous waste dump receives waste from all over the nation. The dump has the required liners and will be permanently off limits to humanity once it is full. I hope someone reminds the lizards, snakes, birds and other animals of that desert area that this means them, too.

Hazardous waste is usually the by-product of industrial activities. These wastes remain dangerous to humans and other life forms *forever*. These chemicals have changed their molecular structure that cannot be undone by nature. Since these are not natural products, they do not naturally biodegrade. Nor do the by-products of chemical weapons testing at Dugway, Utah. Many hazardous chemicals are necessary to create the products of an industrial and highly technical society. As a direct result of manufacturing, the waste products that cannot be recycled must be dumped somewhere. That somewhere now is the West Desert at Grassy Mountain, and potentially some Indian reservation that take the bribes and the deal. The associated problem is that the hazardous wastes buried in landfills will be toxic longer than the liners meant to contain these very dangerous materials. Burning the chemical weapons renders them neutral forever, but the waste by-products remain dangerous forever.

Immediately next to Skull Valley, Utah in the West Desert is the site of a low-level radioactive waste site, the Enviro-Care facility in Clive. It is one of only three active sites in the United States that are allowed under federal law to receive radioactive waste permanently.

The other two are in Hanford, Washington and Barnwell, South Carolina. These radioactive wastes include mill tailings, parts from nuclear reactors, radioactive wastes from hospitals, and other mildly radioactive products. The site fully complies with federal law, and is carefully monitored by the State of Utah and the federal government's Nuclear Regulatory Commission.

Enviro-Care is an absolute blockbuster money-making machine. They have gross revenues of over $1,000,000 per week. The Tooele County Commissioners allowed this facility to be located in the unusable land of the West Desert, at least 25 miles from the nearest population center, the Skull Valley Band of Goshutes. Grantsville, Utah is still at least 40 miles away. Approximately 40 high-paying jobs were created at this site. The facility stores substances that will remain radioactive for at least one thousand years.

There were two toxic waste incinerators in the West Desert. After it became clear that the market for two incinerators was not there, one is shut down. Over 200 jobs were lost and the remaining incinerator may not survive. The market place is just as ruthless as a winter storm 200 years ago. Only the careful and the prepared survive. There was not enough toxic waste at a price that made economic sense to feed two incinerators.

Tribes, rural communities and Third World countries that would want to site toxic waste incinerators must understand that the market place is constantly changing. The companies who were the major corporate players at the turn of the century are not around today. Fifty years is a long time to be in business. Most businesses only last the one generation of the

domineering personality of the founder. Very, very few last past the first
and final generation. This, too, is natural. In nature, very few eggs from
the salmon become fingerlings. Yet few still make it to the sea and home
again. Even fewer reproduce successfully. If a tribe, a rural community
or a small poor country accepts municipal solid waste or a toxic waste
incinerator, they may be stuck with the waste, the incinerator, a bankrupt
company, and environmental liability. The risk is too high.

Low level radioactive waste sites are similar to hazardous waste dumps.
The materials that will be permanently stored are dangerous to humans
and other life forms for more than seven generations. Under traditional
Indian law, any environmental action taken must be safe seven generations into the future. If the proposed action is not safe for at least seven
generations, 140 years, the action is not allowed by the Grandfathers.
Indians protect the future and the past because time is viewed in a circu-
lar manner—unlike the European linear view. Yesterday was today; there
is today, and tomorrow there will be today. Everything we do effects
today.

Radioactive waste is far different than other types of waste. If you
do not fully understand radioactivity, you are not prepared to site a nuclear
waste facility on your land. Even if you do understand the risk, unless the
land is completely worthless and has been the burial site for sheep illegally
buried as a result of nerve gas agent VX accident, this waste should be
avoided. The only site in Indian America which fits this extremely narrow
criteria, and the only Indian government which I am aware of that is prepared to site a nuclear storage facility for spent nuclear fuel in, is the Skull
Valley Band of Goshutes.

How did the Skull Valley Goshutes and other tribes get involved in the
attempt to site nuclear waste? It was by accident. Like most things
attempted which fail, the federal government was behind the idea. David
Leroy, then head of the now defunct Nuclear Waste Negotiator's Office,
sent a proposal out to all communities to site a high-level nuclear waste
storage facility on a temporary basis until the permanent disposal site is
ready.

Being the skeptical leader that he is, Leon D. suggested we look into
what exactly the feds and utility companies were up to, and warn the
Indian community. We needed to find out the truth. We believed there
was a conspiracy that needed to be stopped immediately. That conspiracy
we suspected was between the largest utility companies in America and
the Department of Energy. I had experience as a kid fighting the United
States government with the ill-fated MX weapons system. I clearly knew

the danger of nuclear weapons and had spent my adult life studying them. Given the racism of the Reagan Bush administrations, one could clearly not take lightly a plan to dump high-level radioactive waste on Indian Reservations. Was there a conspiracy between the utility companies and the federal government to target Indian reservations as sites for nuclear waste dumps? Our journey for truth would take us around the world.

10

THE GLOWING GOSHUTES

Radiation is bad.

Margine Bullcreek, vocal tribal opponent to a
spent nuclear storage project planned for her reservation.

Skull Valley, like its nefarious name, is a forbidding place. Located next to the Dugway Proving Grounds and being the site of the most illegal environmental racism that has occurred in the last 50 years, it has sand that does not grow marketable tomatoes. In 1968, over 1,600 nerve-gas contaminated sheep were illegally buried on the reservation. When asked recently by business executives to describe Skull Valley, I simply stated, "picture sand, sagebrush and tumble weeds." The good lands in Utah, that previously belonged to the Goshutes for over 1,000 years, were taken by the Mormons without compensation. This nuclear native's saga began in 1990 when David Leroy was America's nuclear waste negotiator under President Bush. This thankless job involved finding a host community for the site of the Monitored Retrievable Storage (MRS) program. This program contained the federal government's promise to the nation's nuclear industry to store and eventually dispose of the highly radioactive fuel rods that exist in over 72 communities in 34 states at more than 112 nuclear power plants. The utility company executives believed the federal government, and our nuclear power industry was born.

I decided to investigate the aims of the federal government and the nukes crowd. I asked the tribal council for permission to apply for a Phase I $100,000 Department of Energy grant to study this MRS proposal. *The real motive was to gather the data and kill this environ-*

mentally racist proposal.

The first step in any search for truth is to know that you don't know. I *believed* there was a conspiracy, and looked for evidence to support my beliefs. This was improper. I suffered the vanity of thinking that I had all of the answers. After enough confrontations with my assumptions that continually proved to be wrong, I realized I did not really know what I was talking about. The harder I looked for a conspiracy, the less evidence I found. Eventually, it became clear I was just plain and simply mistaken. There was no conspiracy. Always remember that you have a right to change your mind when presented with facts that clearly prove you are mistaken. This is truly what learning and education are really about.

The $100,000 grant was used to interview executives, environmentalists, scientists, crazy people, sane people and Department of Energy employees at several nuclear power plants in different parts of the country. The data that was available was voluminous. Like all data, it could be distorted to state whatever you wanted to conclude. I tried very hard to ensure this did not happen.

The study took us all over the United States. We first traveled to a shutdown nuclear power plant in Rancho Seco, California. We got a complete tour of the plant and their spent fuel pool. From Rancho Seco we visited with Green Peace in San Francisco, California. Green Peace was obviously opposed to the storage of spent nuclear fuel on reservations or anywhere else. They were correct that the problem should have been thought through in the beginning. Their opposition was articulate and sincere.

From Green Peace we immediately traveled to Oregon and attended an environmental conference hosted by the Indigenous People's Environmental Network next to the Columbia River. There were representatives from tribes across the United States, Canada and South and Central America, and their opposition to the project was overwhelming, vocal and at times very emotional.

From Oregon we immediately drove to Hanford, Washington. The damage to the environment from the nuclear work at Hanford in producing nuclear weapons is so vast that humans will never be able to repair it. High-level tritium was dumped directly into the Columbia River. Some of the tanks, containing highly radioactive liquid waste, are leaking and cannot be repaired. Others might explode, and the chemical composition is now unknown. America created the Hanford site to assist in the development of nuclear material as part of our Cold War effort. The original atomic bomb was partially developed at Hanford. The amount of nuclear waste that was released into the environment by the United States government at the Hanford site is beyond our ability to repair. Hanford is a reminder to humanity; sin no more. Like the Cold War, this was a monumental mistake.

The Yakima and Umatillas are all too aware of the environmental damage of the Hanford nuclear activities. Located next to this once top-secret bomb factory, their lands have been damaged by high-level tritium, and the potential for a nuclear explosion from one of the many leaking tanks is great. Their traditional way of life is destroyed forever.

We would never do today what was done at Hanford in the name of national security. Our environmental laws and safety procedures will never allow this type of activity again. We have learned as a society to protect our environment better. However, for the Yakima and Umatillas it is too late. They have to live with waste tanks that are underground and leaking. Despite spending over $1 billion dollars per year to clean up this site, we can see that it is truly beyond repair. The best we can hope for is to stop the spread of radioactive contamination. My friend, Russell Jim, has spent a large portion of his life trying to undo the damage the federal government has forced upon his Yakima Tribe. His efforts are heroic. But the task is overwhelming and beyond the capability of one man; even as talented a man as this Yakima elder.

We wanted to see an operating nuclear power plant with an excellent environmental record. So we traveled to West Palm Beach, Florida to tour the St. Lucie Nuclear Power Plant, meeting the workers and various business executives. This plant is the model of how to manage properly an industrial enterprise. In addition to being museum clean, the workers were also monitored not just on their physical health, but routinely screened on their mental state. Florida Power spends considerable amounts of time and money into environmental causes. They don't pound their chests to call forth a heavenly choir to proclaim their minor deeds. They let their good work speak for itself. And that work is impressive. From saving sea turtles and endangered panthers to preserving habitat for West Indian manatees, this company's extensive efforts is corporate responsibility at its highest level.

After the tour of the St. Lucie Nuclear Power Plant and the meetings with Florida Power and Light executives, my view of nuclear power and the storage of spent nuclear fuel started to change. The executives explained that they needed to institute long-term plans in the event that the federal government did not live up to its commitment and take the spent fuel from them. Florida Power and Light, like all utilities, have an obligation to their customers; when they turn on the light switch, the lights actually go on. These corporate executives are people just like you and me, and are not in the least bit interested in destroying the environment.

We flew next to Surry, Virginia and toured their nuclear power plants. Virginia Power has an onsite storage facility at Surry. This is a miniature version of the proposed Federal MRS facility. At the large storage casks, we found no abnormal reading on the Geiger counters. From the Surry power plant we drove to Washington, DC and met with industry and government officials. We received piles and piles of data.

After Phase I, the Tribal Council and I realized that there is no conspiracy between the utility companies and the Department of Energy. In fact, it was the exact opposite of a conspiracy. The utility companies felt betrayed by the feds.

Yes, the feds ripped off the utility rate-payers for over $15 billion dollars. Our taxes paid for a nuclear fuel storage facility. The money is gone, and there is no storage facility. It almost ranks with the $40 billion dollars the Bureau of Indian Affairs has managed to lose out of their tribal trust funds. Still, this sum does not quite equal the loss of the Black Hills by the great Sioux nations. And it is still smaller than the loss of Georgia by the powerful Cherokees. Nor does this rip-off match the amount of money stolen by defense contractors at the height of the Cold War.

It was one thing to conclude there was no conspiracy. It was quite another to conclude that a spent nuclear fuel storage facility could be built safely and maintained. Other countries had successfully built storage facilities for spent nuclear fuel. Were these decisions in error? Could and should the Goshutes build a dry cask storage facility for nukes? What were the dangers? Who was involved? When would all of this take place? How long would the facility remain on the reservation? Would this violate sacred Native American traditions of respect for mother earth? What about the dangers of giving large sums of money to poor people?

The federal government wanted a quick decision on building a storage facility for highly radioactive spent nuclear fuel. The Skull Valley Goshute Tribal Council does not make quick decisions. They look at what will be the long-term impact of this facility on the people, plants, and environment. Was this in the best long-term interests for the reservation? Some of the material will remain radioactive for over 250,000 years. What is the true potential for harm?

It is one thing to proclaim that something is radioactive, and another to understand what that means. Without obtaining a physics degree, we common people can comprehend radioactivity. Radiation is energy that moves through space in the form of particles or electromagnetic waves. There is ionizing and non-ionizing radiation. Non-ionizing radiation consists of energy particles like radio waves and television waves. Ionizing radiation will harm you if you are not shielded from the particles. These fast-moving electrons can go through your cells and damage them.

Then we must consider beta particles, gamma rays, and alpha particles. Beta particles can go though two inches of wood. Gamma rays are pure energy, and can penetrate through most substances except steel, concrete and lead. With enough shielding, you can stop beta and gamma radiation. The alpha particles are slow-moving protons and cannot move through anything. Your skin layer will stop alpha particles. However, if you inhale one of these particles, eventually you might die of cancer. Many of the people down wind of the open-air atomic tests in Southern Utah and Nevada died of leukemia caused by inhaling alpha particles that were in the dust.

The electromagnetic spectrum is the complete range of frequencies of electromagnetic waves from the lowest to the highest, including radio, infrared, visible light, ultraviolet, X-ray, gamma ray, and cosmic ray waves.

Ultra-violet light, gamma rays and X-rays are ionizing radiation. The gamma rays and X-rays emitted by radioactive materials are waves of pure energy. In common with other electromagnetic waves, they travel at the speed of light and their energies are determined by their frequencies. Alpha and beta particles travel at much less than the speed of light and their energies are functions of their velocities and masses.

Anyone who makes the blanket statement that "radiation is bad" is off base. The term *radiation* includes all forms of energy, some useful and some dangerous. It all can be handled safely or can be harmful in the hands of the ignorant. The energy derived from all forms of radiation and the human intelligence to put it to use are both gifts from God. Whether it is the fire that warmed the hands of Neanderthal man or the chemo-thermal reaction that put that spark of life in the modern computer, radiation can injure and kill or it can foster the human condition and evolution.

The Tribal Council deliberated. They decided to see European and Japanese nuclear facilities for themselves. If the French, Japanese, British, Swedes, Spaniards, Russians, Koreans, Canadians and Finns could build interim storage facilities for spent nuclear fuel, why can't Americans? Could the Goshutes? Are these foreign people so much smarter and better, or more foolish with their environmental decisions? If other people in diverse parts of the world could license and site peaceful nuclear facilities, why not Skull Valley? If it is so dangerous, why are other people building these facilities?

Sometimes you just have to see things for yourself. It is not always enough to read about the glorious deeds of others. You need to be there to ask questions spontaneously and just observe. Is it real? Does it pass the smell test?

11

THE OLD WORLD, EUROPE, AND JAPAN

Vicissitudes of fortune, which spares neither man nor the proudest of his works, which buries empires and cities in a common grave...

Edward Gibbons

Like the Sioux, the Pueblo, the Comanche, the Utes, the Apache, the Cheyenne and numerous others, the Japanese were completely flattened in World War II. Not being successful in obtaining oil and other resources by force, this great warrior nation decided to try another method. They were determined to accomplish economically what was beyond their reach militarily. It worked. In an area slightly larger than Salt Lake County, Tokyo and its surrounding suburbs is the second largest economy on earth.

This ancient culture is certainly one model that can be followed by people everywhere on how to turn absolute military defeat and devastation into complete economic victory. In the information age, it is the only victory that matters.

In the space of 16 hours, we had traveled from San Francisco to Japan on a Boeing Airlines 747 and were half way across the planet.

In the 19th century, it would take approximately three months to make that journey lasting better than half of a 24-hour day. The Japanese industry officials made special arrangements to have the leaders of the Skull Valley Goshutes visit several nuclear facilities and talk with industry representatives. In typical Japanese fashion, waiting at our hotel were color brochures with clear see-through English overprints explaining in detail over the Japanese writing, exactly what these facilities were about, their location, and what functions they could perform.

These nuclear industrial sites were incredible. America invents and Japan perfects the products of the modern age. It is interesting to visit people who have better manners, are quiet in public, have clean cities, infrequent blue-collar crime, and amazing world-class technology.

Tokyo has over 25 million people in an area the size of Salt Lake County, Utah. Crowded is not a proper description. But the entire country has fewer murders than Chicago. In traveling all through Japan I saw two homeless persons. My former secretary forgot her jacket on the bullet train, and a total stranger rushed to bring it back. Everywhere you would see bicycles parked in front of stores unattended and without locks. Babies were laughing, happy and healthy. The elderly were treated with great respect and sought out for their wisdom and advice. The remainder of society worked and worked and worked and worked. At 11:00 p.m., people were still in their tiny offices working.

Despite their unending hours of hard labor, Leon D. looked at me and observed, "They can work their whole lives and never have what I have." That is easy for Leon to say. He manages an 18,000-acre reservation. What he doesn't realize is that he would be successful if his skin color was fluorescent purple. He has brains, guts and discipline. Throughout history, this has always been enough to succeed in any endeavor.

Every portion of Japan that is usable for something is utilized for that function. The sides of railroads were farmed. Parking permits to own vehicles cost $1,000 per month, and you could not buy a car without one. The food was fantastic and healthy.

The Japanese people seemed to be content. They were not ever loud, and you had to look at length for graffiti and overt signs of poverty. I loved seeing women walking alone at 1:00 in the morning through dark alleys completely unmolested and unescorted. Even in boring Salt Lake that is not possible. I felt very ashamed of the behavior in our great country. Our blue-collar crime in America is inexcusable. We simply have very bad manners.

Like everything else on this tiny island, the nuclear program in Japan is taken very seriously. Without any fossil fuels to waste, Japan imports over 90 percent of their fossil fuel energy resources. Despite no indigenous natural energy resources, this island nation is the second largest economy on earth. They are the second largest exporter of automobiles, the largest donor of foreign aid, at the time had eight of the ten largest banks, and was one very rich country with the largest foreign currency reserves of any nation. The 51 Japanese nuclear power plants provide over 26 percent of their electricity. This incredible country has bullet trains, a space program, super tankers, high-energy physics, and a whole host of modern gizmos.

Unlike America where if we can throw it away we will, Japan takes spent fuel assemblies apart and recaptures the fuel through a French process invented in America called reprocessing. They were building a very large nuclear waste disposal site for intermediate waste on the northern part of their island. As one of their physicists explained it to me, "Nuclear energy is a great energy source and a gift from God to mankind." He spoke four languages and was educated at Columbia.

The top executives from several Japanese utilities and industry groups explained in full English the difficulty of siting a nuclear facility. They gave the following advice: "Tell the people the truth. Explain in detail exactly what you are going to do, and leave it at that. Eighty percent of the people will support you. The other 20 percent will oppose your project, regardless of what information you provide. These opponents are so dogmatic that they already know the truth and nothing you tell them and no amount of science will change their mind." If the Japanese can build a nuclear storage facility for spent nuclear fuel, why not the Goshutes?

In between meetings, in the evenings, I did get the chance to play. I visited a small country and western bar in downtown Tokyo with a friend. We actually found Elvis. He is alive. Although he had shrunk, lost lots of weight and did a terrible job with the Beetles' Norwegian Woods, he was still pretty good. The increasingly intoxicated crowd enjoyed him.

The Japanese are a nation to be admired and respected. They have used brains and sheer discipline to accomplish the near impossible on limited resources. Success should always be applauded, not envied. Despite their modern gizmos, their cultural traditions remained intact. They spoke the language of commerce, English, but also retained their unique Japanese heritage.

American tribal leaders need to visit Japan to see that it is possible to retain your culture and survive in the information age. The nation that has the most to fear from nuclear technology is the one who is making the greatest strides to adopt this wonderful energy source. The Japanese learned the important lesson from WWII. Peace is a hell of a lot more prosperous then war. Economic victory is victory.

In our brief one-week stay, we fit in a massive number of tours and conferences. We visited the Tokei Reprocessing Facility outside of Tokyo. The attention to detail was truly impressive. At this major industrial facility, the Japanese take spent fuel rods and cut them into tiny pieces. The recovered fuel is then reused. One scientist was telling about a demonstration that took place outside the facility. There were more reporters then demonstrators. We went on the bullet train up north all along the island. The ride was smooth and short.

Our hotel was impressive. The woodwork on the floors and furniture was perfectly fit and clean. We were in the heart of Japan. All of the tourists who were skiing were Japanese. It was not as crowded as Tokyo. Still, every bit of usable space was used for something.

The people were all slender and exceptionally well mannered. There seemed to be traditions for every aspect of life. From having tea to saying goodbye, the people had a ritual they observed when dealing with each other. The most pleasant part of Japan was the exceptional care they had for their youth and elderly. Children are loved and appreciated. Parents are very patient with pre-school youngsters. The elderly are respected and treated with affection.

I did not experience racism in Japan. Everywhere I went I was treated with dignity and respect. Some places were difficult to get around because of my wheelchair. I saw very few disabled people in Japan. I know they exist because when I play wheel chair tennis nationally and internationally I usually see Japanese tennis players at various tournaments. Despite the great time and good manners, I couldn't get a date in this wonderful country to save my life. These beautiful Japanese women were just not interested in a good-looking Mexican-American attorney with a wheelchair and an attitude.

I would encourage everyone to visit this economic superpower island nation. These myths about Japanese people mistreating their children are not justified. This society is very careful with youth. The social stability that results is reflected in the economic strength and well-being of the nation. The Japanese have the longest lives of any people in an industrial nation. They have taken the power of the atom and used it successfully for peace. Nuclear power is viewed as a tool, not a weapon for mass destruction.

It will be interesting to see how Japan handles a decrease in population over the next century. This crowded country is becoming less crowded as their population becomes older and their work force contracts. Japan is a glimpse of one possible future. The sad part for me was staring at a stuffed bear in northern Japan as I was waiting to check out of our hotel and ride the bullet train back to Tokyo. The wild life in Japan is almost completely gone. Maybe the next century will bring greater prosperity as fewer numbers increase the quality of life. We left Japan amazed by their technology and good manners. From Japan we next flew to Europe and home of some of the oldest nuclear power plants on earth.

We flew into France on a 15-hour flight across Russia. Our United Airlines 747 accomplished in a few hours what took Magellan's crew and my Spanish ancestors five years, luck and good weather to accomplish. We had now traveled three quarters of the way around the world. In five very short centuries, humans have made great technological progress. From wind power on wooded ships that were lucky to make 40 miles in one day to air travel on giant airlines that zoomed across the upper atmosphere at 550 miles per hour. I was sick with the flu from the moment we left Japan. I slept it off and was in good shape by the time we arrived at Charles De Gull International Airport in Paris. The most interesting part of the journey was beginning.

France has 50 over million people, and like Japan, almost no fossil fuels. Without nuclear power, they would cease to be a modern industrial state. At least 75 percent of French electricity is produced by nuclear power. Some of it is exported to the rest of Europe. Since much of the planet's early research in the nuclear field came from the French, they are not as squeamish about the atom as America's anti-nuke, pseudo-environmentalists. The French public understands that if they want televisions, hair dryers, lights and the other conveniences of modern life, they must have nuclear power plants.

The French government arranged tours of their ultra modern nuclear complex at La Hague. In addition to nuclear power plants, La Hague is the world's largest reprocessing facility for spent nuclear fuel. They have dry cask spent fuel storage and well run nuclear related industrial enterprises. Their scientists explained in perfect English exactly how their nuclear power generation system was developed and why it was so important to their survival as a modern industrial nation. At the time of the Arab-Oil embargo in 1973, the French made a decision never to be placed in a position where their energy needs would be held hostage by unfriendly governments. They acted in their own best national interests.

Richard Bear, then tribal vice-chairman, said to me that the place reminded him of the movie, *Star Wars*. It was so modern, technologically advanced and clean. The French executives gave us a well-prepared briefing on the capability of their power plants and their waste disposal systems. In addition to their own spent nuclear fuel reprocessing, the French sell their capability to other countries.

After the visit to La Hague, the Tribal Council and I visited the low-level nuclear waste disposal site at L'Aube. The French do not take any unnecessary health risks with their nuclear waste. In addition to reprocessing, they also have in place a comprehensive program to deal with waste disposal. At L'Aube, the French government and private industry have built a facility that is supported by the surrounding communities, creates employment, and is well managed. Originally, there was political opposition. But after the facility had been in place and people have seen the economic benefits with little health risk, the public accepted it. It is normal to fear and oppose the unknown.

In Paris, the French industry and government officials gave the following advise, "Tell the people the truth, build only what you say you are going to build and do nothing more." The French have taken American technology and built standardized plants. They have used their own science and improved some of our nuclear technology.

I attended mass at the centuries old Cathedral of Notre Dame. Built over an older structure in the 12th century, it is still standing, functional and remains very beautiful. It was raining and the gray clouds added to the haunting atmosphere of Good Friday mass.

One can only picture what Europe looked like several centuries ago when this massive Catholic cathedral was the largest structure in the area. Humans can clearly build structures that will last for several centuries, provided there is proper upkeep and a commitment to preservation.

I had the very brief opportunity to visit the world's greatest museum, Musee de Louvre. The one-day visit could not possibly do justice to so much art. The room with the *Venus de Milo* was the most impressive. There were so many human contributions from so many centuries of great artists that it was difficult to take it all in. This art is as much as thousands of years old. They last because as humans we know the importance of taking care of these items we have collectively produced. I had a great time in France. My French entertainment, Veronica, was kind enough to take me on a tour of the city. Her beautiful brown eyes and long black hair with her broken English were a perfect match for the sidewalk cafes and cobblestone streets of Paris. We shared dinner and conversation. The French have the same emotional problems plagued by all of us. They lack stable long-term love relationships just as their American friends and relatives across the ocean. Veronica was charming, gracious and much-needed great company after weeks without a female companion and the unfriendly women in Japan. Unlike America, we never once watched television. That altar of entertainment was dinner or walks.

The Tribal Council and I were staying at what was supposed to be an expensive hotel near the Eiffel Tower. Nobody changed my room linen during the entire week. Despite my reminders, no one thought it was a big deal. The various hotel workers from North Africa did not think that clean rooms were important enough a function to bother with it on a weekly basis, much less every day. This was typical French attitude on matters of personal hygiene.

In college, I had a French roommate named Christian. He was not the least bit clean, just incredibly intelligent, humorous and nice. He introduced me to good food and great red wine. To this day, every other year (on my drinking years) I enjoy dry red wine in keeping with my Latin heritage. I drink every other year in order to be completely certain I control the alcohol and it does not dominate me. Several of my own family members suffer from alcoholism. I know alcohol is very dangerous. This modicum of self-discipline is a small price to pay to ensure that drinking does not destroy my health and success.

France was proof that you can have a safe nuclear program that provides for the energy needs of your nation without destroying your environment or risking the health of your citizens. Education is the key. The French produce great engineers and nuclear scientists. They do not hate Americans. I was never mistreated by the various French people I met. They hate our arrogance and, at times, very bad manners. I have personally witnessed Americans who mistreat the hotel help, taxi drivers, restaurant workers, and others. Sometimes rich Americans have this feeling of moral superiority that is truly annoying to people in other countries and even here at home. Having money does not translate into moral superiority. We are only one nation that is temporarily the most powerful in our brief 6,000 years of recorded human history. Once the Romans ruled Europe. The Spanish and then the British once had very large empires. Other countries simply recognize that we Americans really are not all that. If we keep reading our own headlines, we had better plan on losing our empire. What is that saying about pride goes before the fall?

From France we took a short flight to London. This magnificent city is still a major financial center and has a pulse of its own. We stayed near Buckingham Palace and the gray skies with the constant drizzle of light rain reminded me of Seattle. I attended Easter mass at centuries old Westminster Cathedral.

This is where one of my heroes, Sir Winston Churchill, is honored. It was his and the English people's sheer courage that helped keep the modern world free from the evil of Hitler's massive war machine. Like Red Cloud and Chief Joseph, Churchill had brains and guts. These attributes are clearly lacking in our political leaders today. Not one person on a national scale comes to my mind as having clear vision, courage, a sense of history, and the brains to carry this massive empire into the next century.

Great Britain reminded me in almost every respect of America—a natural situation given the historical ties and the fact that the majority of white people in America have roots in the British Isles. The trains were one hour late. There was a labor strike by the coal miners, and Irish terrorists were blowing up things to get negative attention. Football scores were the important news after the weather report. And just like our own country, their cities were dirty. The British had massive crime, race and labor problems. My luggage was stolen with all of the sweatshirts and small gifts I had purchased in France and Japan. Yet I absolutely loved this country. Despite the problems, pollution and chronic unemployment, the people I met were wonderful. Britain is a happening place. The women were pretty and quite friendly. The people had a great sense of humor. One of our drivers constantly teased me about America. I told him their entire country drove on the wrong side of the road and they would be speaking German if it were not for American aid in two world wars. He called America "the colonies."

We visited with nuclear officials from industry and government. They took us on a tour of Sellefield where we saw one of the oldest nuclear power plants on earth. We toured the Thorpe spent nuclear fuel reprocessing facility. With technology borrowed from the French and America, the plant was clean and well run. The plant was managed by British Nuclear Fuels Limited, one of the best governed companies on earth. Their company hosts were gracious, and explained in detail the workings of nuclear power, waste disposal, transportation and storage of spent fuel, and policy considerations of siting facilities. The entire complex provides jobs and energy. Despite their previous history of countless environmental problems and actual dumping of radioactive wastes into the ocean, the management and function changed. Now, with proper management, this industrial facility was a wanted and essential part of the local economy. We visited the low-level nuclear waste plant and talked to the workers and local people who lived next to these facilities.

Northern England is so beautiful from the green rolling hills and gray mist of the ocean, it forever leaves an impression on your mind. The country looks very much like the Oregon rain forest, with the constant mist above the green fields and gray skies. Britain is very much like America in their attitude toward energy consumption. They want both clean air and a powerful coal and natural gas industry. Unlike France and Japan, with their North Sea oil and natural gas, the British clearly have enough fossil fuel resources to live without nuclear power. Like America, they are losing their entire nuclear energy industry. This is a sad state given the massive contributions from British nuclear scientists to the development of nuclear technology. From Great Britain we next visited the most environmentally friendly nation on earth.

Sweden, the environmental peace and love nation that is also one of the world's leading armaments suppliers, relies on nuclear power for 50 percent of its electricity. In addition to great food and beautiful women, this small country is so clean that the forests have garbage cans on the paved public walks. The trails in the woods are well-developed and very old. Their cities are concrete and gray from centuries old buildings that are still intact as a result of avoiding the horrendous fighting of WWII. Stockholm has lakes and waterways everywhere. The people are playful and full of energy. They are so confident, that in their society, children are left unattended in strollers while the parents shop in the stores. This was something I had a hard time believing. I thought this well-dressed Swedish lady walking into the store, while leaving her cute blonde hair twins unattended in their strollers, was being irresponsible. So I waited and watched the children to make sure that they were safe. Pedestrians simply either smiled at these happy creatures or ignored them as if this was completely normal. In fact it was normal. Their society is so safe it is expected that a mother can go into a store and not worry about her children being abducted. If only our country had even one tenth the respect they take for granted, this place would be paradise.

The Tribal Council and I stayed in a modern American hotel in Stockholm. Swedes certainly have a different attitude about sex. They show x-rated films on the television and no one thinks anything about it. Violence is shunned. Yet the national defense forces are second to none. Having learned their own lessons from WWII, they are well-armed, well-trained and battle ready. I managed to squeeze in time between classes and meetings with industry and government officials to visit a local city zoo with two teenagers who were happy to show me around. One was from Sweden and her friend was from neighboring Finland.

I flew by myself to visit Anaka Danielson, a friend from Los Angeles, whose pet, Rocky, was a beast of a Rotweiler that hated Mexicans. We had a pleasant dinner with her neighbors and we talked about taxes and politics. They complained about the high taxes. I told them that Americans would certainly not be as adverse to paying high taxes if they enjoyed what Sweden took for granted. The government believes that they are there to serve the people and are very responsive to every aspect of life. From the cradle to the grave, there is some type of government service to assist you on the journey of life. No one watched the television. It was not the center of living like American homes. And no one had any special programs which they had to watch constantly at a certain time of the day or evening.

Anaka took me on a tour of the Swedish countryside. We drove around the pristine blue lake located next to her lovely house. For April, it was still a comfortable 70 degrees outside. We talked about life and the similarities with love relationships and behavior of people everywhere. They pay attention to detail in the homes. They are amazingly clean: a place for everything and everything must be in its place. The neighborhoods had small houses with red metal roofs, and the interiors all had wooden floors with nice rugs. I only saw a few non-whites. There were no signs of poverty anywhere.

After we settled for the evening, I would leave the Tribal Council behind in the hotel and go exploring by myself. Since I was single and adventurous, looking for attractive women proved to be exciting. After several interesting adventures with cocktail waitresses and random targets, I met up with my group at the Swedish temporary spent fuel facility located at Oskersham, a tiny seaside vacation spot. Here Sweden has built an underground wet nuclear storage facility that is located next to their most popular summer resort.

Unlike the proposed and controversial above-ground dry storage facility of the Goshutes, this project survived political hysteria and is completed. The storage capacity is 5,000 metric tons, built at a cost of $275 million dollars. If dry cask storage technology had been available at the time Sweden built their wet storage facility, they would have gone with the American designs. The Swedish industry and government officials all spoke fluent English and helped our film crew with interviews of local politicians. We talked to the local mayor and got some terrific shots of their technology.

The Tribal Council was pleased with what they saw. The advice the Council received from the Swedish government and industry officials was similar to that given by the various other countries we had visited. Tell the people the truth and only build what you promised. After it is built, local public support will come, although slowly. The small vocal people "who already know" and are opposed will never be convinced with any amount of science, data or facts.

Once at a high-level nuclear waste conference in Las Vegas, Nevada, we were having lunch while listening to Nevada's Governor Miller give the anti-nuclear pep talk, knowing full well the media and others were listening. A friend of ours, Hans Forstrom from Sweden, could not believe what he was hearing. He was shocked. Here was a major political figure in charge of a state who was either mistaken about his science or was deliberately lying. "I can't believe he said those things. This is incredible. In Sweden, people would have stood up and challenged him on his facts." I looked at him and replied, "Welcome to America, now you know why we have such a huge problem with nuclear waste and other issues."

After returning from our round-the-world nuclear education tour, we produced a film and carefully explained what we had learned to the tribal members and neighbors surrounding the reservation. The field trips to Japan and Europe made it very clear that storage of spent nuclear fuel could be accomplished safely.

But the question remained; could it be accomplished in America? Could a tiny Indian tribe build a world-class, $500 million, national facility for the storage of spent nuclear fuel in a patch of desert which is now what remains of the once great Goshute Nation? Because the temporary storage of spent nuclear fuel is a real and pressing problem in this country, there comes a time when you have to try something. Doing nothing produces nothing. No risk is great for no loss, but it will clearly not produce solutions or economic results.

If the Skull Valley Goshutes could handle this challenge, they would have the money to buy back much of the land that was stolen from them in the last century. They would have money for medical insurance for all of their members. They would have a small number of jobs to return members to their homeland. They would have directed a major national project that would help the entire nation solve a political, not technological, problem.

12

<u>ENVIRONMENTAL RACISM</u>

All communities and persons across this nation should live in a safe and healthful environment.

President William Jefferson Clinton, February 11, 1994

President Clinton issued Executive Order 12898 on February 11, 1994 to establish environmental justice as a national priority. This was the first presidential effort to direct all federal agencies with a public health or environmental mission to make environmental justice an integral part of their policies and activities. The order focuses federal attention on protecting the environmental and human health conditions of minority and low-income populations.

The term, "environmental racism" leaves connotations of destitute people of color surrounded by garbage dumps, hazardous waste sites and abandoned factories. This is, of course, partially true because this is usually the case. What is this nebulous condition called environmental racism that is inflicted upon poor minority communities? According to Simon Buttin,

Environmental racism is the social injustice represented by the disproportionately large number of health and environmental risks cast upon peoples of color in the communities in which they live. These minorities are the most common victims of toxic landfills, waste incinerators, industrial dumping, uranium mining, and other environmentally detrimental activities. As a practice—whether purposeful or unintended—

*it is often reinforced by government, legal, economic, politi-
cal, and military institutions, because it occurs simultaneously
with other racial inequities—high poverty rate, deteriorating housing and infrastructure, economic dis-investment, inadequate schools, acute unemployment, and poor or inac-
cessible medical services. Thus, environmental racism is not
just an environmental dilemma.*

This is nice rhetoric. However, we have to be realistic about where
industries are sited. The decision is usually made on economic grounds,
not race. I have never met an industry executive who has deliberately
thought to himself, "Oh boy, let locate this facility at a poor Mexican community. We don't like Mexicans." What really happens is that, when
presented with the idea, the comptroller of the company has a smug look
on her face and ever so gently informs the officers, "This is going to cost
what?! Are you guys out of your minds? There is no way you can
economically justify this decision. Damn it, find a cheaper site and close
the door behind you as you leave the room." The officers moan under
their breath and humbly leave the comptroller's office.

The steel, concrete and cement plants of America are not going to be
built in expensive neighborhoods next to the governor's mansion. It is
ridiculous to believe that a magnesium plant will be sited next to the Delta
Center in downtown Salt Lake City. The MagCorp plant, located in the
West Desert in the company-created town of Rowley, Utah, which produces magnesium by adding chemicals to the salt water from the Great
Salt Lake and running an intense electric current through the mix, emits
massive quantities of chlorine gas. So much chlorine is emitted into the
atmosphere that this facility has the dubious honor of being "the most
polluting plant in America." Could this plant be located in a residential
section of a nice city next to a park? Hardly. Is it environmental racism
to locate this plant in Tooele County, Utah, within 30 miles of the Skull
Valley Goshute Reservation and 80 miles from Salt Lake City? The often
unasked question of do we really need this type of polluter will remain
unasked.

The Geneva Steel Plant is located next to Utah Lake. It is approximately 13 miles from Provo, Utah. Now, despite bankruptcy, low steel
prices, unfair foreign competition and encroachment by neighbors, the
plant still exists. Today, other cities have crowded next to the steel plant
by sheer explosive growth. Is this urban sprawl and subsequent encroachment environmental racism? Rather than being a conscious effort at dis-

crimination, environmental racism is merely one more component of systemically racist society; when you tend to treat a people as unwanted and isolate them on unwanted land, there is a tendency also to place your unwanted waste in the same location. Put the trash with the trash is the idea.

It may come as news to leftists and right wing conservatives on the fringes of the political spectrum, but we do have zoning laws. Industrial plants are not zoned in rich residential neighborhoods. Poor residential neighborhoods are usually across the street from industrial sites. We certainly can and should restructure our entire society. We need to do simple things like eliminate lawns, develop more mass transit, spay and neuter our pets, breed children that are loved, and have good manners. However, we have to live in reality land, not in liberal environmental make-believe land or right wing "New World Order" Nazi Land. Reality is hard work, and presently, industrial pollution is part of that reality.

Garbage sites and polluting facilities are located next to poor communities because the land costs are much cheaper and people of color lack political power. I am familiar with communities throughout Europe, Japan and the United States (I have been to every part of the United States except Alaska). The industrial section of a city is usually across the street from poor neighborhoods. These poor neighborhoods have attracted immigrants to an urban environment because the housing is affordable. Having lost the foot race to the cities, they take the least favorable housing—which is the most affordable. This affordable housing for the new urbanites is located next to the county dump, the city steel plant, the concrete plant, the gravel pit and other undesirable locales. There is no question that race is *a factor* in siting these putrid industrial enterprises. *However, it is usually the least important factor*. The cheap land value and rural location encourages the siting of polluting industries more often on lands owned and lived on by minorities and poor whites who are usually single mothers with children.

There are very few Indians who live in the upper east bench in the exclusive sections of Salt Lake City, Utah, or any other city. There are just as few Mexicans and African Americans. Until the great migrations of the turn of the century, the majority of blacks in America lived in Southern rural agricultural communities. After WWII, Catholic Hispanics in the Southwestern U.S. migrated from the rural agricultural communities of the northern New Mexico and southern Colorado to the urban centers of Pueblo and Denver, Colorado, Albuquerque, New Mexico and Salt Lake City, Utah. My parents and relatives were part of that migration. Indians have moved from the rural, isolated reservations throughout the West into the urban centers of Phoenix, Los Angeles, Denver and elsewhere.

It is too soon in history to evaluate the migrations of previously rural, agricultural, hunter-gatherer groups and call their location in the poorer sections of any city or community environmental racism. This social migration urban problem will be partially solved as the move up the social-economic ladder occurs over the next several generations. This move upward will be a consequence of access to education and economic opportunity—exactly the reasons why people move to cities in ever larger and larger numbers.

There is no question that the votes are just not there in the Indian, Mexican and other poor communities to force politicians to remain accountable. Many Mexicans cannot vote because they are in this country illegally. Since over half of the country earns less than $30,000 per year and do not vote, power is held by the moneyed classes who are the nation's ultra-rich minority. Throughout history, there have always been very few rich and many more poor. This is natural. Rich people also know that an honest politician is a politician who is bought and stays bought. So we always contribute to both political parties. This, too, is normal. At the time of the Roman Empire, 80 percent of the population consisted of slaves. Today, with freedom of choice and individual liberty, we, the employers and property owners, hand out W-2 forms. But is this concentration of wealth in the hands of a privileged few an example of environmental racism? Or is it economic and environmental insanity?

The myths that exist in the environmental religion of the nineties are diverse and provocative. As celebrated scholar Joseph Campbell reminds us, myths may at times have some basis in reality. Yes, we have environmental problems. No, we are not going to run out of oxygen in the next ten years. And there are very serious environmental problems and much controversy over perceived problems. There is much scientific debate on the existence and validity of "global warming." Is it real or is it media hype? If real, is it man-made or just a natural warming cycle? The point is that we must find the true source of the problem before committing to a solution.

Racism is real and it is very ugly. I have suffered from vicious racist attacks, both physical and verbal. As a skinny ten-year old, I once faced a big 16-year-old cowboy in Tooele, spitting in my face and calling me a dirty Mexican, laughing and knowing that he was too big for me to retaliate. His sister would call me a nigger. Living in student housing, I experienced an unhappy white lady I had never met, mistake me for Iranian and leave a note on my windshield, "foreigners, go home." So many Mormons have called me a Lamanite, I am no longer offended by this racist remark.

However, racism is a thought process. This bad idea can only be defeated by good ideas in the free market of thought called the first amendment. The ideology of racism needs to be understood and studied. Mormons are among the most racist people on earth. For all of the exposure that they have to other peoples and cultures resulting from their missionary activities, they are amazingly ignorant and intolerant; and worst of all, they believe that they have a divine right to be. But the reason I have no anger or hatred toward them is that I have family members and friends who are either practicing Mormons or are of Mormon heritage. These people show both their love and their bigotry. I do not believe that they know any better. Just as my Spanish relatives are such zealots about their Catholic religion and one is a nuisance with her born-again Christian religion, you have to learn how not to take beliefs too seriously. If your grandfather teaches you as a small child that people's skin color was cursed by God, you will believe him. The fact that he doesn't know what he is talking about does not matter to children. We are all affected by the ideas we learn as children. You have to forgive people for their beliefs and their behavior. Hopefully, you will remember your own fallibility and teach by example.

The problems of racism are far less complicated today than fifty years ago when my hard-working father, who was quite dark, could not get into the carpenter's union and therefore limited to working at the Tooele Army Depot because no other employers would hire Mexicans from northern New Mexico. Racism is not as vicious as 100 years ago when blacks and Mexicans were murdered and no one was prosecuted. With the exception of Utah Mormons and a few white supremacist groups in Idaho and the deep South, the majority of white people in America and throughout the world are not racist as a rule. If the right person were qualified, regardless of skin color or sex, the majority of people would vote for that individual to be the next president of this great country. Whether big business would allow that person to take office is another question. Racism is an excepted way of life in Utah.

The environmental needs of the planet should be extensively studied and understood. By combining one ugly word racism, with one beautiful concept, environment, more verbal power is achieved. A book which is required reading for all Americans with a college education is *Environmental Overkill: Whatever Happened to Common Sense?* by Dixie

Lee Ray and Lou Guzzo. Ray, a scientist and former governor of Washington, is brilliant and unafraid as she examines environmental claims with well-reasoned scientific and political criticism.

It is easy to make allegations against anyone about anything. In America, we call that tacky behavior litigation. The damages that can be done by false allegations are lasting and unnecessary. I honestly cannot count how many clients I have had who were the subjects of lawsuits, just because they had money. Since the losers in American litigation do not have to pay attorney fees and costs for the damage they cause with their words, every corporation that is publicly traded is sued, has been sued or is in the process of being sued.

The Skull Valley Band of Goshutes have been severely criticized for examining the science, reviewing the facts, visiting actual facilities and making a well-informed decision to built a temporary nuclear fuel storage facility. Is the utility's plan to build a nuclear storage facility on the Skull Valley Goshute Reservation environmental racism or a unique economic opportunity for the tribe? Certainly the tribe's sovereignty is an added plus in this decision.

There is no question in my mind that the Skull Valley Band of Goshutes has been subjected to racism. But the racism came from those espousing to protect the Indians from themselves. This racism came from that fact that a minority group took on a major national project, using highly technical science. The tribe reached a conclusion that is supported by six Nobel laureates and 17 of the world's top nuclear physicists. The Tribal Counsel traveled the globe to arrive at an informed and considered decision. If this group of community leaders were white, the criticism would not have been so vicious. Frankly, we must accept the fact that many supposed liberals and environmentalists are closet racists who treat minorities with condescending paternalism and simplicity. They behave as if only white liberal environmentalists know what is best for the plight of minorities and the pristine wonders of nature. The belief that Indians don't know what is best for them is the basic reasoning of the B.I.A.

What if the tribe could buy back a large chunk of their land, preserve their language, provide health care and jobs to their small community, and receive an income stream from the rent and participation in major industry? Is leasing 840 acres for 20 years and being subjected to politically motivated attacks worth it? Remember who is bringing these slanderous attacks and what motive they have in making their allegations. What if a community has studied an environmental problem and decided that building the waste facility was in their best interest? After all, whose problem is it?

This is exactly what East Carbon, Utah, did in building the largest municipal solid waste dump on earth. New jobs were created and the additional tax revenue has been used to fund education and recreational programs. Young people have stayed in their community. This small town has an employer. The consequence is that, unlike many rural communities which lose their youth to our ever-expanding cities, East Carbon will survive.

Across the state of Utah, a small rural militarily dependent Tooele County had to find alternatives after losing their largest employer, the Tooele Army Depot. This antiquated military facility had been the largest employer in the county. The base realignment process enacted by Congress closed this facility in 1994. The depot has been converted to other uses.

There is no other land use that will make money in this desert region. This land is sagebrush with bad water, rattlesnakes, rabbits and a handful of coyotes. The location of the unpopular Hazardous Waste Zone near Grantsville, and Tooele City and the Goshutes' Reservation creates a few high-paying jobs. There is no question that these waste sites continue the ability of industry to produce toxic substances. We subsidize industry when we allow pollution and do not tax the environmental costs of the damage to the ecosystem. However, this is a political as well as an economic and environmental problem. It has very little to do with race. This is just how our industries developed over the last 150 years.

The rural communities and reservations in America and other parts of the world are dying. The young people are moving away because there is no work, less entertainment, and even fewer educational opportunities. In the 1800s, 70 percent of the population lived in rural agricultural communities. Today, over 70 percent of the country lives in communities with more than 30,000 inhabitants. We are now an urban society. Losing one's youth in a community and watching it die because of poor planning might also be considered environmental racism. Many of us who have the advantage of being over forty have seen communities die as the young move out and the old die off.

The population of my hometown of Costilla, New Mexico, has reduced drastically from its 5,000 people at the turn of the last century. The town lost its high school in the 1960s, then it's elementary school in the 1990s. Of the very few remaining citizens, the majority are over age 60. One ski resort, Rio Costilla, provides some jobs if there is snow. But there is not enough to bring this town back to life. In my last visit, there were fewer than 200 beings. The houses were empty and deteriorating from lack of life. The wind blows weeds and dust through the broken glass and open doors. As elderly residents are buried, there are fewer chances youth returning to replace them. There is no work of any kind in the town other than the one lonely gas station next to a highway that takes passersby onward to Taos, New Mexico or southern Colorado.

The hunting and gathering days of the Goshutes and other tribes are gone. However, the reservations do not have to lose their members to the cities. And they do not have to host dangerous polluting industries to create employment. Some reservations are amazingly beautiful, replete with wonders of nature. Others are patches of desert without water or electricity. Remember that reservations located on land that was considered to be wasteland by 19th century values. Some turned out to have oil and timber reserves and others, like Skull Valley, turned out to be no more than salt-encrusted lake bottom. With planning and careful choices of economic projects, some limited employment can be created for rural areas.

The environmental racism imposed on the Goshute stems from the presumption that they know more about an endeavor then the Goshute, and they, therefore, should second-guess their conclusions because the decision makers are people of color, black, brown or red.

Of course nuclear power is dangerous. It is very dangerous. But so is steel production, car manufacturing, coal mining, long haul trucking, law enforcement, nerve gas incinerators, emergency room work, corrections, child abuse investigations, construction and a whole host of modern industrial enterprises.

What Native Americans can add to a modern society is a healthy natural respect for the environment. If we can reduce the hazardous waste created by industrial projects, all of us will benefit. If we can find new ways to deliver products to market, we can reduce municipal solid waste. Remember that 90 percent of all municipal solid waste derives from packaging. If we can find new ways to generate electricity and use less electricity by turning off television sets and getting control over our own lives rather than watching other people live, we can reduce atmospheric pollution. The same results can be accomplished when we realize our transportation systems will need to be completely altered nationally and internationally to reduce air pollution. Charges of environmental racism will not solve environmental problems or racism. But political exploitation of the fact that a minority group has made an informed decision on a hard science issue *is* environmental racism.

True environmental racism is what happened to the Skull Valley Goshutes in 1968. The Federal government dumped and buried sheep killed by nerve agent VX on their land. The illegal burial is described in the Band's Site Health and Safety Plan as part of their contract with the Army Corp of Engineers to investigate properly this sheep burial site. And how did the Band come to investigate this sheep burial?

In 1993, my office received a letter from the Department of Defense requesting permission to come on to the reservation and examine the sheep that were buried there in 1968. I gave the letter to then Chairman, the Honorable Lawrence Bear, who told me, "Quintana, clean it up."

I could have filed a lawsuit under the Comprehensive Environmental Cleanup and Liability Act (CERCLA). However, a lawsuit against the Department of Defense and all concerned would have taken many, many years. I asked a couple of my clerks to pose as graduate students and make Freedom of Information Act requests of the Department of Defense. We did a massive amount of research and prepared for trial. We found a grant program that could solve some of the problem, and I submitted an application.

By chance, Gary Vest, the Assistant Under Secretary for Environmental Security, answered my phone call. He said he knew Utah while working for the United States Air Force trying to site the MX Weapons System.

"So you're the guy," I said.

I told him that I had drafted the Utah State Senate Resolution for Utah State Senator Francis Farley that helped stop the MX from coming to Utah. He replied, "So you're the guy." We started laughing. I told him I just wanted to solve this problem and was not interested in being in court for the next ten years. He agreed, and the Skull Valley Band of Goshutes received the first contract in the nation to investigate an environmental problem created by the Department of Defense in Indian Country. Instead of litigation, we created a national program and a mutually beneficial solution.

This research contract was important for all of Indian Country and the nation. From the research, we concluded that this illegal burial happened for these reasons:

> *In March 1968,* Dugway Proving Grounds (DPG) *personnel conducted an aerial test with the chemical warfare agent VX that apparently resulted in the deaths of up to 6,000 sheep in surrounding areas. Information obtained from a literature*

search suggests that the sheep ingested vegetation that had been contaminated with this chemical warfare agent. In total, 1,728 sheep were buried in a single trench in the White Rock Ranch Area. It appears that the sheep that died at the Skull Valley Reservation site may have died of the same cause. The Skull Valley sheep burial site is located about one mile north from the northeast boundary of DPG. Three trenches for sheep burial were constructed approximately 1.5 miles south of the Goshute Reservation Village and 2 miles east of the county highway. The chemical nerve agent GB and the agent simulant, dimethyl methyl phosphonate (DMMP), are also contaminants of concern because they were reported to have been used at DPG during the same time period.

The Goshute Reservation is located in Skull Valley, Tooele County, Utah, approximately 60 miles southwest of Salt Lake City. The reservation encompasses approximately 18,000 acres of Tribal Land. Skull Valley is bounded on the east by the Stansbury Mountains and on the west by the Cedar Mountains. Both mountain ranges are open to the North as Skull Valley approaches the Great Salt Lake.

The Sheep Burial Site is situated on open grassland in a rural setting in Skull Valley. There are no ponds, streams, or other surface water areas. The terrain at The Sheep Burial Site is gently sloping and is sparsely vegetated by low grasses.

The site has a semi-arid climate with wide seasonal and diurnal temperature variability. The average high temperature during the winter is 40 degrees Fahrenheit (°F), the average high in summer months is 89 °F. Average annual precipitation is 7.5 inches. The prevailing wind direction is from west to east.

The Army Chemical Warfare Service established Dugway Proving Ground on February 6, 1942 to fill the need for testing weapons and defenses against chemical and biological agents. Dugway's projects included the development and testing of mortars, incendiary and flame-throwing weapons, and chemical and biological warfare agents. DPG was the primary field test area for chemical munitions from 1942 to 1947, and again from 1950 to the present. DPG conducted open-air testing of chemical agents and disseminated modified agents as spray from aircraft until 1969. Since that time, only chemical simulants have been tested in open air.

The chemical warfare agents that have historically been tested at DPG include the organophosphate-based nerve gases, VX and GB (Sarin). Dimethyl methyl phosphonate (DMMP), a decomposition product of VX, was also tested as a nerve agent simulant. VX is slow to evaporate and may persist as a liquid for several days. GB is moderately persistent when dispersed as large droplets; it is non-persistent when disseminated as a cloud of very fine particles. These organophosphates are not considered to be persistent in the environment, and it is considered that any of the agents that may have been present at the burial site should have passed through numerous half-lives (i.e., the time required for ½ of the material to decompose). It is unlikely that any of the original material is present at the site; however, some of the degradation products of these agents and simulant may be present in detectable quantities. The degradation products of VX and GB include: dimethyl methyl phosphonate (DMMP), ethyl methylphosphonic acid (EMPA), isopropyl methylphosphonic acid (IMPA), methylphosphonic acid (MPA), diisopropyl methylphosphonate (DIMP), diisopropylaminoethyl methylphosphonothioic (EA 2192), diethyl methylphosphonate (DMP), and diisopropylaminoethyl mercaptan (DESH).

Through my confidential sources, I obtained top-secret government documents which for the first time directly proved that the Department of Defense knew all along it was their nerve agent VX that killed all of those animals. The long-term question of whether or not there were any by products remaining was answered by the investigation. The results of the drill hole samples and literature review, as well as meetings and interviews with experts, were that no VX or any daughter products were found at the site of the sheep burial. After over thirty years, there was no trace of the agents, either because they are so small and could not be detected, or the agents had turned into strong fertilizers. Funding was approved to remove the sheep from the reservation as part of the the United States Government accepting responsibility and being willing to solve a problem they created. This act of environmental racism was resolved by the band and the Army by working together and talking with each other rather than having the courts make a decision for the parties.

A lawsuit would never work in the short run to determine what danger, if any, there was to the reservation. The better solution was to talk and investigate the facts. Filing an emotionally charged lawsuit would not result in an immediate investigation and ultimate removal. Making harsh accusations without a proper basis in science is not only impolite, it is a good way to find sanctions from a court when the case is thrown out as not properly based in law and fact. The sheep were buried on the reservation because of the gross stupidity of the United States government. Extensive research into weapons of mass destruction, including nerve agents, chemical and biological, as well as nuclear weapons, was being conducted right next to the Skull Valley Goshutes' Reservation.

When the accident happened, the sheer luck of the wind changing directions kept the nerve agent in Skull Valley. Had the wind shifted, the VX would have gone over Tooele and Salt Lake Valley and killed thousands of people. It didn't, and to the best of our knowledge squirrels, birds, rabbits and approximately 6,000 sheep were killed. The sheep were buried on the sparsely populated reservation because the smelly decaying carcasses had to be disposed of immediately. Since the sheep were grazing on the reservation under a lease, the Army asked the BIA and was given permission to bury these sheep on the reservation. *Nobody asked the Tribal government for permission to bury these sheep on their land.*

This was crass and illegal behavior, trespassing, and totally disregarding the legal rights of the Skull Valley Goshutes. There is no possible way the actions of the Army would be repeated today. We know better. And tribes have lawyers and tribal courts. Today is a different, better, and in some circumstances, safer world. But the fact remains that this sheep burial was environmental racism. The sheep could have been moved to a site off the reservation at nearby Whiterock where the other sheep burial occurred. Instead, they were buried where they fell without the permission of the Band government. This tribal government is older than that of the United States of America, and despite its small size, has been in existence for a long time.

There are people today who believe that using rural communities and poor areas as sites for dangerous activities is justified because the land has a low dollar value. This attitude reveals environmental racism. The only way this attitude will change is by increasing the land value of these areas and thereby making it economically unattractive to use them as dumping sites. Improving the value takes careful work and study. Rural areas have, as a rule, lower land value than urban areas for simple economic reasons. But rural life has its own special value. When you travel the back highway behind Utah Lake or go on the Lincoln Highway to Fish Springs National Wildlife Refuge, you will see many hawks, eagles, antelope, wild horses, and beautiful unmolested natural formations. These natural wonders have substantial irreplaceable value. There are over 250 different types of birds at Fish Springs National Wildlife Refuge. And they are breathtaking in their beauty.

It is in the best interest of the planet to keep people from moving to urban centers. The cities are already overcrowded. The crowding creates crime and pollution. The last thing the cities in America or anywhere else need is more people. If we can create more reasons for people to return or remain in the rural areas of this country, maybe we can solve some of the massive urban problems that now exist. We need planning. We need to view reality differently. But there is hope.

With television, telephones and the Internet, moving to a city can have some advantages. People can work at home and telecommute. We will still be required to produce and transport food from the large corporate farms to the urban centers. In this new age, two percent of the people feed the other 98 percent. So farmers, truck drivers and mothers become especially important. The rest of us push paper and pretend we are important. After all, farmers actually grow food. Truckers deliver the food to market. Good mothers ensure healthy babies that are loved and nurtured. Without good mothers, we could get a generation of sociopaths.

Environmental racism is a very strong allegation. However, will this allegation withstand close scrutiny and criticism? It was politically expedient for several elected officials to call the plan to build a nuclear fuel storage facility environmental racism. They each had their own motives. But close examination of this charge requires a dismissal of the claim as frivolous.

As our society rapidly transforms from the nuclear age to the information age, our reasons for military expansion and conquest disappear, hopefully forever. All of human history is now being completely transformed by the Internet. The question is not whether tribes going to be destroyed by environmental racism. The real question is how will tribes and all of us survive in the information age.

13

TRIBES IN THE INFORMATION AGE

Never take a knife to a gunfight.

Old cowboy saying

Today, 556 federally recognized Indian nations exist within the United States with a combined population of approximately two million. Over 65 percent of this population live in urban environments and use English as a first language. Native Americans have survived the invasion of their homelands in the first 400 years, but they won't continue to survive without conquering the Internet.

Every person on earth will be touched by the Internet, the most revolutionary change in human history. At your fingertips lies all of recorded human history. This is the largest library ever. With a mere computer and a phone line you can visit Rio De Janerio or Paris. You can research nerve agent VX or a substance abuse hospital in Orlando, Florida. There at your fingertips are unbelievable music, sights and information. You can listen to samples of songs and do incredible reports for school and work. You can learn. I suspect no human alive today will survive the impact of the Internet. Like fire and electricity, all will be touched.

Most importantly, the Internet levels the playing field. No longer do you need to travel half way across the country to an expensive university at a cost of approximately $150,000 and five years of your life. Data is now available at a cost of less than $1,000 for a computer, and a connecting fee of $20.00 per month. What is the magical mystery of the Internet? Basically, it is the connection of computers and the worldwide telephone system. The data on each computer can then be shared with anyone you want to have access to your site.

Web site after web site exists for people to share with the world who they are, what they do, what they are selling and their views on drugs, sex, rock and roll, gardening, politics, and anything else you can imagine. Universities are on the web. Studies on the flow of water in Red Butte Canyon and the possibilities of life on Mars are there to be explored. Name it, think it, imagine it, and you will find it on the Internet.

Each day more information is added onto the information superhighway. This data is multiplied as more people read the new material and learn from this information. In turn, more knowledge is shared with the world. We can find so much knowledge from so many on virtually everything and everyone. Reports that took months of my time are accomplished in one week.

This technology, for the first time in history, provides information to all. Information is what is valuable. Information was only available to the upper classes of society throughout much of history. Now, with the Internet, all of the data publicly available on line is available to the public. Information is the key to upward mobility, and the Internet is the tool that provides this opportunity to every individual. This means that you can no longer use racial discrimination as a crutch. You are no longer excluded from society because you are deprived of the knowledge that previously came only with a college degree. Go to the public library and log on to the Internet. You will have to do the work to gain the knowledge, but then again, those people with degrees from Harvard worked plenty to get them.

There is also quite a bit of disgusting junk on the Internet: from sick, child pornography to vicious messages of racial hatred. It is up to you to separate the wheat of knowledge from the shaft of useless and destructive information that can be found on the Net.

We can do so much with technology. We can make weapons of mass destruction or works of absolute wonder. If you have ever been to a nuclear power plant and seen the amount of electricity produced without air pollution, you can appreciate the nuclear age. If you had to worry about your child's life because of the very real possibility of nuclear war, you appreciate the importance of peace.

The nuclear age for war is over. With the exception of the handful of humans who will always hate others, the threat of total nuclear destruction by an all-out nuclear war between the United States and the former Soviet Union is gone, for now. The two competitors are now collaborators on something far more important, space exploration. One key to the successful exploration of space is the combined knowledge of nuclear energy that was derived during the cold war. As you read this book, our astronauts and Russian cosmonauts are living peacefully in a space station together. Where we once pointed missiles at each other, today we launch space ships together. As we come to know more and more people from other parts of the world, there is less reason to hate each other.

The information age is the explosive growth of access to computers and the World Wide Web in the hands of millions. Tribes, poor rural communities and individuals can use this wonderful device to connect their people into the same knowledge base and better communicate with them. It should be the goal of every tribe to have every member hooked up to the Internet to their very own tribal web site. This connection will enable tribes and their members to be competitive in an increasingly smaller world.

You cannot afford to miss changes in technology. It can mean the end of your means of survival or even your culture. Let's face it. Tribes have lost many of their people, much of their land, and are now losing what is left of their language and culture. The tribes who survive and prosper in the information age will be the ones who place a computer in the hands of every tribal family. Tools of war and peace cannot be ignored. Information is the tool that will enable tribes and everyone to survive and protect their lands, culture, heritage and people. The information age has the potential to be the ultimate Golden Age of mankind. It can also be used to create new super weapons even more deadly then the nuclear, chemical and biological instruments of mass destruction we have had to endure thus far. And this will happen.

The tribes in the information age have the potential to share their rich knowledge of nature with us all. This knowledge, at least what is left of it, will enable us to prosper. Unlike my Spanish ancestors who burned the sacred books of the Mayans, Aztecs and Incas as works of the devil, we cannot burn the Internet. Ancient knowledge was destroyed at the hands of religious fanatics throughout history. In the free market place of ideas, the communication of knowledge will enable good thoughts to defeat the messages of violence and hatred. At least that is always our hope. Despite the control of the mass media by a handful of very rich white males, there is enough real data out there to allow for truth to defeat rumor.

Each month, more than 100,000 new web sites are created and added to the information superhighway. With each additional web site, there are more and more books that are replaced by electronic data. Electronic mail is so much cheaper and faster than regular mail, it is fast becoming the preferred method of communication.

What the Internet does provide is the ability to preserve language and culture by communicating internally within the tribal group. And some tribes have already adopted this language tool as a cultural preservation method. They are using their Internet sites to enable members to re-learn lost culture and language skills. Once, tribal members and others in European, Asian and African villages lived in close proximity and were able to visit and work actively together. Today, everyone is spread out over vast stretches of land covering many states, cities and countries. One of my sisters is a judge in New Mexico. Another lives in Denver, Colorado. A third lives in Saudi Arabia, and the other family members live in Tooele, Utah. All can communicate via the web.

The necessity of earning money drives all of us, from small closely knit family units out of villages and reservations to our many crowded and vast cities all over the world. We now have the luxury of sending e-mail across numerous miles, to distant lands to other family members—for free. Many tribal members do not attend important meetings at reservations because of distance, costs of travel and other family and employment commitments.

It takes quite an effort to travel hundreds of miles to attend tribal meetings where people are bickering and screaming at each other. Simple communication by e-mail or phone will work. In this information age, we must manage tribal governments like small public corporations. Tribe's books and records should be available for inspection with a secret password issued only to tribal members. With the Internet, management of tribal resources and getting out the message to the masses is much easier. This process is especially important on very large complex projects.

The Skull Valley Band of Goshutes was losing the propaganda war with Governor Leavitt on their plan to lease 840 acres of their land to a private utility group to store spent nuclear fuel. A group of 124 people were no match for a slick politician armed with racial hatred and an agenda. So the Band developed a web site to explain their project to its members and the world: http:www.skullvalleygoshutes.org. It clearly helped. This idea for an Internet site came from the constant barrage of politically motivated criticism of Utah's politicians. Truth, which travels slowly by mouth, cannot overcome the lies, which can travel via television and radio waves and newspapers at the speed of light.

So vicious were the attacks on the Skull Valley Band of Goshutes, that Professor Richard Wilson from Harvard's physics department called me to ask if he and his friends could be of assistance in bringing truth to this political hysteria. I arranged for the Chairman, Leon D., and the tribal secretary, Rex Allen, to travel to Harvard to meet with this esteemed scientist.

At Harvard, I was amazed to watch Dr. Wilson call his Nobel laureate friends. With mere phone calls, Dr. Wilson arranged for six Nobel laureates to take the time to contribute their very real knowledge of science to educate the public on this important issue. The scientists went through each hysterical claim of Governor Leavitt and set the scientific record straight.

Now, each time Utah's former, crazy Congressman Merrill Cook or some other politician makes an outrageous claim about the storage of nuclear waste and how this is morally wrong, they are simply referred to the web site. If Utah's politicians want to express their racism, let them vent themselves at their personal computers. We don't have to sit there and endure them. The Goshute's web site is not for Utah's politicians anyway; it is designed for thinking minds which don't have to consult with the Book of Mormon to see the truth. Distorted dogma and a jaded view of reality will not protect you from spent nuclear fuel. Fortunately the Goshutes have done their homework, they asked the experts.

Professor Wilson is one of the world's great scientific minds. He has been a source of great relief in bringing scientific honesty to such political hypocrisy. His writings on physics and other subjects cover several decades. He and his friends have important knowledge that adds to the human database. This knowledge can be shared economically via the net.

One of my client's, Junior Whiterock, is a world-class artist whose artwork is so precise and difficult to produce (made entirely of original materials) that it is best displayed and sold with beautiful pictures on the World Wide Web. At our first August Art Auction for the Indian Walk In Center, he sold all of his beautiful hand crafted pottery. The Internet is being used by numerous tribal artists to sell their beautiful work to the world. This arrangement enables them to stay on their reservations and earn a living at the same time.

Like guns in the last century, the primary users of the Internet are white Americans, upper-class Europeans, and the Japanese. The Internet has not yet filtered its way down to communities of color as quickly. This greatest tool of learning is something to which every community on earth should have immediate access. The biggest hindrance is the lack of money for a computer and phone service in the poorer areas of Indian America. Presently, tribal members on the Navajo Reservation and other parts of the country do not have running water or electricity, much less phone service. And $2,500 for all of the equipment necessary for Internet access is beyond the reach of families who have an average income of $13,000 per year. The hook-up charge of $20 per month is too much for large segments of the world and Indians here in America. Here is where corporate America, the federal government and rich tribes need to step up and just purchase the computers for those who can not afford them. All tribes can and should work together to develop their Internet resources.

The large companies, which have been the greatest vehicles for economic and technical growth, need to work with tribes and other indigenous groups to ensure access to the net. There is no economic reason to prevent companies like Microsoft, Intel, IBM, Cisco, Dell, Qwest and others to coordinate their efforts with tribal governments and indigenous people and help them. Microsoft has a market capitalization of over $350 billion. This sum is larger than the entire Russian economy. They have over $38 billion in cash just sitting around for use on any type of project legally available. Intel has a market capitalization of over $207 billion and over $11 billion in cash just available to do deals. The largest American companies make more money then many countries. All of these companies are very rich and can afford to help tribes and others to gain access to the information superhighway. It is in their best interest as well, because economically healthy tribes means more customers for all of these well-managed companies.

What the Internet provides is a gun in a gun-fight of the information age. This gun has to be used by tribes and rural communities to protect their resources from people who have an altogether different agenda. This requires carefully watching for con artists. For one smart con can wipe out years of hard work. And cons are particularly attracted to unsuspecting young people (like you), the elderly and Indian Country.

14

CONS, CON ARTISTS AND INDIANS

You cannot do good business with bad people.

Warren Buffet

In addition to garbage dumps and gaming, tribes are routinely the target of very clever con artists. The schemes range from over priced equipment deals to municipal solid waste sludge, oil scams, leases with blind assets ... you name it. The scam does not matter. Poorly placed trust does. Historically, tribes have been sold poison meat, blankets with smallpox, rifles that would not fire, over-priced machinery, and a host of other frauds. What tribes and all of us need to learn is how to spot a scam. We are not taught these skills by our parents, coaches, law professors or others. We certainly did not learn this insight to human behavior from our grandparents.

A business deal has two important elements: the people in the deal and the market. The first element is the most important. The people in the deal make or break you. Business deals are transactions designed to make money. This requires knowing people, not just goods. Good people make a deal and bad people can destroy a venture and a lifetime of work. Business deals are made in the heart with honor. The contract is written to remember what it is you agreed to and how you are going to accomplish this transaction. If a dispute occurs, you go to lunch and straighten it out.

However, knowing what I know now, I clearly understand that if you believe even for one second when money is involved, people are going to tell you "the truth, the whole truth and nothing but the truth so help you God," make sure they are sworn in properly at their depositions after you have lost your or your client's last investment dollar. Even nuns will sometimes mislead you when money is involved.

Con artists and child molesters work slowly by winning your trust. They will groom you like pedophiles luring small children with candy until they have won your trust. Then they steal your entire life savings. These people are sociopaths. It does not matter what you have in writing. *Con artists do not respect anything verbal or written.* Their goal is to obtain illegal money.

How do you spot whether or not someone is a legitimate businessman or a con artist? There are several warning signs. If you take the time to look and are very, very careful, you will spot them. In nature, venomous snakes hide behind rocks and are rarely out in the open waiting to bite you. If you leave them alone they won't bother you. If you try to handle them and don't know what you are doing, they will bite the hell out of you. They might even kill you. The same is true with con artists. If you don't do business deals with them, you will not lose your money. First, like advising children about sex offenders, don't trust strangers. Question the motives of individuals who are asking you to invest your hard-earned money. These individuals are being very nice and polite trying hard to win your friendship. Why are they so friendly?

Con artists are some of the most clever individuals around. They enjoy the chase and pride themselves at stealing without being caught. *The most glaring red flag is that they will present deals that have higher than normal returns.* Being greedy, full of pride and arrogant is the best way to attract these creeps. Greed is believing there is a fast way to make large rewards for smaller effort. For most of us, it can't happen. Money is usually made carefully, slowly and in small amounts over a period of time. Remember, most legitimate business deals earn between two and nine percent profit. Look out for the flashy deals that offer the quick large returns of greater than nine percent. If the deal offers greater than nine percent profit, stop and watch your posterior. The majority of deals that earn returns greater than nine percent are either selling drugs or not paying taxes. In either event they are probably illegal and when caught by the law, you and all involved will lose and lose big. Jail is an awaking experience. I suggest that all of you spend time there to learn what loss of freedom and dignity really mean. When the cold gray steel bars close behind you and you clearly realize you need someone's permission to leave, the reality of politics and law wake you up quickly.

If someone is intent on ripping you off, this person will have a history. Believe me, you are not so special that cons are interested in you and only you. They are interested in your money. On any investment greater than $10,000 ask for a written list of every business deal they have entered into their entire lives. All we own is our time. All of us have to account to someone for the actions and inactions of our lives. We all worked somewhere, spent money, lost money, possibly went to jail, attended college, were sued or we sued someone.

References either check out or they do not. A snake remains a snake despite the lies he will tell you. By taking the time to check on their prior deals and actually talking with the people who have done business with them, you will get some truth. If you were ripped off by John the Con and someone called you about doing business with him, you will tell them about your unpleasant experience. Due diligence is daring to ask the financial questions that make people uncomfortable and may, in other circumstances, seem to be impolite. But when someone is trying to get you to part with your money, all questions are polite and everything is fair game. Ask the impolite questions.

Just like a sex offender, John the Con moves carefully and slowly. He wants to win your confidence. After all, he is John the Con the Confidence Man. He knows just what to tell you and is very friendly. He will make extra efforts to win your friendship. If you are raising money for charity, he will be the first with a contribution. That is easy enough, since it is someone else's money he is contributing. If you drink, he buys and makes certain you have the time of your life. Do you like women? That pretty girl you just spent the night with may have been a prostitute. If you like football or the symphony, he will make sure you have tickets. He will go out of his way to make sure you trust him. He knows it will merely be a matter of time. He is always willing to wait. If it takes six months, a year or two or three years, this is fine. *No only means no right now.* Trust takes time and time happens slowly.

What John the Con wants is your investment. Once he has your money, you are done. As one con artist I helped bring to justice, John the Con Chivers, so aptly stated, "I have his money. There is nothing he can do about it now." No legal document is binding.

What we are talking about is fraud. What exactly is fraud? When does mere embellishment become fraud? It is a question of intent. When the misrepresentations are made to induce your investment and the person making the false statements clearly knows these matters are not true, this is fraud. It is the big difference between the white lie and lying to take your money. Remember the advice of St. Thomas Aquanis: *"A lie is deliberately withholding information from someone who has the right to know that information."* Fraud is usually directed at naïve new investors who suddenly came upon money, sleeping insurance companies, unsuspecting banks, and other financial institutions and people with money.

The really good con artists will hire top-notch professionals to hide their fraud. Attorneys and accountants are routinely used by cons to do their dirty work. The public is much more likely to believe a con artist's attorney than John the Con. An attorney is an officer of the court. When I first started practicing law 19 years ago, that actually meant something. With the exception of federal court, it rarely means anything anymore. Yet most members of the public still trust professionals. The new investors, who are fresh money, do not expect professionals to mislead them in financial matters.

Just because an attorney is in a deal does not mean that the business transaction is real. I learned that expensive lesson the hard way when I believed some opposing attorneys. If an attorney lies to you and it is not in writing, you are out of luck. Even if the lie is in writing, so what. Does the attorney who made the representation have any assets? There is such a glut of attorneys that most make under $30,000 per year. On average, good experienced legal secretaries make more money than half of the Utah bar members. Suing a poor attorney who was used by a con artist will not recovery your money. Many attorneys don't even have malpractice insurance. And even if they do, it may not be enough to cover the fraud.

If you see that other people have invested in a deal, this does not mean the business is real, or better yet, a good investment. In the John the Con Chivers' deal, other contractors were already conned long before my clients invested one dime. It could very well be they were suckered first and you might be next. Just because others were foolish or greedy does not mean you should follow in their footsteps. Do your own due diligence. So you have visited the industrial plant. You saw the equipment, the busy blue-collar workers performing labor services, the long-term contracts with the county government, the joint venture agreement with the large national company and contractors doing their thing. This is not evidence that the deal is real. It is only evidence that others are in before you and may already have been fooled or foolish.

In *Skull Valley Band of Goshutes v. John Chivers, aka Owen Chivers, aka John D. Chivers, John R. Chivers,* the equipment had been moved from state to another state without the permission of the banks. Some of it was, we believe, stolen. The workers were all under contract and their quarterly taxes were not being filed, much less paid. The facility was built on the come by the various contractors who had been or soon would be stiffed. The contractors were told my clients were already in the deal, which was a lie and John the Con Chivers knew it was a lie.

If you see politicians are involved in the transaction, this is not evidence the deal is real. Many politicians are involved in fraudulent deals or have been used by con artists. It could just mean the politicians were conned first. Politicians generally do not get to the top because they are nice people. They do not always hang around nice guys. Once in office, they will reward their friends with jobs and contracts. In the Bonneville Pacific case, investors lost millions of dollars. Major Utah politicians were involved. None went to jail.

More money is stolen in the United States through white-collar crime than could ever be stolen by blue-collar crooks robbing grocery stores and banks. The big thieves steal several hundred thousand dollars and sometimes millions with their scams. They don't waste their time with little money like armed robbery. White-collar crime like white-collar work, rewards those involved with the very healthy wages and benefits. Cons are always willing to wait for the real money. Suing them will rarely do any good. The money will be hidden offshore in Europe, at the Isle of Man, the Cayman Islands, in other companies, or in other bank accounts. You will usually not find it and you will not have the resources to chase lost money with good money.

The best protection from John the Con is to know we all have a past. Some of us are proud of our past. All of us have made mistakes. Our past is the best record of our future. Again, John the Con will have cheated others before you. He will have been sued before and failed in other ventures. These failures were not mere coincidences, changes in the marketplace or even bad luck. John the Con failed in business because he lied and cheated. Like professional basketball, after five fouls you are thrown out of the game. Cons do not honor any contracts with others and will not honor them with you.

John the Con clearly understands that *it is very easy to cheat honest men*. Because honest men have this silly belief that just because they would not lie to others in matters involving money or most other things, others would not lie to them. This is so noble, yet so naïve and so very, very wrong. If money is involved, John the Con will lie to you. So will your relatives, priests, bishops and nuns. I don't know the character of your grandmother, so I'll pass on her behavior. But she might lie to you too, so be prepared for the worst. At least your mom won't lie to you.

If you do not want to lose your hard-earned money that took you years to accumulate, then watch every single move of the people who want you to invest in anything. Why does John the Con and his friends keep coming back after you have already told them no. They want you to invest? Why you? Why your company? Why your tribe? Why your small government? Why won't banks fund John the Con's deal? What are they really going to do with your money and how do you know? Are they really going to use your money to complete this deal? Really? Have you checked on the use of your money? You were told it was going to be used to pay contractor debts. What if it is going into John the Con's friend's trust account in New York, to pay his American Express Card, loans to his girlfriends, payments on child support and fancy dinners? This is exactly what occurred with John the Con Chivers.

That Scotsman is one brilliant man. He is one of the smartest men I have ever met. He does not have a law degree, yet his legal pleadings were of very high quality. He is not licensed to do engineering anywhere. His engineering skills were superior. He does not have a business degree, but this was one well-planned operation. In the end, his greed and arrogance finally caught him. I could not be a witness and an attorney in my own case. I hired one of the nation's best fraud attorneys to track and nail him.

Jerry Mooney was decorated in Vietnam and graduated at the very top of his law class at the University of Utah. Chivers was so accustomed to winning against other attorneys and victims that he was certain he would win this one, too. He totally miscalculated the resolve of a small stubborn tribe and of one of the nation's best trial attorneys, Jerome Mooney. When the jury returned a verdict of fraud and awarded the Skull Valley Goshutes $625,000 plus interest for a total judgment of $970,000, Chivers was no longer the smiling self-assured macho man. It took five years of litigation, but Jerry Mooney brought John the Con Chivers to justice. But even this did not stop Chivers from being a con man. He even worked as the site manager for Utah's Olympic Village housing project; he just expanded his scope of potential victims from the Goshutes to the Utah taxpayers. Given the nature of how Utah bought the Olympics, this is truly poetic justice.

Do you want to chase away con artists like John the Con Chivers and his friends? Require the following on every important business deal: an opinion of counsel from a reputable law firm that the representation made by John the Con are true and correct to the best of their knowledge, and they have investigated these; an accounting report of audited assets and debts by a reputable accounting firm; a background list of *every* business deal this person or persons have entered into their entire lives; a confession of judgment for the entire amount of the investment so you will not have to chase John the Con; titles to all of the assets claimed to be in the deal; a litigation check with every court you can think of on the number of times John the Con may have been sued in every state or country he has ever lived which is signed off by John the Con and his attorneys; a securities check with the Securities and Exchange Commission on whether or not John the Con is being sued for securities violations; a quick FBI check on any federal charges; a bankruptcy; check to determine whether or not John the Con has previously filed bankruptcy, and finally, a credit check with Dun and Bradstreet.

Like almost everything else I learned in life, unfortunately, my lessons came the hard way. I have several clients who were hurt by very clever con artists before I had the opportunity to check their deals. I chased the money after it was already lost. Chasing lost money is not fun. In the long run, if you survive financially, being stung by a crook is sometimes a positive experience. Without that education in human behavior, how will you be able to spot real deals? Now that you have been bitten by a snake, you know how to spot them. Without John the Con Chivers, I never would have made real money for any of my business clients. He taught me how to play ball in the big leagues. The moral of the story is trust slowly, and only those who prove trustworthy. In the words of the immortal Ronald Reagan, "trust but verify." In other words, check every single representation made and be certain your investigation was accurate.

Here are some of the more common Utah scams that pray on Mormons and non-Mormons:

Utah is the white-collar con capital of the nation. From polygamist Joseph Smith being chased down by the state militia for fraud, to Mormons later selling westward bound pioneers overpriced goods, to the Mountain Meadow Massacre, Utah has a rich history of deceit, fraud, and even murder with those who do not agree with them. That tradition continues to this very day. The recent Olympic scandal is the rule, not the exception, of how business is conducted in the Land of Zion. Some of the more clever Utah hustles are legal, but have little chance of success.

A common one is the dubious multi-level marketing scam. If you get in first on the ground level and build this tremendous down line, you will become very wealthy. Others will sell their products and you will be supported by their efforts. Oh, by the way, you need to pay $125 for the materials, and the seminar to show you how to build your down line will only cost you $500. I cannot even count how many Utahans are engaged in multi-level marketing. Although barely legal, it is a scam. I have never met one person who has made any money on a multi-level marketing deal—except, of course, the people who dream up the scam. Several have called forth a heavenly choir to proclaim their very small down lines. None hit pay dirt. Other states frown on this glorified Ponzi scheme.

Most people clearly do not have the type of personality or lust for money to build this terrific down line. It is just not going to happen. Many people are so shy they have trouble asking a store clerk for change, much less asking others to sell hair products, new skin treatments, phone service, water purifiers, cleaning solutions and various other overpriced products to be part of this wonderful multi-level financial empire.

Salt Lake used to be home for the infamous penny stock market. These deals involved using a shell corporation with no assets and only shareholders to merge with a real corporation and real assets. The promoter who created the shell usually had all of his friends, relatives and even dead people from the grave who would rise to vote their stock proxies. The stock certificates are then gathered and put in a box. After the merger with a real or semi-real company, the real shareholders from other states are buying stock based upon the news releases coming out of the company. The promoter and his friends sell their stock while the real shareholders buy blue sky and thin air.

These "box jobs" became such a plague on the securities market that Salt Lake won the distinction of having a branch office of the Securities and Exchange Commission. After the promoters and company would sell their secret stock, the deals would usually end up in bankruptcy. Although some have, I never saw one penny stock deal survive in 19 years of practicing law. All were so speculative they might as well have been fraud. Having been lured by my own greed, my office has numerous stock certificates from these failed ventures. The market place can never protect you from your own greed.

Then there are the new inventions scams. Sometimes these deals have real and unusual inventions. However, the financial statements of these companies would have boxed stock that appeared out of nowhere. In one stock fraud case I recently settled, the inventor has a new product that will revolutionize transportation—an electric car that has zero emissions and can travel long distances at 70 mph without recharging. They also claim to have purchased a diesel production plant in Mexico with stock from a subsidiary and to have been awarded large contracts for the production of electric bicycles with China. Really? I constantly see news releases that flash this new deal and that new merger. When you pull up the Form 10K's and 10Q filings with the Securities and Exchange Commission, you see that these mergers and acquisitions are being accomplished with stock that is worth less than one cent per share and total assets of $1,000. The money was used to pay the Salt Lake City south state street accountant and for the new yellow pages attorney. I took stock for fees because they could not pay the judgment I obtained against them. Since I knew the company did not have anything, I slowly sold all of my stock into the market and got out quietly. The financial statements, that are publicly available, reveal the company has nothing. *Carefully read the financial statements of every company that wants you to invest money.* If the financial statements are not audited, don't invest anything. Let someone else lose money.

One of the best cons to come out of Salt Lake was a major book fraud. A local author wrote a book with a very similar title to a best seller. He would call various bookstores around the country and order his own books. Then he would tell them that a seminar was being held in that town and he needed 100 copies for Idaho, 300 copies for Montana, 200 copies for Iowa or whatever figure or whatever state he was using that particular day. He would fly to these states when the books had been shipped and buy back his own product. Since he was the one shipping them, he had a pretty good idea on when the books would get there. He would arrive at these various towns all over the nation with a check in hand and pick up his very own books. Then he would sell the same books to the next town. He did this enough that he was picked up on a bestseller list and was offered lucrative speaking engagements all over the nation. Now that was a very clever scam, and he got away with it.

A more common Utah fraud is called a bankruptcy bust out. A new business opens up and immediately starts taking orders for goods and materials from all of the surrounding communities. The vendors are paid for the first order to win their trust. On the second order the payment is less then the full amount. After that the new company is filled with so much debt that it cannot possibly survive, so it files bankruptcy and the cons go to the next scam. The vendors are left in bankruptcy court looking for their merchandise, which is sometimes on a van traveling out of state to a storage unit to wait for the statute of limitations to end.

Then there was the great Utah diamond caper. A local shark convinced investors that he had discovered all of these diamonds in some foreign country. The first diamonds were real and were sold for a profit. The investors having been convinced that they were buying real diamonds at a discount, invested their money with him. When they went to sell their newly purchased jewels, they discovered all they had was zirks. Zirconium is commonly used to lure nice-looking young ladies into bed. When the young ladies discover their diamond does not cut glass, the romance usually ends.

Foreign investors have frequently been the target of Utah con artists. Hiding behind the Church of Jesus Christ of Latter Day Saints (you know, the Mormons), people in Germany and Asia have been targeted and hit with stock scams and other investments. They were sold shell corporations with no assets or assets that had been moved immediately after the sale had taken place. Beneath the cloak of the LDS church and all of the communications companies that promote the wholesome image, people will sometimes hide a very small network of con artists that target Mormon and non-Mormon communities. These individuals, like some Southern Baptists preachers, hide behind their claimed moral superiority to fleece unsuspecting investors. The main victims are their own people. Remember, those closest to us will often cause us the most harm.

Then there are the forged documents cases that were sold by convicted Utah killer, Mark Hoffman. He was able to fleece investors and the Mormon Church for tens of thousands of dollars. The documents would cause a great deal of embarrassment for the church, so they were quietly purchased to keep the illusion of purity alive. He killed two people in cold blood, but he had so much evidence against the church that in exchange for life imprisonment without the possibility of parole, he did not have to testify and was given a life-saving deal. One of the bombs he exploded was on my floor in the Judge Building where my law office was located in Salt Lake City, Utah. His documents later proved to be forgeries.

Of course there are always the phony government contracts to the suddenly new minority owned firms. I was the executive director of the Intermountain Minority Contractors Association. While I would try to work with government agencies to get work for legitimate minority contractors, others were trying to use minorities for money. White Mormon con men would convince Indians and others to put together a front minority company. Contracts are bid on using the federal preference given to minorities. Sometimes the work is completed and the profits go to white players who are working the deal behind the scenes. These front companies take work away from emerging and real minority businesses. Then they go into bankruptcy, and everyone loses except them.

A common scam all of us have encountered is the charity for needy, the poor or some unfortunate group or project. One charity wanted me to be on their board of directors. They claimed to help 2,500 homeless children annually. As it turns out, their inflated figures did not mention that there were five to seven kids per day on average over the period of one year. The executive director was paying herself $35,000, her assistant director received $30,000, and the director was receiving $25,000. It is hard to say just how much money actually went to the actual care of the children since the organization also had volunteers and free rent for the daycare. I declined their offer.

When I got out of the hospital after my bout with transverse myelities, which left me partially paralyzed, I asked the Multiple Sclerosis Society for some assistance. They offered to rent a wheel chair. I explained that I had just got out of the hospital and was on welfare and could not possibly pay any money for a wheelchair. I still remember the words, "Well I guess we can't help you then."

Some of these non-profits raise millions of dollars. Where does the money actually go? How much money actually goes to heart research, cancer research, homeless children, hungry whales, uneducated Indians, horny lions, missing trees, and every other cause that is out there seeking your hard earned paycheck? Read their financial statements and check with the local authorities to see if there are complaints or even lawsuits. Inspect the place for yourself .

The final scam you need to be aware of is contributions to religious organizations. True religion is in the heart. We know God from our own life experience. It is a very special relationship that has nothing to do with money. The larger the church, the greater the finances. The Catholic Church has real estate worth billions of dollars. The Mormon Church with a mere 15 million members, has gross revenues of over $10 million daily. Watch these television evangelists: they have the money hustle down to a fine science. In the United States, religious extremists can scream, yell, jump up and down and outright beg for money in the name of the Lord. This is sad and bad luck. The Great Spirit has little tolerance for individuals who use religion to steal from others. I sit on the vestry of my church. This is similar to the board of directors of a public or private company. We watch the finances like a hawk watches her nest. The budget is so tight, every dollar counts. We have a food program for Utah's ever expanding poor and do our best to keep our facilities properly maintained. If your religious organization won't disclose the finances, what are they hiding?

The wonderful reality of the sweat lodge is that there are no books and records and no tax-exempt number from the Internal Revenue Service. It is real religion. I am not advocating you to suspect every single motive of every individual or organization before you contribute or invest your money. But having seen the con men in business, charity, government and religion, caution is the buzzword when dealing with finances.

Leave investment banking to investment bankers, charity to the rich and TV religion to pencil heads. Don't play investment banker on other people's deals. Invest in your own deals. By creating your own deals with your own money, rather than investing in other people's hopes and dreams, you have control over your own economic destiny. This is what really will give you the greatest hope for a secure future. When you make your own money, you have control over your own life. These are the deals you need to consider carefully.

15

TRIBES IN THE MARKETPLACE

We are still hunting bucks. But they don't have horns. They have dollar signs.

Honorable Chairman Leon D. Bear

Most people do not understand the marketplace or business. This is especially true of the people on the far left of the political spectrum. When I was a kid, my political views were so far to the left, I was right wing. We continually hear from leftists, including myself when I was a mere child of 19, about these scary corporations that are trying to take over the world! All of the environmental problems, all of the problems with the arms race, breast cancer, low sperm counts, even male impotence is the result of the irresponsible behavior of those rascal Corporations. Really?!

Fear is the unknown. Because people do not understand the marketplace, business and what corporations are and what they do, there is a tremendous amount of unnecessary fear. What are corporations? Where do they come from? What do they do? How long do they live? How can you kill them? Can they kill you? What power do they have, and how can you overcome that power? Do they really control the world and are they responsible for cancer and AIDS, the military-industrial-complex, and the New World Order? In a word, no!

Corporations are make-believe persons, otherwise known in the lawyer trade as legal fictions. These rascal corporations are the modern equivalent of the ancient hunting parties. In the time of Chief Tabby, the Goshutes and other numerous tribes had hunting parties. Some were quite large with over 100 warriors chasing game for miles. Others were two or three people with good skills and a hard work ethic. The hunting parties were careful with inventory and did not waste game. Herds were not slaughtered only for sport. They were careful with equipment and kept their tools sharpened and bows strung tightly. They were honest. They did not inflate game figures; the villagers were relying upon their reports to eat. They were tough, knowing whom and when to fight. Other tribes did not take their game. And they protected their resources. All of these habits still apply in business today.

Modern corporations are groups of people who are organized together for the purpose of hunting and gathering money from the marketplace. These legal fictions have whatever power you give them under state, federal or tribal law. When my son, Isaac, was quite young, he had make-believe friends, Johnny and Gina. He did not slam the dog's tail in the door; John and Gina were responsible.

The MagCorp plant in Tooele County, Utah, which emits highly toxic chlorine gas into the atmosphere, is a make-believe entity. The president of this company and the plant employees did not emit the chlorine into the Utah sky; their imaginary friend, MagCorp did. The people who operate this massive industrial enterprise know exactly what they are doing to the environment. The chlorine exists because the chemicals are created by the individuals at this plant.

We can hide behind make believe people like General Dynamics, General Electric, Boeing and the other top 100 corporations which consume the bulk of federal tax dollars in the defense sector. But these corporations are just people. And they are just good, very good, in fact great, hunters. They hunt and gather successfully hundreds of billions of dollars from the marketplace every year.

Dow Chemical and the centuries-old Catholic Church exist only in our minds. General Electric is just a large group of well-organized hunters. As one of the largest and certainly most successful money-making machines in human history, these boys know how to rock and roll. In fact, I personally believe that GE is the model for capitalism in the modern world. In my opinion this is the best-run public company in the history of the world. They are a charter member of the New York Stock Exchange, and were the only member around to hear the ring of the bell on its 100th anniversary. They were the only company that survived the last century. This hunting party has been in existence for over 100 years.

What do the people who are organized as General Electric do to make money? How big is this hunting party known as General Electric that brings good things to life? More than 239,000 people go into battle as

General Electric. Until recently, they were led by the Michael Jordan of capitalism, a brilliant man named John A. Welsh. They gather over $100 billion annually. This is the fifth largest corporation in America and one of the top 20 largest corporations on earth. They adapted to the changes in the marketplace and survived the last century. As they like to proudly boasted on their Internet web site:

> *Industrial giant GE operates a wide array of businesses, from TV network NBC to power plant parts manufacturing. The fifth-largest US corporation, it produces aircraft engines, electronic appliances (kitchen and laundry equipment), industrial products and systems (lighting, electrical distribution, and control equipment), and materials (plastics, silicones, laminates, and abrasives). Financial services arm GE Capital Corp. is one of the largest financial services companies in the US. The corporation has almost 150 manufacturing plants throughout the US and Puerto Rico and over 100 plants in 25 other countries.*

No tribe in America has 239,000 members. The Navajo nation that controls a reservation larger in land area then West Virginia has approximately 200,000 members. The entire national $6 billion income from gaming, and the budget of the Bureau of Indian Affairs ($1.3 billion), is substantially less than the net income from General Electric.

General Electric also makes the internal components for the warheads for nuclear weapons. They make the engines for the fighter planes. They make nuclear reactors. How do they do this? Each person in this corporation has responsibilities. To be hired by this major company you have to be a very good employee. They only keep the best. Unlike government employees, if you don't pull your weight with this hunting party, *you will be replaced.* Hundreds of thousands of people will be waiting in line to take your place. This is true of most major corporations. Like hunting parties of old, if you don't pull your weight, you will be left behind.

How are corporations formed? Hunting parties are formed by a group of hungry young men and now women deciding to feed themselves and their families. Corporations are formed by people who have decided to make money to feed themselves and their families. In the old days, hunting parties had a name: the Eagles, the Bears, the Moons, the Bulls and others.

Modern corporations pick a name and file the paperwork with the appropriate government. Some corporations have their origins in Europe, Japan and Delaware. Others begin their legal birth in Utah. A select few are organized on tribal reservations that have business codes. Like hunting parties who kill game for their members, corporations are organized to gather money for their owners, the shareholders. Tribes have organized tribal governments to protect and further the interests of their members.

Like corporate shareholders, tribal members have an ownership interest in the tribe and its management. Some tribes have fantastic resources like timberlands, plenty of water, oil, natural gas, and cattle operations. Others like the Skull Valley Goshutes, have good leadership and a patch of desert with sheep killed by nerve gas illegally buried in their soil. The Navajos near Shiprock, New Mexico have patches of desert. All of the good land with the forests and water was taken from them at gun point in the last century.

As some of you are aware, tribes have to make money from their business activities. They don't have the tax base like other governments because their very few members are financially poor. Tribes can compete with corporations in the modern marketplace of money. This competition involves really good organization, knowledge of law, and common sense in their business deals. What can tribes do to make the money they will need to protect and further the interests of their members? Learn from the corporations that already exist and imitate their behavior.

The path to success is to follow the successful. There is no reason to re-invent the wheel. Tribes, like corporations, need to compete for money to survive unless they are completely traditional, have a sufficient land base, natural resources and the reservation is off limits to the public. Only the Zuni and a small handful of Alaskan tribes meet these limited criteria.

Some tribes have tried to go into manufacturing. One tribe made cattle guards and failed. Another tribe made parts for Department of Defense and failed. Why did these tribal business ventures fail? There are several reasons, but the most common is that they did not manage their money properly. This is the same reason corporations of every kind fail every day. And it is the same reason hunting parties failed in the old days. They didn't pay attention to what they were doing, they lost their weapons, and starved or were killed in battle.

Forming a corporation involves choosing your hunting partners, identifying a market or markets, and deciding where to file the paper work. Since most tribes do not have corporate codes, they end up having to file their articles of incorporation with states. Remember, the tribally formed corporation, whether in a state or tribal jurisdiction, is a separate legal person. This new, make-believe person has the ability to buy and sell property, to hire and fire employees, to pay taxes, to sue and be sued. The only things corporations cannot do is have sex with your wife or girlfriend and vote for corrupt politicians. They can and do contribute money to corrupt politicians.

Being a successful corporate, tribal, sports, military or any other type of leader requires many of the same qualities. Leadership is not a popularity contest. Hard decisions must be made on firing people, going after new markets, and changing directions of the group. This means other people are not always going to like what is decided. I absolutely hate to fire people. But I also hate looking into the faces of the contributing members of the organization and trying to explain to them that they are not going to get paid. If left with no other choice, I terminate employment as a last resort. Over the last 21 years, I cannot recall how many people I have let go. Some showed up drunk to social events my law firm was sponsoring. Others refused to do what they were ordered after being properly warned. Each supplied a reason and a cause. I have remained in business by keeping people on my team that helped with the workload and were not a financial burden.

To build successful tribal and non-tribal businesses we need honest, tough, hardworking leadership. Without thoughtful leaders, everything else will fall apart. The leaders of the Fortune 500 corporations that produce the majority of the goods and services in this country and most of the world are among the toughest, smartest and certainly the greediest people on the planet earth. They are not drunks, drug addicts, lazy or dishonest. Some of these people are so greedy they would put poisonous dirty water in children's milk to make money. They have sold and are selling baby formula to Third World mothers knowing thousands of babies would die from using dirty water. The Reagan Administration did absolutely nothing about this horrible behavior.

Other members of the Fortune 500 were responsible for the development, production, and sale of weapons of mass destruction. Again these corporations are composed of individuals. Some are honest. Others are less honest. All are human with the faults and flaws that accompany our species. We all make choices on what we will do for game, or money. Killing children with dirty water is a choice. But when we die, the Great Spirit does not provide us with attorneys.

Every product or service in America is produced or made by a business. If Europeans, Japanese, Russians and Latin Americans, and African Americans all can create corporations that produce products and sell services, so can the Native Americans. The paperwork is not difficult. The difficult part is making the product, delivering the service, and having a profit at the end of the year. From this computer I am using to this chair I am sitting on, to my tennis wheel chair, the television in the background, the cup that contains my water, the peanut butter sandwich I just ate ... every product or service is made by some corporation out there some-where. If the product or service does not make money, the corporation will eventually go out of business. Like hunting, you either kill your game or you starve. In business, you either make money or you die in bank-ruptcy or civil court. In both cases, you and your family do not eat. How can you or your tribally owned corporations actually make money? Watch, listen and learn.

16

SPANK YOUR MONKEY, INC. AND OTHER TRIBAL ENTERPRISES

Gold is a wonderful thing! Whoever owns it is lord of all he wants. With gold, it is even possible to open for souls the way to paradise!

Christopher Columbus, 1503

Let's create a simple state or tribal corporation. We choose our hunting partners carefully. We have learned from being ripped off that whom we do business with is as important as what business we are doing. We pick an honest, smart president, a good hard-working vice president, and a cheap, penny pincher that is good with paperwork for the secretary-treasurer. We are careful about hiring good employees. We are careful with whom we contract. We know that contracts are promises in writing to perform in the future. Who makes a promise is as important as what we promise to do in the future. We remember that a contract with a con artist is a lawsuit, not a business deal. And finally, we pick a name for our company that will get and keep people's attention.

Let's call our tribally chartered company, Spank Your Monkey, Inc. The purpose of the company will be to perform gay marriages on the Skull Valley Goshute Reservations. The Utah legislature recognizes marriages performed by medicine men. There is clearly a market. The LDS Church, [you know, the Mormons] and every other self-righteous religious fanatic group has come out against gay marriages in Hawaii, Alaska and now California. We are attempting to help people who otherwise would have to suffer by not being able to formalize their union with wedding vows.

We are filling a market need. For a mere $5,000, happy homosexuals would be forever bound in matrimony and live happily ever after or until they changed their minds and get divorced. Ten marriages per month is $50,000 in gross revenue. We do the math on all of the labor, taxes and all other costs and then do the work. At the end of the day we deposit money in our bank, pay all of our bills and what is left goes to Spank Your Monkey. We become very successful and word gets out nationally.

The State of Utah sues us. Religious protesters with signs picket the entrances to the reservation. The media overwhelms the nation with its stand on this newest exercise of tribal sovereignty. Pat Robertson and Jerry Fallwell introduce legislation in Congress to prohibit Indian tribes from performing gay marriages. Like abortion, and tribal gaming, gay marriages on reservations become a huge national debate. This helps with sales and the notoriety brings customers from all over the world. We win at the US Supreme Court because of the sovereignty of the tribe and the fact that Utah had previously passed a law recognizing marriages performed by medicine men. We sponsor music events and college scholarships. It becomes successful—wow, what a great idea for a business.

We know Spank Your Monkey, Inc. is a make-believe legal person that is providing a valuable service to a large segment of the population whose legal needs are unmet. Corporations, unlike real people, can live forever. Therefore, you can Spank Your Monkey forever. This is how the big boys on Wall Street do it.

Success requires knowledge of people as well as of hunting grounds. It does not make sense to form a business to perform gay marriages on reservations if no gays want to get married. And if you calculate that it is going to cost more in gas, labor, rooms, and attorney fees to fight the State of Utah forever or until your retainer is depleted, then the money you are going to make by selling gay marriages…*Don't sell gay marriages.*

How do you know people are going to buy gay marriages and what price are you going to charge? These are the decisions business leaders make every day. These were the same decisions that were made by your great grandfathers and great grandmothers in the old days when they went into the field to hunt deer and gather pine nuts. They did not charge for the marriage ceremonies, with the exception of gifts for the spiritual leader. The old tribal and non-tribal leaders must have made good decisions. Your being alive to read this book is evidence of their sound judgment.

It is not possible for all of you to re-invent the wheel every time you want to start a successful business enterprise, just as it was not necessary for your ancestors to develop a new type of bow for each hunt. To succeed, imitate the successful. Look at the annual reports of Fortune 500 companies and learn. Some contain amazing information. John Welsh's 1999 report to shareholder should be required reading for every financial minded person on earth. He directs this massive GE industrial enterprise toward new markets. He knows how to find game, and he direct his hunters to the various fields.

Tribes—and most of us—cannot compete head to head with these Fortune 500 giants. However, you might be able to convince the boards of directors to locate a plant on your reservations or small rural communities and train some of their members in jobs that are challenging and rewarding. There are small enterprises that can be farmed out to rural communities that can keep people there and away from cities. With computers and the Internet, there are few reasons to have travel to urban centers and sit in front of a desk when you can do most of those things from your own home. Some rural business proposals can be controversial, yet very lucrative.

Several very large utility companies are trying to store their spent nuclear fuel on the Skull Valley Goshute Reservation. The combined revenue of the utilities proposing to build a spent nuclear fuel storage facility is over $50 billion. They can clearly afford to take Native Americans from several tribes and teach them about power generation.

How can you get these lily-white male corporate executives and tribal leaders and rural community leaders to do business together? Introduce them to each other. There are approximately 556 federally recognized tribes and thousands of rural communities. The golden Fortune 500 are the cream of American industry. Corporations can adopt tribes and rural villages and work with them to protect their mutual interests. The Fortune 500 clearly has more money then several nations. American tribes in rural communities are the poorest of the America's poor. Tribes have some sovereignty, mineral, and land resources, that if properly developed or maintained, can ensure employment and economic opportunity. The Fortune 500 has technology, world-class business expertise, and more money than King Solomon had gold. Tribes still have knowledge of the environment that must be shared with the pollution factories of the Fabulous Fortune 500 club. The two are a natural marriage.

What tools do you need to hunt and gather in the marketplace of today? Do you need a business plan to start a business? This is the written plan on how you will conquer this hunting ground. (Hundreds of business plans are available on the Internet.) Some business plans are written on the back of a napkin over coffee. And they obtain the credibility they deserve. Others are elaborately typed on high quality bond paper and have financial statements reviewed by certified public accountants. Remember, if you learn nothing else, the formula for business is Revenue - Expenses = profit. You also know that in most instances, if your profit margin is greater than nine percent, you are either selling drugs or not paying taxes.

Ask yourself again and again and again… do you really have a market? Is there game out there beyond that ridge? In business, we call this a marketing plan. In hunting, we call it spotting game.

There could be so much competition that the profits would not be worth the effort. Nationally, we have more than 2,000,000 attorneys. We have more lawyers than all of the other nations in the world combined. And we have the largest prison population in the history of the world, of approximately two million. There are over 9,500 attorneys in Utah from Ogden to Provo. More than half of the attorneys in Utah make under $30,000 per year. There is so much competition for the same game. So it is crazy to believe that going to law school is a good investment idea for young white males. The law schools remain open for the benefit of the universities and their tenured law professors. The principal market for Indians and Mexicans is representing poor people who have a very difficult time paying you.

What then can tribes and rural communities sell in the marketplace to make money? How big is your imagination? Where buffalo once roamed the plains of the Midwest, some tribes live in squalid poverty. Others raise buffalo and sell the meat to distant markets in Chicago and elsewhere. The meat is grown by Native Americans with no preservatives and all natural substances.

It does not matter what product or service is chosen for the purpose of the business. The fundamentals are the important aspect of the business. The rest of the decisions are simple math. You are in business to make a profit. Will you make a profit in the proposed enterprise? Let's assume you are selling lumber or cattle instead of gay marriages. Are you managing a destination resort, complete with a restaurant and hotel and an exclusive golf course? Or you are managing an eco-tourism enterprise? Do you have a simple casino, or a tribal store, or a construction company, or possibly a bank. Is it a family business previously managed by your parents? Whatever the legal entity, the numbers have to work. You must have more revenue than expenses. You absolutely must have a profit because if you don't, you will go out of business.

The most interesting projects I have been involved in with Indian Country have been business deals with the Internet and eco-tourism. These deals require the careful application of my fundamental rules of business. My three golden rules of business are:

1. It is going to take longer than originally planned.
2. It is going to cost more than originally estimated.
3. It will make less money than the projections.

Why will it take longer than planned? People talk, and like our obnoxious friend, Aaron Nelson, constantly reminds us, mis-quoting Confucius, "for every one thousand persons who talk, one will do." Good hunting partners avoid delays. However, even with good hunting partners, delays are sometimes inevitable. In the old days you did not need licenses. Today you need a host of licenses for everything. You plan it. Reality delays it.

There are several reasons your project will cost more than you originally planned. In fact, I have never seen a pro forma lose money. When you first put together your cost estimates, you looked into the vast wilderness we call the future and anticipated all possible ways you were going to spend money on this venture. You listed them: taxes, rent, equipment rental, phones, and labor. But there were hidden costs that you just missed or underestimated, like taking prospective clients to lunch, bad secretarial help, broken equipment, customers writing you bad checks, and lost time because one of your kids was sick with the flu. We can try as hard as possible to guess the future. Sometimes our business plans are like crystal balls and have great clarity. Other times they miss the mark by miles.

What about the last golden rule, that our business venture will make less money then we estimated? This is normal. After the delays and the cost overruns, of course the deal will make less money than projected. What if you fail?

17

FAILED HUNTING EXPEDITIONS

The lust for money is the root of all evil.

Jesus Christ

What happens if we fail at hunting? And I have seen so many business failures. Over the last 21 years, I have seen more people fail financially than succeed. This too is normal. Thousands of new businesses are started each year. Only a handful will live to age two. And even less will live to age five. Of the tens of thousands of companies that are alive today, only a few are able to qualify to sell their securities publicly on a major exchange. Even less will pay dividends.

Look back and carefully think about your choices. The 70 hours per week you are spending to make this business survive is time you are not with your family and friends—unless you've made the mistake of hiring them. True wealth is good health and family and friends who love you. Love takes a time commitment with people and other beings you care about. If you love money more than friends and family, you might be careful what you pray for. Sometimes you get it. So put your pursuit of business and money in perspective. It truly is only money and nothing else. These are numbers that are assigned meaning by society, are an important tool, and nothing more. Money is not more valuable than health or family and friends who love you.

Whether we call our hunting party corporation Spank Your Monkey, Inc., Valley Girls Car Center, or some more formal name, if we are not good hunters making money, we will soon be out of business. We won't be hunting for ourselves as owners in our own corporation with our own hunting party. We will hope others are buying our labor and we will be helping them to hunt.

In any endeavor, you are taking risk. With risk comes gain and loss. How does one overcome a loss of revenue? After you have been beaten by the ruthless marketplace of capitalism and lost all of your money...now what? This is not 200 years ago where you will go hungry. Today, if you fail in the hunting grounds of capitalism, we produce enough food as a society that you will not starve. There are food banks and jobs.

We have many options. Look back at the business venture you tried and ask yourself, why did it fail? I only know success because I have failed and hopefully learned from my lessons. I remember why my purchase of an apartment complex as a business venture failed. My ex-wife made it explicitly clear in the beginning that she did not want to be actively involved, and that was her God-given right. "Danny, you are going to fall on your face. I don't want you to invest in these apartments. These people in this part of town will not pay their rent, and you will lose all of our money." I hated it when she was right. I am a good trial attorney. I did not know beans about owning and managing an apartment complex with welfare tenants and heroin addicts and single mothers with cats and boyfriends.

My partner was not interested in evicting tenants, making repairs and collecting rents. The market was not going to turn around for apartment space in Salt Lake for another nine years. Unlike today, supply was much higher than demand. You had to beg tenants to stay in these units. Then they wouldn't pay their rent. Then the tenants would steal refrigerators and dishwashers after they had been evicted and moved out in the middle of the night with no forwarding address. Then tenants would have shootings while fighting over heroin deals. Then they would move out and leave their cats. As my ex-wife predicted, the business venture failed.

I remember one nearby business failed because the president of the company hired his relatives as officers and directors in his construction company. He now had vice presidents. Through his tremendous efforts he increased sales from $4 million per year where he was clearly making a profit, to $16 million per year almost overnight. The problem was that not all of his officers and directors had his business sense and work ethic. They did not spot problems on jobs, and grossly underestimated the difficulty of some projects. Some went bowling instead of watching construction jobs. After the cost overruns on some jobs reached several hundred thousand dollars, the company was forced into bankruptcy. Keep your friends as your friends and your relatives as your relatives. Do not assume that others will have the same level of interest in your business that you do.

After the business closed, my friend started out small and succeeded again. He just plain and simply has guts and did not quit with a failed venture. He did what he had to do again, but this time without relatives and partners. Success comes to those willing to pay the price. He was and is willing to pay the hard, difficult price of success. Smaller can sometimes be much better. You move faster and can pay more attention to detail.

Another business failed because the owner was far more interested in investing in his massive home, complete with a swimming pool, hot tub, orchard, luxury boat, motor home, satellite television, expensive furniture, airplane, luxury car and his pretty young wife. But he refused to pay his bills, and he was sued by more people than anyone I had ever represented before or since. In fact, this horribly dishonest businessman was sued by more plaintiffs than all of the other clients I have ever had. He filed bankruptcy. One of his adversaries sued me because he felt that I was responsible for my client's dishonesty. He lost, but it cost me money to defend.

One businessman had a good invention. But he refused to add valuable people to the board of directors that could have greatly expanded sales. Among the people he failed to add was a retired Air Force general who knew the procurement process. The threat of success was too much. Fresh blood with a new insight will sometimes help get you over the final hurdle. All that was needed was sales. Numbers make or break any business. You can have the greatest product on earth. However, if you are not able to sell the product at a profit or even make sales, then the business will just plug along indefinitely. Yes, some people are genuinely afraid of success. They are so used to the struggle and toil and scraping to pay bills, the prospects of actual success is sometimes not bearable. The product this company was producing is of very high quality. The market niche is clearly there. However, the prospect of having someone on board who would help reach the market was too frightening.

Deal with people who are ultimately not afraid to win. Making money will only change you if you believe that because you are rich you are better. I've tried poverty; there's no money in it. My financial goal in life is to be rich enough to afford my leftist views. One friend reminded me, "Danny, John D. Rockefeller did not have that kind of money."

One business refused to follow the license procedures of the state agency. By believing they were above the law, the licensing agency got tired of the complaints from the public who was receiving these services and shut them down. No one is above the law. If you don't like the law, run for office and change it. Or better yet, work with your politician and change the objectionable law. Having worked with the Utah legislature to change laws that harmed the public, I know that change is possible.

The marketplace keeps all businesses on a level playing field. The law is the referee and will penalize us for fouls. Too many fouls and we are thrown out of the game. We may not like having to complete this form and pay that filing fee. Either file the form and pay the fee or run for office and change the requirement. As many of you will find out, some regulations are duplicative and unnecessary. The only purpose they serve is to offer social employment for the unqualified who cannot work in the private sector.

I remember one individual who became convinced that the IRS was unconstitutional and that taxes violated the fifth amendment. We should be on the gold standard, and the world was controlled by the Trilateral Commission and the New World Order. His theory of constitutional law did not fly. Give unto Caesar that which is Caesar's and unto the Lord that which is the Lord's. Pay your taxes and keep very good records. Taxes are just simply a cost of doing business. Never under any circumstances cheat on taxes. There are many things you can expense out. Avoiding taxes is clearly legal. That is what employs armies of accountants. Evading taxes is not.

My accountants are Deloitt & Touche, a world-class accounting firm. They make certain that the numbers crunch properly and keep me out of trouble with the Internal Revenue Service. They are brilliant accountants and save me much aggravation over worrying about whether I am doing things properly.

If you want to go out of business quickly, get in a fight with the IRS. They have the resources of the most powerful nation on earth on their side. The IRS will absolutely slam you into a wall, hold you upside down, and take every last drop of blood out of your body before they throw you into the streets of poverty. Further, if you cheat on your taxes, it makes the tax burden for the rest of us much higher. You live in this most wonderful country, and taxes are part of the price of admission to playing ball in the marketplace of capitalism. If you don't like taxes, vote out politicians who will raise them. Don't expect the rest of us in the marketplace to pay your taxes just because you believe that taxes are unconstitutional.

Casey Stevens, a friend who is very talented in project management, introduced me to some friends of his at Hartford Steam Boiler. We met with the Tribal Council of the Skull Valley Band of Goshutes about building a national energy institute at the now-abandoned Tooele Army Depot. We put together the proposal and were going to walk through the transfer of property to the Goshutes. After all, the Depot was built on the Aboriginal winter camping grounds of the Skull Valley Goshutes. Everything was proceeding as planned. Then we ran into the BIA under the failed leadership of Ada Deer. The land and buildings were to be transferred to the Skull Valley Band of Goshutes under the Base Re-Alignment Process set up by the Clinton Administration.

The idea was to build a national energy institute in conjunction with the University of Utah and Hartford Steam Boiler. This energy institute would train companies and tribes about electric power generation. Hartford insured approximately one third of the utilities nationally. They did not want chaos in the marketplace. The University of Utah would have provided the engineering. Everything was in place to make the project work. The empty facilities at the Tooele Army Depot were perfectly suited for this project. We met with various public officials and took the proposal to the BIA. It fell into a black hole and never surfaced.

I was at the office of the property division of the BIA and asked for assistance with the application process for the land and building transfers. The bureaucrat could not process my client's application because she was too busy. There were so many stacks of papers everywhere. I was aghast. I worked until the wee hours of the morning and did the paperwork for them. The next day, after an exhausting evening, the same young bureaucrat refused to help me because she had a training session to attend in the afternoon. She was learning how to write a resume. I threw my briefcase and screamed at her. I was thrown out of the BIA headquarters. The deal failed, and the entire national Indian community missed out on facilities being transferred though base re-alignment.

This was a tremendous opportunity that was lost because of incompetence. If you have valuable facilities, you can attract companies to your communities. The real losers were the Indian community. Having valuable and empty military facilities transferred to Indian tribes made very good economic sense. The facilities could then be converted to profitable businesses with the help of major multinational corporations, like Hartford Steam Boiler. It is difficult to pull yourself up by your bootstraps if you don't have boots.

I learned that if you are dealing with losers and bureaucrats who place their personal time and jobs above the interest of your project, it will fail. You cannot put your business idea or project in a position where a weak player has control and the ability to tell you no. If a license can be held up by a petty bureaucrat or small-minded politician, expect the permission to be denied or withheld. Politicians and bureaucrats like the word *no* because no is safe. No means no risk of failure and continued job security. The fact that nothing is accomplished is irrelevant.

All this deal needed was the transfer of an empty building and small block of land to the Goshutes, and the entire Indian community would have had a national energy institute. The land in question was clearly Goshute aboriginal territory. In fact, this land had been the winter camping grounds for this tiny stubborn band of people. Tribes would have received training about becoming energy self-sufficient using their own wind, water, oil and gas resources. The local community ended up having the facilities transferred to them. Penske Trucking bought the facility we were trying to obtain for a song, and today there is no national energy institute. The BIA's ineptness managed to lose out on the entire base realignment process.

My office also pursued building a small reservoir for the Skull Valley Goshutes Reservation. The Bureau of Reclamation developed the engineering plans and a budget. We took the proposal to Congressman Jim Hansen, in whose district the Goshutes are located. His staff was polite but cold. After five separate trips to Washington, DC and various letters and phone calls, the response has been silence. The entire project would cost less then three million dollars. In addition to irrigation, the water is needed to fight the raging and dangerous range fires of August in Skull Valley. The project has not succeeded because of lack of public funding. But all of the white local communities have received funding for reservoirs.

This reservoir has not been constructed because the Skull Valley Band of Goshutes did not have the political muscle to get the assistance of their congressman to walk through this tiny amount of funding. If a politician can kill your deal for his political gain, he will. Jerry Mooney once observed, "Danny, politicians are usually cowards." He is right. If you can deliver significant sums of money, politicians will listen to your proposal and work with you. But if you have that kind of money, you do not need federal funding.

If the Skull Valley Band of Goshutes are successful in building their proposed storage facility for spent nuclear fuel with their utility company tenants, they will be in a position to build the reservoir themselves. I believe Congressman Jim Hansen is a racist who perceives Indians as Lamanites. According to Mormon theology, their skin color was cursed because the Lamanites killed another mythical lost tribe of Israel, the Nephites. Because Indians are evil Lamanites, he is not obligated to help them at all. A responsible politician would have walked through the funding on this project. Since the Goshutes did not buy Jim Hansen with massive campaign contributions, they received nothing from him. You will have your runs of bad luck by being dependent on the Jim Hansens and BIA bureaucrats of the world. Endure the bad luck and move on. Formulate ways to fund your projects that are not dependent on racist and or incompetent politicians and bureaucrats.

Other business deals fail for the simple reason that the people involved finally drag it down to defeat. One businessman had a partner who was the absolute kiss of death. He refused to be bought out at a reasonable price, and took the company under with him. People are young and old, but they are consistent.

I don't know whether some learn from the lessons of youth. It would be nice to have the knowledge I have now when I was 19 years old like those of you reading this book. The warning signs on the lousy partner where there early. He refused to put up his own house and own hard money in the deal. Well, this tells you how much he believed in the business.

Your partners should be people who have as much to gain or lose as you do. If someone is not willing to give the same level of effort, get him out early. The problems you see now will expand 100-fold when the business venture becomes financially viable through your massive efforts. Suddenly the people who have contributed very little will want it all. It amazes me how no or little effort suddenly becomes important when the venture is successful. It reminds me of sports, when you lose you lose alone and it is all your fault. But when the team wins, it is surprising how so little effort will claim so much credit.

Sometimes you will suddenly look at what you are doing and realize I am spending $2,490 to make $2,500. It is taking me so much time to make $2,500 that I am really earning $1.00 per hour. Is the level of effort to make the money you are making really worth it? What about the headaches involved in managing employees? I have one friend who sold his company of 30 employees because he got sick of playing baby sitter and payroll manager. He was running a profitable ship. But the gut work of hiring and firing employees and ensuring that they remained productive and competitive was just not worth it. One male employee grabbed a female employee's behind while she was walking by. My friend got sued. Are you really in business or are you just baby sitting expensive help? Are you working for you or to keep your staff in paychecks? Look carefully at your situation. Who really owns this business, you or your employees?

Do you really need all that help? And is the help actually helping? Remember, small can be very efficient and sometimes far more profitable. You cannot be small and produce automobiles. However, you are probably not planning to produce automobiles. Do you really need the employees you are just about to hire? Remember, each employee is a separate life and mouth to feed.

More often than not, the fewer employees the better. Having professional employees is like herding cats. They clearly have their own minds. You have to ask and still they may or may not do what you want them to accomplish. Most are pretty stubborn. A few understand the importance of numbers and the reality that paychecks don't just have magic numbers. Bank deposits are also required to make them negotiable.

Failed hunting expeditions occur because there is risk. The risk is failure. So what. The only way you will consistently avoid failure in hunting is not to hunt. You can be the most careful hunter, the most prepared, the most knowledgeable, and still not kill any game. What happens if the marketplace has changed so much and conditions are so tough, no one is successful? Look what happened to the various plains tribes when the buffalo were deliberately killed off. You could be the best buffalo hunter on earth. But there were no longer any buffalo to hunt. Then what? Hunt something else besides buffalo. Go after ground squirrels, snakes, birds, deer, elk—anything but buffalo. In a capitalist society, markets are going to constantly change. Get used to change and adjust to the new markets. Understand that change can be good. The Internet will change everything.

When you do fail at business, close the company down, take your lumps and pick yourself back up. ***Success in a particular market does not last forever.*** The companies in the last century that were selling wagon wheels and cannon balls either stopped selling these products or are now out of business. The market for wagon wheels is not quite what it was 150 years ago. To the best of my knowledge, the Department of War no longer exists and the new Department of Defense no longer buys cannon balls.

You will fail in this life at many endeavors. Loved ones will die or leave you. Friends will move away. Your health will not always be the best. But if you realize that just because life is very hard, always has been and is certainly not fair, it does not mean it is not worth the effort of living. Try your very best. And if you fail, accept defeat and try again. The only way you will get over your fear of failure is to fail. We can only overcome our fears by facing them.

I've failed so many times in my life that calculated, well thought-out risk is something I welcome. My biological mother died when I was two-and-a-half years old. My father was killed by a drunk driver when I was ten. I lost the state championship in wrestling when I was 18. I ended up in a wheelchair because of a rare nerve disease, transverse mylities, when I was 21. My divorce was final in 1990 when I was 34. Losses will happen. Pick yourself up after you are knocked down. Get over it and move on. Your loss was yesterday's news. It is like a bad shot in tennis. That was your last shot. It is not your present shot or your next shot. What are you doing today to improve your game? What is your life like now and how does it fit in with the well being of the planet?

My life has also had wonderful blessings. I have a smart, healthy good-looking wonderful son, terrific family and friends, and I've also made some money practicing law, traveled around the world, played wheelchair tennis in exotic places, had beautiful girlfriends and won important cases.

I now have Laura, a wonderful woman. Since I accepted her offer of marriage, I have so many pets and plants in my small house. You will like her. She has a tremendous love of life and a great sense of humor.

Risk always means you might fail. But the real failure comes from doing nothing or not trying your very best. Not taking a risk is the ultimate failure in love, sports, business and life. It does not mean being reckless. Just look at the possibility of success and ask why not. There is this excitement from playing. Whether it is sports, money or love, playing is much more exciting than watching.

I have seen clients get so discouraged by failure in love and business that they simply have wanted the pain of life to end. They wanted to kill themselves. Some did kill themselves. What they really wanted was the pain of their thoughts to end. You can change what you wish to think here and now. If you want to think peaceful thoughts, it is up to you. It is only hunting. It is a sport. You will win and you will lose. Compete and enjoy. Some people are participants, others are spectators. What are you? Do you watch sex videos or do you actually have sex? Do you read about nice places or do you actually travel to faraway lands and beautiful beaches?

As long as you saved some money and risked only what you could afford to lose, you will be all right. If you risked it all and lost it all, start over. Yes, it will take you several years to save another $20,000 or more that you lost. Sometimes you may never recover all of the money you lost. Did you lose your health and family and friends? If you retained your integrity and did your best, you will still have people who care about you. If you lied to succeed, the people close to you know that the success is phony and not real.

No one respects cheaters, in sporting events, love and business. Ill-gotten gain is still ill gotten. It is like buying your own trophies rather then owning them through competing. How many people really respect men and women who cheat on their mates? You remember the class cheater who received an undeserved higher grade. Did that person really win anything? He or she lost respect. When we lose our reputation, then we have failed.

If you failed at hunting and can no longer afford to take the risk of going back into the marketplace, put the loss in perspective. Understand that in every endeavor in life the majority of people will not succeed. Only one team will be the super bowl champion, and very few companies will survive competition in the marketplace. Every one of the players on championship teams will sooner or later retire. And every corporate executive will one day retire or die. Despite their best efforts, they cannot take it with them. So put your life in perspective and ask yourself, is what you are doing worth the price of your health and love of your family and friends?

When I attended my tenth-year class reunion from law school, I saw so many attorneys who had ruined their health for money. It is not worth it. I have been rich, poor and middle class. Nothing in this life is worth ruining your health and compromising your integrity. No amount of money can buy you happiness. They are just numbers. I have rich clients and friends who are miserable bastards. Nothing pleases them. Things, which will soon be thrown away, are not happiness. You chose to enjoy life. *The absolute key to unhappiness in this life is to compare yourself to others.* Yet I constantly see clients, friends and relatives measuring their wealth, toys, and looks to others. You are only going to live a certain amount of years, between 60 and 80. If you spend all of your time hunting money and comparing your self to others, you have completely wasted your life. There is so much more to life than hunting and gathering money. There is also enjoying the time you are here.

Enjoy hunting and gathering. But clearly understand, it is only hunting and gathering. There is also time spent exercising, praying, having dinner with family and friends, and appreciating God's wonderful creation. But where is there game in this new century?

18

WHERE THERE IS GAME

We are not without accomplishment. We have managed to distribute poverty equally.

Nguyen Co Thatch, Vietnamese foreign minister

Sometimes out of nowhere a large elk or deer will appear. Luck... and the harder and smarter you work the luckier you will be. Why does luck favor the strong, the alert, the energetic and brave? Lady luck is attracted to winners. Her favors of love and affection lean toward the quiet, strong and good-humored charm of the successful. And sure enough, the friends and relatives you will suddenly have when you have bagged a large game and are financially successful.

You can set your goals and reach them by realizing that if what you are trying does not work, try something else. Arron Nelson defines insanity as "doing the same thing over and over again and expecting a different result." I am so amazed when I see people with the look of death on their face pull that slot machine handle one more time. Having already lost their rent money and car payment, one more pull and they will get it all back. There is no game in a casino unless you own the place.

Where is there game in this new century? What are the new markets? Markets happen for a variety of reasons. With computers, the need to share information on a national and international basis has created an ever expanding consumption of keyboards, monitors, hard drives, software, and the other gizmos that we use every day. One market can open for Native Americans if they couple their respect for the environment with the technological skills of the scientific community. The Skull Valley

Goshute dead sheep case resulted in the first contract in the nation between an Indian tribe and the Department of Defense. The sole purpose was to investigate and repair military activities on Indian lands. This contract has led to several tribes' obtaining funding for clean up of Department of Defense activities in Indian Country. The Oglala Sioux have developed a comprehensive clean up of a bombing range, and thereby reclaimed some of their land. Other tribes are cleaning up rivers, bases and training their members in the expanding field of environmental science. Our environmental problems resulting from weapons development, industrialization, urbanization, mass consumer production, and worldwide military bases will require an extensive labor effort and hundreds of billions of dollars to repair. The game in the new century will be repairing the damage we have inflicted on the environment in the last two centuries of industrialization, urbanization and overpopulation.

The current budget of the Office of Environmental Security of the Department of Defense is approximately $5 billion dollars. Out of this money must come the funds to clean up all the US military facilities worldwide. This is not enough money. In addition to the clean up of shut-down military facilities like the Tooele Army Depot, there are the past clean up responsibilities like the nerve gas accident at Dugway Proving Grounds. The clean up of Hanford, Washington in 1987 was estimated at approximately $47 billion dollars. Even at one billion dollars per year, this radioactively contaminated site will remain a problem for many decades to come. And remember that clean ups usually mean taking garbage from point A to point B.

What are the environmental problems of the nation that are not hysterically stated and need to be resolved? How can the Native American community and rural communities and you take advantage of these opportunities, if they even exist? If we provide a model for behavior for the rest of society by living simple lives and not buying all of the plastic, paper and glass garbage that eventually ends up in the environment, maybe we can start to make a dent in the problem of municipal solid waste at its source.

The market of being the world's janitors is a large and unglamorous task. One of the jobs of environmentalists is clean up. As Native Americans and as environmentalists, we are all too aware that nature was never broken before, and therefore there was no need to fix her. We humans, not mother-nature, created the messes that now require clean up. Nature works well when people do not tamper with her. Those days of an unspoiled environment are gone forever. Now we have to determine the best methods to resolve the horrific damage to an ecosystem created by overpopulation, air pollution, over fishing, deforestation of rain forests, loss of water, and disposal of hazardous wastes.

The respect that is truly held for the environment by indigenous people worldwide prior to overpopulation and electrification is a value that is important for human survival. The Paiutes have knowledge of plants in the deserts of southern Utah. Goshutes and other tribes have their knowledge of medicines and animal behavior. Not all of the knowledge of the past has been lost with the genocide of the last centuries. These value systems can be marketed and sold. Explanation of how plants can be used for medicines and food is very important. People in the rain forest of the Amazon have cures for various ills. They have extensive knowledge that must be preserved or lost forever, like the writings of the Mayans, Aztecs and Incas. The rain forests of the world are the lungs of the planet. The bio-diversity in them is so extensive that we are only beginning to tap this tremendous database.

So the game in the new century is in developing, implementing and marketing an environmentally friendly way of life, a way of life that involves simplicity, modesty, and moderation in the consumption and accumulation of knowledge, finance and power.

Simplicity and moderation in consumption means you buy only what you need and take care of what you buy. When we buy clothes, we should expect them to last for long periods of time—not only as long as they are in fashion. It amazes me that Americans are so wasteful. We build storage sheds next to our homes to provide shelter for plastic junk purchased on the spur of the moment. We have annual summer yard sales to rid ourselves of all our junk. We waste incredible amounts of food.

Approximately 15 percent of all food that is purchased goes into the garbage. Our eating habits are so unhealthy that approximately 40 percent of us are seriously overweight. This excess weight leads to a host of diseases like heart attacks and strokes. The battle cry of the new century should be "who needs it."

The game in this new century is in understanding technology, finance and knowledge. Money and power exist between the right ear and the left ear. These are mental concepts that, if properly understood, enable people to have peace of mind and prosperity. If you are not all stressed out by paying for all of your stupid toys, and therefore are working to enjoy life, not to pay for plastic gizmos, you will be physically healthier. It is damn stressful paying for a motorcycle, a truck, a car, a motor home, and a huge house.

One client was earning a decent wage. He was working 50 hours per week to own the trappings of material success. He had a truck, a fancy car, a motorcycle, a large expensive home, and many appliances. He had unbelievable debt payments to support this American Dream lifestyle of the near rich and almost famous. He was so stressed out from his recent business investment, which was fast turning sour, that the anxiety was now reaching heart attack level.

He did not like my advice, but followed it nonetheless. I told him to sell his toy truck, fancy car, and motorcycle, and cut his debt level significantly. Several months later he visited. He was so much happier. He found that at his wage level, by living simple and not having as much debt, he actually had extra money to invest, which he did carefully. He will one day be able to retire and actually enjoy the fruits of his labor.

Why would a warrior kill or horde more meat than he needed to satisfy the needs of his family and tribe? It would be unhealthy to gorge himself on the excess. It would be environmentally unsound to deplete the herd unnecessarily. And, it would be disrespectful to the Great Spirit to deprive others greedily. Gratefully taking only what is needed and ensuring that nothing goes to waste is an Indian wisdom that needs to be learned by the rest of industrialized society.

In this new century, the game will be in teaching people to own stocks, bonds and property. This means not investing in depreciating assets like durable goods that break or one day end up at the landfill and thereby cause more environmental problems. It will mean there will be a market for creating products that will last for several years and not just long enough so that a new product can be sold to you. Most of you have noticed that car companies deliberately produce cars and trucks which are sold to the public with payment terms that will take at least three to five years to complete. Once the vehicle is paid off, it is time to buy a new car.

The creative individuals and companies who produce products that last several years will have the most success with the environmentally friendly marketplace. As more and more people adopt the attitude that having less things means you have time for more adventure, buying will require an emphasis on quality. I buy clothes and appliances that I expect to last several years. I have been wearing the same jacket to court for the last 15 years. One of the buttons is missing. And if I had my way, I would never wear this jacket again. Why? I can't stand to dress up for court, weddings, funerals or anything else. I like being in my shorts without a shirt and just my headband and cross earring.

We need to get over this addiction to constantly buying more and more stuff. The new game is to spend less and save more. It means not having so many pieces of clothing that we have constantly to get rid of extra sweaters, coats and other items. It just sickens me when I see people who constantly shop till they drop. They have clearly bought the materialism myth. This myth could destroy the earth.

Once I was having lunch with three millionaire friends. One understood the necessity of having less. He got rid of all of his extra homes, cars, and other items. "It is ridiculous to have all of these things," he said. "People seek you out for what you have, not for who you are." He is over 80 and understands the importance of life and time. One of his children died; that wound still pained him. No amount of money could ever bring back this loss.

Wealth, once accumulated, must be used with wisdom. Where the game is in this new century is getting the people who own the world to use their massive wealth to solve the problems of overpopulation and pollution among others. These environmental and behavioral problems are certainly not insurmountable. We merely have to reduce the number of people. This will happen as the people in the Third World have clean drinking water and the reduction in health problems translates to lower birth rates.

One of my clients comes from a village in Mexico that is so poor no person has an automobile, indoor plumbing or telephone. No one has a television. He has a wife who loves him and their two healthy children. He is healthy. He came to America to work long enough to save one thousand dollars to take back to Mexico to build his wife and children a home. Three drug dealers offered him a place to stay when he was sleeping on the streets of Salt Lake. He is serving time for drug distribution charges and could spend the next ten years in prison. The game in the next century is to convince the minority populations not to get involved in the drug trade because the American government will kill or incarcerate them.

The clear reason so many people use drugs and alcohol to alter their mental state is that they cannot stand their lives. As one of the priests in my church so aptly stated, "If we love our neighbors as ourselves, we are going to be in big trouble." The game in this new century is to develop a society where people are physically and mentally healthy without the use of legal and illegal mind-altering substances.

Again, there is great joy to be found in appreciating the wonders of nature. My wife and I enjoy bird watching. It is inexpensive, good exercise, and gets us out there with the trees, fresh air and cool breezes.

Before television and the mass entertainment that has been developed as a result of leisure time created by urbanization, people did not get bored. I firmly believe that only people who watch television get bored because they have never been taught to entertain themselves. Not knowing how to make furniture, baskets, pottery, paint, cook, garden or much of anything else, too many of us depend on others to entertain them. This unfortunate state has created so much leisure time that people seek relief from their bored existence with alcohol and legal and illegal drugs.

When our politicians are lazy and stupid it is to be expected that this model of physical and mental ill health will promote policies and lifestyles that harm the body politic. The game in the new century is to hire politicians who promote physical and mental health. Approximately one half of Americans do not bother to vote. They have lost all confidence in the political system. People who do not own property do not vote. They are under the mistaken belief that their vote does not matter. If you vote, you hire the people who take your money in the form of taxes. Since you are going to pay taxes or go to jail, you should choose who is going to spend your money. Because the reality of life is if you do not like how Congressman Jim Hansen is spending your money, he is your employee, you can fire him by voting.

There is game is in the development of the economies of South and Central America, Asia and Africa. This development must result in economies where moderation in consumption is a value. This means that the corrupt governments of Mexico and other countries will have to start being accountable to their people. It means using American tax money to build mass transit, clean water systems, access to health care, education and population control. It is just stupid to believe that having six billion cars serves the public interest of the planet. It may do wonders for General Motors, Ford, Toyota and other auto producers. But the last thing the planet needs is more automobiles. Native Americans can set the example by leading the way. Urbanization does not have to mean environmental destruction. It can mean living in a simple and modest apartment or home, and carefully investing money for emergencies, travel, even retirement.

The game in this new century is bringing better water, food, transportation systems, access to education, better medical care, and the Internet to the countless villages of the Third World. This too is not impossible. In Lima, Peru garbage is piled in the streets next to a river that is so filthy, it is scary to think about the diseases carried. When the Inca's ruled this once magnificent city, it was clean, and the citizens had great health. There was no army of unemployed.

184

But the economies in small countries are not going to turn around without massive assistance. This assistance should not be just financial. In fact in most instances, financial aid increases existing problems. With corrupt leaders, the financial aid often ends up in bank accounts offshore in the Cayman Islands and other tax havens. Their economies are often so small and so dependent on agricultural or energy commodities that the fluctuations in world prices puts them in very difficult positions. Peru's entire gross national product is smaller then many American corporations.

The last thing Lima, Peru needs is more people moving to their already overcrowded and filthy city. The corrupt government does not have the waste management capabilities of richer nations, so their streets are full of paper, glass, plastic, and metal. Of the seven million people, approximately one million are completely unemployed. They moved to the city in hopes of finding some job offering tiny amounts of money for the sale of their labor. But if no one is buying their labor because of oversupply, they are forced into abject poverty.

Since America rules the world, it is imperative that we assist Peru and all of our colonies with their environmental problems. Peru and other countries are so poor they can't even pay attention, much less their massive debt to our banks. The total foreign debt of the poorest African countries consumes their limited government revenues with the interest payments they are obligated to our banks. Debt forgiveness is in both our best interests. Exporting our consumer lifestyle will only create more problems like more urbanization and more municipal solid waste that ends up in the streets of Third World Cities. Garbage service in the United States and other industrialized countries is a luxury poor countries often cannot afford. This municipal solid waste ends up seriously damaging their fragile ecosystems and delicate environments. Sea turtles, fish and birds cannot digest paper, plastic, glass and metal. And these beautiful creatures do not have the brain capacity to know these substances are not food.

Along with debt relief, world powers (with America leading the way) must quit using Third World countries as their dumping grounds. Global restrictions must be placed on corporations that either directly dispose of toxic wastes in poor countries or who transfer ecologically unsound manufacturing facilities to these areas in order to avoid national regulations. Protection of the environment is a global issue and corporate polluters should be hit in their global pocketbooks. The game in this new century will be to build a global society where people respect nature and each other. We can win with knowledge and respect for nature and the laws necessary to control the disrespectful.

One thing that always impressed me about Richard Bear was his great patience. His manners were something he stresses by example. The game in this new century is learning patience and the cultural mores of the hundreds of other people out there. Collectively, it takes all of us to make up humankind. It requires studying the various habits and history of our neighbors in the other parts of the planet. We sometimes offend others by accident. The game in the new century is studying the languages and cultures of other people, and using eco-tourism as a means for economic development. This is clean and usually harmless.

We provide employment for people in other parts of the world by being amused and entertained by their way of life that is compatible with nature. Eco-tourism is one small economic solution providing interaction with people from other parts of the world. There will be problems, as people will not always understand other people. And diseases can spread very quickly with jet travel. But this small economic solution can provide great benefits for all of mankind. Travel, if planned properly, can be very interesting and the memories always last longer than the things we buy at the various malls and stores that infest America.

We can only control how we behave individually. We can chose to be moderate or we can buy into the consumption myth. We can be very careful about buying what we need and needing what we buy. Or we can live at the shopping malls that would better serve the public if they were located next to the landfills.

Many people have lousy jobs that contribute very little to society. What are we going to do that will not create more garbage? Moderation in consumption will mean that people will be laid off because no one is buying the junk they are creating and selling. Approximately two thirds of our economy is based on consumer spending. If we buy fewer cars, fewer toys, fewer clothes, fewer televisions, what will happen to all of these workers? Should they simply starve? If they killed themselves, would it help solve the problem of overpopulation?

The game in this new century will be to find meaningful work that does not create more garbage. This will be quite a task. We will really have to think things through to get this planet in line with human work and the environment.

A friend just returned from Mainland China. He was aghast by the total disregard for environmental regulation. Raw sewage was dumped directly into major rivers. The air is so polluted that people wear masks to attempt some protection for their lungs. But products (junk) are produced and shipped to various parts of the world in an attempt at providing employment for over one billion three hundred million people. In India, the bodies of unwanted children are dumped in piles of garbage. Despite the heroic efforts of Mother Theresa, this human dumping is common throughout the Third World. There are so many, many people that there is not enough water, food and certainly no access to education.

Throughout history, over population has been modified by war, famine, or disease. If mankind does not voluntarily curb its exponential population growth, it is a certainty that one or more of the foregoing will. When too many people live too close together, resources and nerves are stressed to the breaking point. I presume that each of us has as much right to propagate as anyone else, but it must be remembered that nature is not obligated to respect anyone's right to propagate, or live for that matter. Everything in nature is in balance. As a product of nature, humankind and human population will be kept in balance by nature, war, famine and disease.

How will we interact with other cultures without destroying the world? It is so easy for the altars of entertainment that are controlled by a handful of corporations to advocate the total destruction of Iraq and other countries. This tiny country bought over $50 billion dollars in arms from the U.S. when they were fighting Iran in a war Iraq started. However, poor people in Third World countries can use chemical weapons on American population centers. These chemical and biological weapons are the poor man's nuclear weapons. They are simple to make and even easier to release on innocent victims. With most of these weapons, it is merely a matter of having access to the ingredients. Most of these substances are readily available at hardware stores and supermarkets.

There is game in bringing the Internet to the non-white world. This will be quite a task. The gateway to the world's largest learning tool will create data applications that will be truly intriguing. This in turn will result in English further becoming the world's language of business and education. This will also mean that the entire world will need law to survive.

People have no idea of the profound impact that the fall of the Roman Empire had on humanity. Picture it this way. Imagine that all of the police and army troops in the United States pulled out all of a sudden. What if disputes could no longer be resolved in courts of law? What if law did not exist any longer because people no longer believed in the legal system? How would we survive the chaos of rioting crowds? Without law, there is total violence and a new dark age lasting another millennium will come about. Law exists because we believe living with it is better than living without it. What if we stop believing?

With a worldwide system of enforced international law, more business will mean more employment and more peace. The challenge in this century is to develop a functioning international legal system for the common man. This means that the 20,000 foreign nationals in America's massive prison system will be treated as humans instead of like animals. This will mean that we will be forced to become tolerant of other cultures.

We have one worldwide currency, the dollar. All international monetary transactions are based on the dollar. We have one United Nations to try to provide information about the planet and to resolve disputes. We have more international trade than ever before in human history. We have international trade agreements and regulations that threaten workers with the cheapening and globalization of labor. We have more tourists than ever before. Clearly we have a new world system of education, travel, money, and health care.

The game in this new century will be in developing a massive human effort to colonize Mars and the inner solar system. Space exploration will require total global cooperation because this will be a truly massive endeavor. No nation standing alone has the resources to colonize Mars. We will require total peaceful cooperation between the industrialized world and the Third World. New opportunities for individuals and companies willing to work to develop new propulsion systems will exist.

There will be opportunities for individuals and companies who are willing to try to find new ways to develop environmentally friendly homes and methods of electrical generation. Some are doing that now. Contractors are using new materials for increasing the insulation of walls and roofs in order to get more from the resources we now exploit. As we restructure our cities to make them less energy intensive and more transportation friendly, we will create jobs in this area of the economy. The only real danger is the possibility of the escalation of violence through war. What if there is a very big war? Then what are we going to do?

19

WAR

You have your law, I have my sword. We shall see who shall prevail.

Adolph Hitler

We are approximately one thousand seven hundred years past the fall of the mighty Roman Empire. The collapse cost the planet the loss of rule of law and resulted in over one thousand five hundred years of ignorance and darkness. Europe fell apart, and only today is finally reuniting under one set of laws with the European Union. One idea remains: war was an instrument of politics.

Many scholars have studied this tragic, but sometimes necessary human impulse. Karl von Clausewitz calls war "continuation of politics by other means." Cicero defines war as "a contention by force." Hugo Grotius says "war is the state of contending parties, considered as such." Thomas Hobbes notes that war can be an attitude, "By war is meant a state of affairs, which may exist even while its operations are not continued. Denis Diderot states, "War is a convulsive and violent disease of the body politic." As long as great nation states have the ability to destroy others militarily, there will be war.

Our ancestors were brave but had poor technology and sometimes even poorer judgment. They took spears and knives to gunfights. Guns are and always have been for cowards. Our warriors looked an opponent in the eyes before they stabbed them in the heart. Today's cowards are unwilling to face their enemies in combat and fight like warriors. Instead they rely on weapons of mass destruction to slaughter helpless men, women and children. Human flesh is no match for planes loaded with jet fuel, chemical, biological and nuclear weapons, or bullets. It does not take courage to kill a man or any animal on the ground from the air or from a distance. It only takes political decisions made either by men who are too gutless to face their perceived enemies—or by young men unwilling to think for themselves.

Unlike the great Roman Emperor Trajan, the fierce barbarian Attila, the ancient Jews who defended their temples from attack, the intelligent warrior Red Cloud, the rebel Communist leader Che, and others who actually led their men into battle and killed people, today's politicians are technological cowards. The Nazis killed women, children, and unarmed old men. Timothy McVeigh was so gutless he blew up unsuspecting men, women, and children. In the Gulf War of 1991, Iraq troops were gunned down by allied forces on their failed invasion to re-conquer territory that the British stole from them. The Iraqis used chemical weapons not only against their own people, but also against Iran. A man I grew up with has the dreaded Gulf War Syndrome. He has lost his health.

In this century, cowards disperse biological weapons through the mails. Other cowards flew passenger planes loaded with jet fuel into the World Trade Center towers. One day cowards will use nuclear weapons on helpless victims on the wrong end of a political cause. Now we have war. Unlike the recent Gulf War of 1991, Vietnam (1945-1975), Korea (1948 to present), World War II (1939-1945), and World War I (1914-1919), this new war against international terrorism will be the most intellectually challenging engagement in our brief 225-year history.

If you want to survive in this new age of cowards, you better have a real and thorough understanding of the Imperial American Empire. We control the world and God help the person or nation who opposes our way of life. Ask General Manuel Noriega. His attorney, Jon May, is a courageous man who has an unpopular client that once worked for the CIA. Noriega fell out of favor with Washington and will live out the rest of his life in prison. When he was no longer useful to our foreign policy and bit the hand that kept him in power, we sent in our Special Forces and that was the end of his dictatorship over the poor terrified peasants of Panama.

Are we required to fight for Pax Americana? Hell yes! But understand what you are fighting for. This is not World War II. Are you fighting to protect the ability of Americans who represent less than five percent of the people to consume energy resources and produce approximately 25 percent of the world's greenhouse gases? Are you fighting to protect the rights of fruit companies to establish dictatorships in Central American countries? Are you fighting to protect the industrial world's right to consume massive quantities of oil?

Our empire circles the entire planet. No nation or group of nations can defeat us militarily. Every nation is required to pay homage to the new center of the universe, Washington, DC. Once all roads led to Rome. Today all political and economic roads lead to Washington. Our drug policies jolt farmers in Central and South America and Southeast Asia. Farmers in poor countries choose between growing profitable cocoa plants and opium poppies or far less profitable coffee and other agricultural products. America is the central piece of the world economy. We sell products that help and clearly harm other people. Sometimes these products are banned at home.

American tobacco corporate farmers, like Phillip Morris and RJ Reynolds, are protected by American law. The corporate officers are not imprisoned when their products kill tens of thousands. When foreign governments object to tobacco imports or other dangerous products, the American government applies diplomatic and economic pressure.

Our military industrial complex, in conjunction with their former partners in crime, the now defunct Soviet Union, planted tens of thousands of land mines in over 80 countries. The lives of hundreds of thousands of men, women and children have been ruined by these vicious land mines hidden during the Cold War. Over 20 million wheelchairs are needed by people in these poor countries. Friends of mine created a nonprofit organization to provide wheelchairs to people all over the world. The Mobility Project, along with numerous other groups worldwide, is working diligently to undo the damage to lives in poor countries from war.

A simple change in interest rates by our Federal Reserve Board affects economies in the rest of the world. The entire global economy is tied to our consumer and financial markets, our interest rates, and our dollar. The economic and environmental effects of the American market place on the planet is staggering. Millions of workers internationally work in dangerous and poor-paying labor positions or are unemployed as a result of American policy. Nations pay their debts to American banks or are impoverished without any control on their limited economic environments. Our largest corporations make more money then most nations. Remember, Microsoft has a larger market capitalization than the entire Russian economy. They have billions of dollars in cash just sitting available for use in business ventures. This company and others like General Electric are monoliths.

American planes, ships and guns can bomb countries back to the Stone Age. In 1998, we bombed the Sudan and Afghanistan in retaliation for the terrorist bombings of our embassies in Kenya and Tanzania. The attacks were authorized by President Clinton who was undergoing a Republican attempt to impeach him. Under the Reagan Administration, our country mined Nicaragua's harbor in clear violation of international law. We have aircraft carriers with bombers and airborne troops who can land anywhere in the world at a moment's notice.

Our present defense budget of over $345 billion is larger than the entire economies of all but six nations. This bloated defense budget was approved after the horrific September 11 attack, and imposed on the American taxpayers without any thorough political discussion. If even one hundredth of this budget were used for peaceful pursuits, our world would become a better place. These troops, ships and planes provide billions in profits for the merchants of death who claim respectability as defense contractors. Politicians justify the spending to "keep the peace."

The Imperial American Empire works well to preserve our hedonistic lifestyle. We rule the world unlike any empire in history. But we do not rule it well. We do not develop the economies of the nations in our realm. When people in Third World countries are in rebellion because their leaders are corrupt, brutal dictators who refuse to protect their country's resources and hoard all the wealth, we need change. Should you participate in wars against non-white peoples in the Third World?

Will you be fighting to protect our ideals of freedom of thought and liberty of expression? Or are you fighting to protect our wasteful luxurious way of life. This "luxury" is the right to live in large, environmentally harmful homes, with lawns in deserts, eating beef that consumes protein and large amounts of water.

It is possible for everyone on earth to have freedom of thought and liberty of expression. And it is our duty to preserve these ideals. But there is no possible way that the rest of the world can live in 1,900-square-foot homes costing $150,000 while enjoying recreational vehicles, swimming pools, private airplanes, hot tubs, and all of the trappings of "wealth." These are the hard political choices of our time in history.

War will not solve the environmental political issue that no one is talking about. The world is running out of fresh water. The Ogallala Aquifer took over 30,000 years to develop. America's wasteful depletion has drained it by over one third in the last 50 years. We cannot reverse overpopulation and overuse of natural resources soon. However, we Americans can set an example. That is true political leadership.

Because our world has become so small, wars in this age are against ourselves. No amount of media propaganda can change the reality that people in other parts of the world love their wives and children as much as we do. The human animal is the same the world over. That is the one lesson you will learn when you travel all over this small planet. We all have the same emotions.

Do we really want to kill the people in Asia, Africa, South or Central America because it might be in the best interest of some politician who is currently using hatred to be re-elected? Would you kill someone for Congressman Chris Cannon who blames the problems of blue collar crime in Utah on the Mexican community?

If you learn nothing else in life or from this book, learn to say no. It is the most important human act you will ever undertake. Say no, especially to children, relatives and politicians. No, I will not march into France, Russia, Egypt, Italy, Vietnam, Cuba, Panama, or any other part of the world to kill people I do not know. Hell no, I will not use nuclear, chemical, biological, or other weapons of mass destruction against people I have never met and will never know. No I will not become a suicide bomber. No I will not murder Jews, gays, Mexicans, blacks, Arabs, cowboys or anyone else. No, I will not kill people because you think it is a good idea and will support your popularity as a politician. No I will not lend you any money. No I will not let you spend the night at your friend's house. No is real power.

War is an outdated political institution. International police actions to keep the peace and chase down alleged criminals like Osama Bin Laden are important and unfortunately necessary. Justice is an institution handed out on a case-by-case basis. This is why after grand jury indictments it is so important to have trials and apply law to the facts and circumstances of individual actions. Timothy McVeigh got a fair trial. So did the terrorists who blew up the Pan Am airliner over Lockerbee, Scotland. So did the first World Trade Center attackers. Trials are important because, despite the public cynicism about our legal system, it works. Because the Taliban government would not surrender Bin Laden and his alleged accomplices, America is engaged in an international police action against these alleged terrorists. When some of these individuals are captured, they will be tried before military courts. And if they are found guilty, they will be treated better then the victims they murdered. They will be afforded attorneys and will be vigorously defended within the limits of the law. Trials give the public confidence that justice has been served. We dominate the world militarily. But it is important that the rule of law be applied over the entire world.

However, one political problem we face is that American military domination is no match against the ability of large, multinational corporations to move capital to several countries at a moments' notice. With 24-hour financial markets, capital does not have national loyalty. The nation state is becoming obsolete. Historically, the nation state is a fairly new political concept. From Napoleon with his citizen's army, the nation state has been with us for a mere 200 years. It is time now to move beyond the nation state. What we lack is a world government that can control capital, develop economies, protect environments, provide law, and eliminate conflicts between nations.

Capital is loyal to capitalists. Money will find the solution to whatever you wish to accomplish: drugs, child porn, weapons of mass destruction, name it. Labor is limited by geography. For reasons of history and geography, workers are usually stuck in or near the place of their birth. Throughout recent history people have migrated to other lands hoping to improve their lives. From the massive migration of Europeans and Africans to North and South America in the last five centuries, to the present movements of people worldwide looking for work, peace and homes, labor can no longer compete with capital. Factories will be shut down if the labor costs can be reduced either with automation or by moving the plant elsewhere on this small planet. Your labor is merely an expense on a financial statement. Expenses will be reduced, and you might be one with the blue slip on the unemployment line. This is why you *must* save money and invest it properly. When you lose your job and you have savings, you will survive in our urban environment. War will not solve the worldwide problem of too many workers and not enough jobs.

Military war creates many more problems than it solves. In another age, Cortez with the help of hundreds of thousands of allies and the use of smallpox, defeated the Aztecs. Not only did he replace the empire, he also established a completely new system of governance in Central and South America. He gave Spain untold riches and temporary superiority over the known world. The use of brutal military force worked with military precision.

But that was over 500 years ago before the age of 24-hour capitalism. The foreign policy of corporate America is the bottom line on the financial page that shows increased assets from foreign investment. American companies compete with foreign firms for business in Iran, the former Soviet Union, and the rest of the planet. Should you fight to protect the right of people in Kuwait to own five homes in several parts of the world while their Muslim neighbors in Africa and Central Asia are starving? At the time Kuwait was invaded, one third of the people were out of the country on vacation.

Do you really want to fight to protect our empire interests in Africa, Asia, or South America? Some of these governments are so corrupt that their citizens hate them and are constantly seeking ways to overthrow them. Without American military and financial aid, many of these governments would collapse. From Saudi Arabia to Egypt to Taiwan, our money and military might keeps our empire intact. Meanwhile, many of us claim to be Christians.

But does our foreign policy fit our view of Christianity? Can we be a good Christian and kill people on behalf of the American Empire? Will war bring lasting world peace without human hunger and environmental devastation? Only you can decide if fighting for Pax Americana is worth risking your life. It is rarely a good idea for poor people in a rich country to fight to protect the assets of rich people.

Most who volunteer for our armed forces enlist for economic reasons. Rich people attend our many fine universities and colleges. Poor people attend our many fine workplaces, armed forces, and prisons. Some say that there are more young blacks, Indians and Hispanics in prison or on parole then in college in America. Our armed forces provide racially neutral environments for non-white Americans to succeed. This is one reason so many of our well-trained troops are non-white or poor white. All protect Pax Americana.

Pax Americana is merely the present corporate and American military empire that rules this planet. American imperialism replaced the British Empire. The political power vacuum created at end of World War II resulted in the United States becoming the most dominant world power in all of human history. So we survive and prosper while millions are homeless and hungry.

Our ancestors fought for survival. They did not fight for the profitability of the United Fruit Company in Central America, Bell Helicopter, the top 100 defense contractors, American bank loans to corrupt South American governments who depend on the drug trade to repay bad investments, and the other Beltway bandits who survive with political contributions to corrupt politicians. Poor people do not give money to politicians. Indians, until gaming, did not make political contributions. Consequently, no grease, no access and no ability to influence policy. But it is your life. Make your own political decisions about your future.

Always put political decisions involving your future in a historical context. In the beginning of our fine republic, poor white males who did not own land could not vote. African Americans were slaves until the 1863 successful conclusion of the Civil War. Actual civil rights did not occur for over 100 years. Women did not receive the right to vote until 1919. Equality in the workplace would wait another 80 years. Indians did not become citizens until 1924. Finally, equality of opportunity is beginning.

The founding fathers were rich white slave owners who limited voting to white males who owned land. These world-class intellectual slave owners would be aghast at the thought of Mexicans, Jews, blacks, Greeks, Italians, poor whites and women voting—much less holding public office. But the 2000-year-old idea of Greco-Roman democracy clearly works. The founding fathers understood history and made the most revolutionary change ever. America may have started as an ideal utopian society for rich white male landowners. But the inclusion of both sexes and people of color has created a more perfect union and a political revolution that changed the world.

Before you go off to some strange country and start shooting your gun or even shooting off your mouth, remember the Americans who are our working poor. Even with our prosperity you will still see them in the streets, homeless, hungry and wanting hope. Picture the world's poor, and imagine just how far they have to walk for water and food. Killing is the most important political decision you will ever make. In the end, killing another human being is wasted effort. God, not man, is empowered to take our lives.

God is not on the side of murderers. Our foreign policy has been and is a disaster. But this fact does not excuse murder and cowardly actions. On September 11, 2001, angry young men with a cause and the claim that God was on their side committed cold-blooded murder. Nothing, absolutely nothing can possibly justify this senseless slaughter of innocent people. Religious extremists on the right argue that because of our policy on abortions, God punished Americans. Political extremists on the left argue that our misguided foreign policy caused this slaughter. But say what they must, those young cowardly men committed murder. Any coward can kill. The world is full of cowards. This does not mean you have to be one. Be brave enough to say no.

Now our mass media is consumed with our war in Afghanistan. A handful of companies control what people see, hear and read if you are unwilling to study and read between the lines. Where was our mass media when the United States government was supporting corrupt dictators like the Shah of Iran, Saddam Hussein in Iraq or Somoza in Nicaragua or Marcos in the Philippines or Bautista in Cuba or Sukarno in Indonesia and many, many others? Our list of killers and terrorists over the last fifty years reads like a who's who in terror and corruption. We have trained some of the most brutal killers in modern history. At our academy for homicidal maniacs, also known as Ft. Benning, Georgia, military leaders from all over the world have received education in military control and political repression. The graduates have murdered tens of thousands of people to protect American interests.

To bypass American media bias, go on the Internet and read the many foreign newspapers. See what other people in other parts of our small planet think about what is happening in the world. Read and learn about other cultures by studying their newspapers. This is a cheap way to overcome the massive media power of America's corporate power elite.

Before retiring, I had clients from all over the world. They talked to me about situations in their countries. Some were from both sides in the Guatemala conflict. Our government trained the Guatemalan military. They killed over 150,000 peasants with American weapons. Some clients were former Iraqi soldiers who tried to kill Saddam Hussein and spent four years in a refugee camp in Saudi Arabia. Some clients were from countries in Africa. One spoke six languages and was a math wizard. Others were from Southeast Asia. All had their stories, their cultures and traditions. All came to work and to be educated in our great land of opportunity.

One of my college roommates was from Tehran, Iran. He is brilliant. When he finally realized I was not with the secret police, he and I would openly talk about what was happening to his great country. "You cannot just kill the Shah. They will just replace him with another Shah. The institution of the Shah has to be overthrown."

Extreme politics throughout history have produced extremist politicians. The Shah was a killer, but he was our killer. The great Persian people with their culture that is approximately 4,000 years old overthrew our puppet dictator. Today, Iran has a democracy and elects moderate intelligent Islamic rulers. Other countries have not been so lucky.

America's power elite know Afghanistan. During the Cold War, Russia and America really made a mess out of that and other countries on this small planet. Millions worldwide have died or been wounded as a result of our competition for power. The Cambodians and the Congo, Central America and Eastern Europe suffered from our Cold War competition. Along the way we have created some pretty ruthless killers. One of our killers, who is currently on our most wanted list, is political extremist Osama Bin Laden. Like Saddam Hussein, Bin Laden is a political opportunist. He is taking advantage of the poverty in the Third World to preach his message of religious intolerance and hatred. He is a religious Nazi. Bin Laden's goal is power and nothing more or less. Religion is his excuse— not his reason for lusting power.

Bombs will not kill ideas of hatred. Only good ideas can defeat bad ideas in the free marketplace of thought. We have to address Bin Laden's arguments. We cannot just call him evil. Bin Laden has appeal in the minds of millions of poor Muslims world wide. Remember, Hitler came to power because of extreme German poverty created by the aftermath of World War I. In 1932, a stable middle class Germany would never have elected Hitler. A stable middle class Muslim world would never support a Saddam Hussein or a Bin Laden.

Bid Laden and Saddam Hussein and various other political opportunists understand that if the idea of America did not exist, there would still be world poverty, suffering and homelessness. America is not a place that can be destroyed with bombs and bullets. America is the concept of freedom of thought and liberty of expression. Fighting to protect this idea both intellectually and, if absolutely necessary with armed forces, is a just use of force.

The intellectual framework of this idea we call America comes from antiquity. Without Islam, there would not be an America or a West. After the fall of the Roman Empire and after Europe had entered an age of total lawlessness, the Muslim world preserved the knowledge of antiquity and expanded civilization. The knowledge of ancient Greece and Rome were carefully preserved at the Universities of Baghdad and Cordova. These centers of learning flourished while the rest of the Western world was in a dark age of lawlessness and ignorance. Islam's great scholars gave us the foundation of math and science. These ideas of freedom of thought and liberty of expression that were an intricate part of the Muslim world have helped create our Western democracy.

To understand the hopelessness of war today, picture the earth as a large cruise ship with one thousand people. In the first class cabin there are ten people with a computer. Nine of the ten are white and Christian. You are probably one of the ten. Two hundred and fifty passengers have jobs, enough food to eat and a place to sleep. We sleep in the upper deck in first class in large opulent suites called America, Europe and Japan. Most of the first class passengers are white and Christian.

Six hundred passengers are employed, have a small place to stay, and are sometimes hungry. Some wonder about the ship without work or a place to lay their heads. Most are brown-skinned Hindus, Muslims and Buddhists. Many are Chinese. A few are Christian. They live in the secord-class crowded dirty quarters we call Asia, India, South and Central America.

The rest of the passengers are so poor that they live on less then $1.00 per day. They are truly beyond third class and hang out wherever they will not be killed by the other crowded passengers. They hide in the boiler room and janitor closets. Their skin color is brown or black. They are Muslims, Hindus and pagans.

A fight is taking place in the poor part of the ship. This fight in the lower decks is a place seldom visited by rich white passengers. A fire is spreading. The poor people are angry, frustrated and tired of seeing the rich people throw perfectly good food into the garbage bins. The few rich people have very powerful guns and know thugs that will kill any poor passengers. The poor non-white passengers quietly sit back and wait. One day they will have their chance, and they will kill a rich person. And that rich person will be an American, European or Japanese who has ventured into the poor part of the ship.

It is a really bad idea to have a fire on this small cruise ship we call earth. Only law and justice will provide lasting peace. No amount of arms and troops will protect the fewer rich people from the more numerous poor people. Time is on the side of the world's poor. Remember, because of our diet and poor exercise habits, approximately 40 percent of all Americans are overweight to the point of obesity. Go to a casino and look at the health of the gamblers. Go to a grocery store and watch the shoppers. Just look at them and you will see gluttony and avarice.

Six months after we buy the various consumer goods produced in poor countries that are sold in our shopping malls, the items end up in our landfills. Yet 750 of the 1,000 passengers sometimes go hungry or even starve. We spend more on dog food and makeup than on foreign aid. For the price of one fighter plane, we can buy over 1,000,000 wheelchairs for the world's poor amputees.

The earth is a tiny row boat in comparison to the other planets and stars just in our galaxy. We no longer have a choice about being careful with our environment, both physical and financial. We are *hours*, not months, away from the tens of millions of poor. Our oceans no longer protect us. Viruses from other parts of the world can spread like wildfire as rich and poor travel throughout the ship. Even without war, millions of people might die from the squalid conditions and diseases that have mutated and become stronger. Knowledge is our only security. More arms will not bring more peace. More arms will bring only more suffering. We have seen this suffering, and all of us understand it.

What frightened us so much about the evil of September 11, 2001 is that humans have collective memory. Our collective memory saw this evil in the eyes of Hitler's troops as we were the attackers and the attacked. We remember the eyes of the slave owners as we beat the slaves until they passed out or were beaten until we screamed in terror. We knew the eyes of the European conquerors as our horses and swords slaughtered innocents. We saw the blood in the streets from the wrath of the Crusaders. The anger and hatred in their eyes said it all. We remember being there and afraid, quiet and hidden unless we be discovered and murdered. We told our children what we witnessed. And they told their children. We were the Mongol warriors who burned cities and libraries of the Muslim world. And we remember running in terror, telling our children. We could see the eyes of the Huns and Goths as they killed without mercy and destroyed our Roman Empire. *We have all lived on the same planet so we have all experienced the same events.* We even killed the Son of God.

In the largest slaughter in history, we believed Indians were evil. We took their land. We all know genocide because we have all been participants. With germs, guns and steel we killed at least one hundred million Indians because we believed they were evil. We understand war because we have been participants and spectators. This is why we are afraid. We know fear from our collective memory. But only knowledge will protect us.

20

ARE INDIANS EVIL?

The Indians presented an interesting dilemma when a dispute between the clergy and the military arose around the identity of the Indians. Bartolome de Las Casas, a priest, circulated accounts of Spanish cruelty which were published in Western Europe and eventually became a source of embarrassment to the Spanish crown. The crown then ordered a debate before the Council of the Indies to settle the question whether the American Indians were indeed human beings possessed of a soul, and therefore, rightfully the charges of the Holy Roman Catholic Church, or, as some conquistadors asserted, sub-humans who had no rights whatever. The conquistadors hired Gines de Sepulveda as their attorney. He argued forcefully that Indians are sub-humans. Las Casas argued they had souls and intelligence and can be socialized to be servants of both the crown and the church.

John Mohawk—Seneca Nation

The popular justification for the crimes committed by humans against other humans is that they were evil. What exactly is this evil that would cause suffering, death and destruction to so many?

Make no mistake about it; objective evil exists in this world. When I worked at the Utah State Prison, there was an element of fear in the atmosphere. Some inmates had killed others just to see the look on their face when they died. There were many who were so mentally ill, they had no business being in prison. They should have been in mental institutions. Some Indians believe the devil lives in prison. The devil is objective evil on earth. Whatever name is used to describe this force, evil exists and is real. And if you seek out the forces of darkness be careful what you pray for. The occult is very, very dangerous. Glorifying the worst in humankind is always bad.

What is evil? It is the ability of humans to do harm to others without reason.

We are all genetically composed of the same material. In the final analysis, we are all disintegrating molecules. The belief that Indians are evil has its origin in the guilt of the conquerors for the absolute horror inflicted on the conquered. Some of the brutal killing was expedient, but completely unjustified. When we have committed so much evil against others, we have to come to terms with our actions.

The surest way to justify our actions is to claim that the other person was completely evil and what was done in killing them was for the overall good of God, country, king or some other excuse which easily comes to mind. We need to come to terms with our guilt, own it and forgive ourselves for the collective harm all of us have done to others throughout history. It is not always possible to forget, and we should not. But it is always possible to forgive. Forgiveness is the essence of all religion, especially Christianity. Without forgiveness, we can never really know love and God. As one of my favorite Episcopal priests, Father Pablo Ramos, so eloquently stated in one of his fine Sunday sermons, "When we do not forgive, we are trying to take the place of God." We must forgive each other over and over and over again. We do this to help ourselves. This is how we heal. We let go of all that anger and bitterness.

Indians and other people of color are not more evil than Swedish women or German teenagers. This silly belief held by Mormons, Baptists and others that skin color is cursed by God is not only false, but extremely dangerous. It justifies the suffering and harm we inflict on others whose land we desire and wealth we wish to exploit. It is easier to steal from or kill your neighbor if he has been labeled as evil or inhuman by your bishop or priest or mullah or rabbi.

The evil and fear of humanity is reflected in our ability to produce weapons that might destroy all human life on the entire planet. These weapons are so horrible that no amount of propaganda will enable us to justify their use. It was once acceptable to murder Indians because they were not American or Spanish citizens and were considered evil by the religious fanatics who killed them. After Indians were granted citizenship in 1924, the killing of savages became the legal murdering of citizens who were savages. And these murders would not necessarily be prosecuted because they were now citizens. In fact, today, Indians are killed in the brutal streets of our cities, and the killers are often not prosecuted. Sometimes the killings are simply forgotten.

You will have to learn how to suffer fools when encountering people who, for religious or other reasons, believe that Indians or any other people on earth are intrinsically evil. The best course of action in dealing with fools is to humor them and have the patience of Job. Understand that you can never argue with fools because they are so certain that they are right. No amount of fact or science will ever convince them otherwise. Intelligent people change their minds when presented with facts that are clearly in opposition of their beliefs. It is easier to believe people's skin color was cursed by God than to accept the possibility that, on an individual level we are all the same—which the evidence of cold hard science supports.

Evil is purely a human event. It could be Kit Carson murdering Navajos, or Custer killing women and children on the plains, or Nazis marching into Russia and murdering millions, or the slaughter of buffalo hunters to see the look on their helpless faces as they fell. These individuals knew they were slaughtering other living beings. They justified the killings by labeling the human victims as evil or not having souls.

With all of this evil that inhabits our planet, is there a God? If there is a God, is Jesus the son of God? There are many people in the Indian community who are justifiably angry at the conquerors, who for over 500 years of ill behavior, claimed to be Christians. Believing that Jesus is the son of God can only make sense to someone who has grown up in this religion and been immersed in the tenets of Christianity. It is not something I personally believe. It is something I know. It makes perfect sense.

Had my Spanish ancestors believed that Indians were humans and had souls, they would not have been able to murder millions of people indiscriminately. Eventually there was great religious debate in the Catholic church over whether or not Indians had souls and were human. When, after much intellectual Catholic discussion, it was decided that in fact, Indians were human and had souls, the wholesale murders were replaced with political domination in South and Central America. Here, in the heart of our now present empire, the murders continued, in part because the other Christian denominations had not yet accepted the fact that Indians are human. And there was also the lust for land that accompanied Manifest Destiny.

The Mormons maintain that Indians are the evil descendants of the lost tribes of Israel. This is a historical impossibility. There is not one shred of scientific evidence that in any way supports even one theory or fact in the *Book of Mormon*. These cult beliefs were formed by the vivid imagination and ability to seduce women by the charismatic Joseph Smith, who was convicted for fraud by a New York court and killed by the state militia while resisting arrest after burning down a publishing house.

The Jews have been a separate identifiable people for at most 6,000 years because there are approximately 6,000 years of recorded history. The Native Americans, or "Indians," as they were called, have been in North and South America for at least 12,000 years. Some of the carbon dating even goes back 40,000 years. All of the bloodlines, the linguistics and genetics go to Asia. But despite science and history, Mormons continue to preach that Indians are the evil ancestors of the mythical lost Israeli tribe, the Lamanites. Blacks are similarly cursed in Mormon and Baptist theology as having the mark of Cain.

Joseph Smith was living in Missouri prior to the Civil War, and needed to take a political stand. With the Indian tribes of the plains not yet conquered and having grown up in the "burnt over" district of New York, an area where there was tremendous religious fervor, this bright young man invented this myth to further his political hold on his religious followers. His ridiculous cult beliefs survived because of the tremendous efforts of the gullible Brigham Young who likewise embraced polygamy, racial differences, men becoming Gods in their own heaven equal to God himself, and the idea of women folk being married to a God. Since history, science and logic have nothing to do with fanatical blind religious faith, the initial Smith followers now have over eleven million members worldwide. The continued preaching of blacks as having the mark of Cain and Indians as being the evil ancestors of the make-believe tribe of Lamanites still inspires young men and women to travel from their homes and become missionaries throughout the world. If the Mormons do not get you to convert in this life, they will baptize you while you are dead. This polytheistic religion is completely contrary to the teachings of love and spirituality of Jesus, the Son of God.

Why we are here on this lonely planet that has abundant life and fragile ecosystems is the great mystery. Since force builds resistance, many Indians do not believe Jesus is the son of God. Nor do any of my Muslim, Buddhists, Hindu and Jewish friends. Islam has great respect for Jesus and believe he is a great prophet. In fact, Jesus is mentioned more times in the *Koran* than Mohammad. This world view of lack of acceptance of Jesus as the Christ is to be expected. Given the sins of my Spanish ancestors and the actions of others in the name of Christianity, it is easy to understand the resistance.

Jesus' message is not complex. The essence of Christianity is love, charity and forgiveness. This human script of love your neighbor as yourself and love God is simple because it works. Jesus did not espouse the

Madison Avenue myth of consumerism and materialism. It is silly to believe in all of the ownership and demands for keeping up with the Joneses that is such an inherent part of American life. God owns the planet and all of creation. Never forget this simple fact. All we own is our time.

We need to pray before each hunting and gathering adventure not only for good luck, but to thank the great mystery (whom I call Jesus) for the opportunity. Indians are not evil. Whites are not evil. No human culture on earth is evil, not even the Iraqis. Hatred of other humans is evil. Hunt. Gather. And respect the great mystery. No one can force you to accept Jesus' message of love. You have to find this message from your own experience and life research. Always remember that Jesus did not own anything except his love of the earth and all of creation. Jesus was a homeless environmentalist. Despite the millions who have been killed in his name, the message was and is one of peace. The irony is that so many people were killed in his name. Will war be a useful tool in saving our hunting grounds?

21

CAN WE REALLY SAVE OUR HUNTING GROUNDS?

The fate of the living planet is the most important issue facing mankind.

Gaylord Nelson

The question facing humanity is can we really save our hunting grounds—the earth's environment? What good is money without clean air, water, and good health? All of our efforts to save the earth are doomed for failure unless we recognize the root cause of environmental problems. In the 1940s there were over 40,000 sea turtles that swim annually to the shore of Mexico. Today there are fewer than 500. Despite the international bans on the hunting of these precious, beautiful animals, over the next 50 years, they will not survive if we don't change our attitudes. There are fewer then 4,000 Bengal tigers in the wild. They, too, will become extinct. The same can be said of snow leopards, several species of sturgeon, salmon, tuna, whales, sail fish and a whole host of other exotic creatures. Continued over fishing to support ever larger human populations who demand fish burgers will kill many species forever.

We have passed law after law, held international conference after conference. We have changed industrial practices in many areas. We have banned the use of certain chemicals and materials. Yet, some of the environmental damage continues to escalate. The various national laws of the United States and the numerous international treaties will not be restated here. These bandage efforts to stop the bleeding might give some relief, but there is one huge problem that ensures their failure: overpopulation.

Over population in the United States and other parts of the world is not a popular political issue. You can't even discuss the reality of too many people without some religious and or political fanatics firebombing your office. "It is God's will" that we have more children then we can feed or give attention to properly. In Utah, where every sperm is sacred, five children are expected if one is to get into the highest level of heaven. India has over 950 million people, and they are still increasing their population. China understands the problem of having 1.3 billion people and is making serious efforts to control their ever-expanding population. Several of their massive cities are already running out of water. Will their efforts at population control be enough? We have over six billion people on our small planet. As you read this, 72 people were born. We will not be able to pass enough legislation on any level that will stop the extinction of rare plants and animals if our population increases to 12 billion over the next 50 years.

We buy more goods in more stores at more malls; the result, more municipal solid waste, hazardous waste, low-level radioactive waste, and land and sea pollution. Our efforts at saving the earth are like chasing the sunset or a rainbow. Without controlling the population, we will always have the environmental solutions beyond our reach. Over population wipes out our environmental repairs in a very short time as demand for resources overcomes the need for protection of wildlife and wilderness.

Short of using the horrific weapons we have invented, one solution to saving our hunting grounds is to have no more than two children and preferable just one. This approach is not only more affordable, in a world with ever-increasing child-care costs and expensive housing, but it also gives each child more parental time. It is far better to have fewer, high quality children who know they are special and loved than several who are lacking in individual attention. It is not the silly American ideal of giving each child more material things. It is the idea of giving each child more time. There is no greater harm to society than to give birth to unwanted children. We can reduce the world's population by accepting the concept that fewer children means a better future for them and for the other plants and animals that also have the right to exist on this lonely planet we call our home.

We had better accept the Native American ideal that other forms of life have every right to exist. We are a mere part of the earth. We are not the most important part. The two-legged ones, the winged ones, the four-legged ones, those that crawl on the earth, those that swim in the waters, have an absolute right to live and prosper. Humans are merely the earth's maintenance man. We are the janitor. Our job is to ensure the health and well being of the whole of God's creation.

We must re-forest the various areas that have been cut down for firewood and furniture. As the bumper sticker points out, "Trees are the answer." Plant ten billion trees and you will have more oxygen. Our environmental problems cause political instability as in Haiti where over-population has ruined islands that once were filled with natural beauty. In many Third World countries of Africa, overpopulation has resulted in de-forestation and drought with crop yields that have not been able to sustain the hunger of too many mouths. Overpopulation has created a tinderbox in the Middle East with the need for water exceeding the supply. This lack of adequate water supply is one of the biggest obstacles to peace. In the nineteenth century, a potato famine in Ireland led to more than one million people starving to death. An ecosystem can only support so many life forms. Too many people living too close together results in death from famine, war or disease. This is the human story throughout history.

One solution is to use America's massive prison population of 2,000,000 people. Put them to work rebuilding the environment and working actively on environmental issues. This subsidized labor can shred America's 400 million plus tires, sort out metal and paper from waste streams for conversion and use in a recycle economy.

We have seen that the drug war is a complete failure and a cynical lie. Let us use the waste of human life for public good. By having the inmates study environmental issues with computers and the accompanying access to the Internet, we can utilize this brain power of over 1,000,000 political drug prisoners to help us out of this massive mess we have created. The planting of trees by these prisoners of war and the cleaning up of our filthy cities and those of the Third World will enhance the inmates' self-esteem by giving them a place in our society. It will also make them employable after prison.

There is no reason to be pessimistic about the future. Saving our hunting grounds is not beyond our human reach. It will take approximately 50 years if we begin in the year 2003 to make a concerted effort to reduce the planet's population to three billion people. This is one half our present estimated world population. If everyone throughout the world limits reproduction to one child, and at most two children, that golden child or children will have a high quality future. This is a future with other animals, plants, clean air, drinkable water, and healthy food. The future is not out of reach. It is just not politically popular to preach that fewer people mean fewer problems and less damage to the environment. It is important to have buffalo, condors, wolves, tigers, ancient forests, blue fin tuna, and the whole host of God's creation that exist only on this planet. People in other parts of the world are concerned about survival, not the environment. We need to give these people hope.

The world is an unforgiving place for species that over populate. Various viruses might kill off millions of people. Our problem of over-population might solve itself if some virus like that which killed a third of Europe in the Middle Ages obliterates a portion of humanity. AIDS is currently killing millions in Africa. We can only hope nothing that extreme will occur to ensure a better way of life for all of God's creation. Having fewer children is an act of generosity and courage. It ensures the success of the survival of other creatures and is an insurance policy for a higher quality of life.

A one-child policy for the entire planet will buy the time we need to repair the damage we have already done. If you want more children, you can always adopt. We have millions of children who desperately want healthy parents. It saddens me when I see couples that do not qualify for adoption because of income or sexual preference. What we need to be good parents is time and love.

One small solution in this country is to require mandatory birth control for all persons who are receiving any kind of entitlement from the federal government. If we are going to have a lower class, at least do not subsidize their breeding habits. Some of the people I have seen in court on child abuse charges have had four different children from four different fathers taken away from them because of drugs, neglect or abuse. Our current politics is to pay the lower class to cause social problems and reproduce. If a person is receiving social security disability, or any type of welfare, we should force them to be on birth control. This is not cruel or right wing. It is just that the carrying capacity of the middle class to pay for all of these people on social security and other social welfare programs is being stretched to the breaking point.

If we keep breeding a larger and larger lower class, at some point the tax burden on the middle class will be so large that our society will collapse. How many more people are we going to put in prison? How many more are we going to have in crime-ridden public housing? How many more abuse cases and neglect cases are we going to tolerate before we realize that unwanted children are a plague and not a benefit to society? At what point do we continue to kill off animal and plant species before we realize that enough is enough?

Our thinking has to change from consumption to co-existence with nature. We must redirect our thinking from more is better to less is more.

22

A HEALTHY, HAPPY,
FUTURE THAT WORKS

*I call heaven and earth today to witness against you: I have set before you
life and death, the blessing and the curse. Choose life, then, that you and
your descendants may live.*

Deuteronomy 30:19

The Communists won. Today, the public owns the means of production
in America. Over half of Americans now own some kind of interest in
public companies. When you as an employee invest in your 401K retirement, this money is invested in stocks and bonds. This means as shareholders in the means of production, you can vote and demand that the
corporate leaders properly pay attention to environmental issues, labor
problems and the various other issues I was so concerned with when I
was a young Communist of 19. This is the most exciting time in human
history to be alive. If you are young, in good physical and mental health,
and live in North America or Europe, you have more opportunity in more
areas of life and more liberty than any generation of people that has ever
lived. We have the Internet and wheel chair tennis.

But what will your future be like? In my lifetime, I never imagined the
Iron Curtain coming down, the Cold War ending, the Soviet Empire dis-
solving, and the raging Republicans displaced from the Oval Office and
then back again. Nor did I ever dream my life would turn out the way that
it has. At age 21, I was in perfect physical shape. Two weeks after I
walked on to the University of Utah's wrestling team, I was in a hospital.
Now, age 40 plus and having spent over 20 years in a wheelchair, I've

learned to take the good with the bad. I have no idea what my life will be ten years from now. Today and next month appear to be just fine.

The future will be fascinating. How much control we have over our lives and our future is left to philosophers to debate. Politically, we do have choices. The planet has a unique opportunity. The end of the Cold War between greedy capitalists and power hungry communists has given humanity a real chance at a lasting peace. From 1945 to 1995, America spent over two trillion dollars on tools of war. Our side lost over 100,000 dead and wounded between Korea, Vietnam and the various other colonial wars fought on behalf of the empire. At least one third of the casualties were non-white. Pax Americana has replaced Pax Britannica in the ever-futile attempt to rule the world. In 1969, at the height of American imperialism, we controlled the world financially and militarily while landing men on the moon. Then we started reading our own headlines and became arrogant.

Our pride defeated us. A poor rag tag nation of courageous Vietnamese fighters, with massive help from their Communist allies, defeated the most powerful military in human history, despite our dropping more bombs on this poor country than all of the munitions used in World War II combined. We used chemical agents to destroy their forests. Humility is important. Vanity is Satan's favorite sin. It is truly vain to think that with military and financial might, we Americans can force the rest of the world to obey. America's future does not have to be linked with the forced subjugation of other people in order to protect our standard of living. This standard of living is measured by the conspicuous consumption of energy and entertainment. There are other ways we can succeed as individuals, nations and as a planet.

If we can link traditional cultures with the science and technology of the modern information age, our future will be terrific. The two are not incompatible. In fact, the two cultures are a natural fit. The respect for nature of traditional cultures and the information on the Internet of the modern world will transform humanity to a golden age of peace and prosperity. It is the small things that are done individually by a large number of people that have the greatest impact for change. Three lifetimes ago, there were no toothbrushes, toilets, Toyotas or televisions. This massive consumption by individuals has caused our environmental problems. These environmental problems, which are primarily waste streams of excess production and consumption, can be solved in the same manner. Do simple things like buying many houseplants and owing a variety of spayed and neutered pets. By surrounding yourself with live beings, you become more conscious of all of God's creation.

In my house, we have four dogs, two cats, a blue and gold Macaw, dozens of tropical fish, and more plants than I can count. We also have a garden and an outdoor fish pond. In my next house I will not have a lawn. Kill your lawns. Recycle all of your newspapers, aluminum cans and plastic bottles. These are individual acts of environmentalism that will work on a local, national and global scale.

Mankind does not know what adventures God has in store for us. We live our lives and sometimes are surprised by unexpected gifts and saddened by sudden losses. We try to plan ahead financially to enable survival in a hostile world. Sometimes events clearly beyond our control will affect our future. If we are prepared, we can act rather than react. This is why we must plan finances carefully. If the economy turns sour and you lose your job, a large client, or a contract, but have plenty of money saved up and very few debts and material possessions, you will be able to swim safely in a sea of economic turmoil. Always remain calm in times of financial or political trouble, for it is by remaining calm that you are best able to act in your own and other's best interest. It is always those who are prepared for hard times that nature treats the best. By being prepared for the hurricanes of life, we better appreciate and enjoy good weather.

A future that works requires careful planning of what lifestyle we try to sell others. Our American life style of consumerism is not attainable for the majority of the planet and is clearly not compatible with the fragile ecosystem. As people in Asia, Africa and Latin America get tired of living under what we in the West consider grinding poverty and buy into the Madison Avenue materialism myth, we will sow the seeds of a nuclear, biological, chemical and environmental holocaust. China, India, Pakistan and Indonesia have over 2.7 billion people. It is not realistic that they can all live in 1,900 square foot homes and own two vehicles. Where is all of this oil going to come from? What about the greenhouse gases that will be created from all of the additional air pollution? What about the property crimes that will result from an increase in materialism?

At what point does life become meaningless because it is so abundant that it is infinitely cheap? You will recall that prior to the last century the Goshutes were a small tribe with adequate resources, good physical and mental health and astute leadership. Each member was and is important because there were and are so few of them. What if there were 1,300,000,000 Goshutes? Would their lives be worth less then the few who exist today?

Whatever road you must travel over the course of your lives, if you are young, manage your money carefully, exercise, eat healthy foods and always be honest with yourself. Regardless of how others behave, carefully govern your own behaviors. By being honest with yourself you will wake up each day and look in the mirror after you wash you face and realize that the world has a new adventure in store for you. Your life will be filled with excitement, good friends and great memories.

But if you take the path of fools and lie and cheat to try to obtain a temporary advantage, expect hostility and disappointment at every turn. You will have few true friends and many enemies. If you cannot trust yourself, do not expect others to trust you. You will never be financially successful because you will lack the discipline to save for a mere short vacation, much less a trip to other parts of the world. You will consume drugs and alcohol to take the sting off your failed existence.

In every area where I have seen my clients succeed or fail, their own behaviors were the deciding factor. From prosperity to prison, from the blessing of good health to bankruptcy, from long healthy lives to early deaths from over-eating and suicide, to drug overdoses, my clients and friends and relatives usually chose their paths with their behaviors. Each day, look in the mirror. Ask yourself what you are going to do today. What plans do you have in the short run that will improve your quality of life today and over the long run? Do you want a companion? Are you lonely? Is your health poor? Are you in good spirits? Do you love yourself enough to love your neighbor?

What is a future that works? It is in understanding that there is a difference between self-love and arrogance. Self-love means we care about our physical and mental health above money and materialism. When you are in good physical and mental health, other people will want your time and company. The reason is that you are probably good company. But if you are so addicted to heroin and alcohol and cocaine and other legal and illegal drugs, expect to be lonely. Expect others to want to stay away from you.

If you want to see the various futures that God has to offer, there are models available. There are people like my deceased Mexican grandmother, Ramonsita Quintana. While growing up in New Mexico, she was such a delight to be around, we always had company. I do not recall a weekend when we failed to have visitors. I mean there were always people over and dinner was always there for everyone. It was wonderful. I remember my Utah Mormon step-grandfather, Hyrum Adams. He was a very sweet and caring individual. He was interesting to be around and was a natural with children. There is Laura's terrific grandma, "Me ma." She is 94 and still going strong. There is the warmth and love from my stepmother, Wyona Adams Quintana. She taught me to stick things out and not be afraid to hit homeruns. There was the intelligence and patience of my friend, Scott York's grandfather, Harrison Brothers. Mr. Brothers founded banks, a successful brokerage firm and was a Colonel in the military. His high standards set the level of success everyone should aspire to achieve. *None of these people are consumed with the need to have more and more things.* It is their contributions, not their possessions, which have caused so many people to love them.

Now contrast their good manners and charm with old grumpy men and women I know from my practice. There are few things more pathetic than an old, tired, out of shape, whiny, overweight, complaining, financially broke, cranky individual who has to burden you with his or her problems. Having lost their health from years of poor diet and lack of exercise, now they want you to hear today's complaint. Everything is negative and they want you to hear about it. They are usually broke and it is everyone's fault but their own for failing to properly plan and use money.

It is very hard to have friends when you do not respect the person in the mirror enough to carefully plan for tomorrow. And when you are not careful with finances or your health, it adds pressures to an already stressful life. For life is always full of stress of some kind. The key to happiness is to take on only the stress you can handle and never under any circumstances compare oneself to others. The key to hell on earth and a lifetime of unhappiness is to measure your success or failures to others. Every one of my clients who have not managed their physical health and/or wasted money usually also wasted their lives. The only part of the future you are able to control is your behavior. You have no control over the behavior of others. To try to control other people's behaviors is like trying to drive a car by honking the horn. Lead your own life and don't follow other people.

What will your future really be like? *You are living your future each day.* By carefully seizing the moment and being honest, working hard, praying to thank God for food and shelter and good company, you are living. This is it. Today's actions are tomorrow's memories. Make those memories good ones by enjoying and utilizing every moment that each day has to offer. If you had a bad day, you did your day wrong.

Another future possibility is that of my clients and relatives who, at age 28, are still in jail. They just did not get the message. They chose using drugs over taking care of their children and managing their resources properly. Some work long enough to collect unemployment. Others refuse to work at all and live off whoever will take care of them. If you choose to sit on your lazy ass and borrow money from relatives by lying to them or steal from a store to get enough money for beer for your next drunk, expect to have a miserable day....and more likely than not in jail.

How much stress can you take? Is it worth it to live in a foreign country and not speak the language like some of my clients? It is your choice. Is it worth it not knowing where your next meal will come from because you have been unemployed for over one year? And now nobody trusts you to lend you any more money. Do you really like having to live with relatives because you are too lazy to make your own mark in America? Hate your job? Well if you do not have any savings and are trapped by debt from credit cards purchasing goods you do not need and you do not have the skills or courage to go elsewhere, looks like you are stuck at that horrible smelly job.

What is your future? If you assume you have freewill (which is a big assumption), then you control your time. If you want a mate to share your time with you, then offer time to a potential mate. Not asking someone out is an invitation to be alone. After all, being alone is the result of choices you make in how you treat yourself and others. But it is better to be alone then to be around abusive people who are such asses they try to take their bad day out on you.

For young men and women, never take pretty girls and pretty boys serious. All they have to offer is their good looks and the allure of sex. Are you really going to get laid? Or are you going to be played? Just exactly what do "pretty people" have to offer? I have seen some of the most abusive, dishonest, outright tramps who had but one quality. They were pretty. But talk about scum. Their boyfriends would be watching their children while they played another guy for his money. I can't count how many men were stepping out on their women while they were working and at times with their own friends. If you want a good mate, be a good mate. Always let the other person screw up. Because then when you dump them, you leave the relationship free of guilt and can move on to a new one. The liars, cheats, verbally abusive, physically abusive, drunks, drug addicts, financially irresponsible, chronically unemployed, trashy to the point of embarrassment... let someone else be their mate. What is your future like alone? Look around you. More and more people are alone. With divorce rates of upwards of 50 percent and relationships taken for granted, of course there are a lot of people who are alone. People also live longer. Old people live alone and usually die alone or in lonely nursing homes. Will you be alone forever? If you do not ask others to join you or attempt to belong to various groups or just form groups yourself, then expect to be alone. I have dozens of single friends. Why are they single? Most of them should be. Some of them prefer to be.

Many people have been so hurt by bad relationships they are unwilling to risk being hurt again. Well there is that risk that you will have your heart wounded by someone else who will lie to you and cheat on you. So what. This is how they choose to behave. In life there are always more losers than winners. If someone is going to behave like a loser, then their behavior has demonstrated they are not good enough to be with you. And when you leave them, go gracefully as friends. Never say anything bad about them as they have their reasons in their minds for their behaviors. Few of us believe what we are doing is "wrong" and we naturally justify any behavior.

How can we love ourselves? It comes from recognizing that we have inherent worth regardless of how anyone else on earth feels about us. I remember one time being alone in my office on a Saturday, crying because some disgusting tramp had lied to me and hurt my feelings. Looking back, I can clearly see why all of her ex-boyfriends and ex-husbands of her two children from different fathers beat the absolute hell out of her. I still took the risk of dating other people, regardless of the poor behavior of the various whores I met over the last ten years. After a while, it became amusing to watch how long it would take in dating someone before they would tell me some lie or play some mental game to try to anger me. Usually after three months I could see what they were really about. I could not control their behaviors. Again, you can only control how you will behave. You are only half of the relationship. If your partner is a liar and a cheat, you have a burden, not a buddy. The world is full of charity cases and whores. This does not mean you are obligated to take care of them. Enjoy their company and if they misbehave, get rid of them. Don't ever try to change them. That is a sign that you really do not accept them the way they are. At a minimum, your mate should have education and religion, age and health in common with you.

Will your future have good physical and mental health? I hope so. You probably have relatively good health now. This is great fortune. Want to keep it? Study a lot about foods and their effect on the body. Keep your body weight within ten pounds of what is normal for your frame. Put the cigarettes and alcohol away. Never do illegal drugs. If you do drink and smoke and cannot go every other year, without alcohol and drugs, give it up all together. If I can give up alcohol and cigarettes every other year and my Indian and Mormon friends can live completely without these substances, so can you. I admire my Mormon, Indian and Muslim friends. Many of them don't ever drink alcohol. It really is not a big deal. It is just alcohol, illegal drugs and cigarettes. If you are, you are doing illegal drugs, you had better hope God will help you. And he will if you ask. A rehabilitation program might, but don't hold your breath. There is nothing about methamphetamine, cocaine or heroin that justifies these horrible substances being legal. Sniffing glue will clearly cause brain damage. There is so much out there that will harm you if you chose to become involved in illegal activity.

Will you be financially rich? If that is your goal, hoarding for the sake of hoarding, be careful what you pray for. You might get it. Any fool can make money. Not everyone can use money in a responsible manner. The annual budget for my church is $300,000.00 per year. We carefully use every dollar. Fools and their money not only soon part, but they create problems along this path of temporary plenty. Money is just a tool, quite like hammers, computers, x-ray machines, bulldozers, copiers, fax machines, and arrows. Your future will have some money. How you choose to use this important tool is between you and God.

I know of a tribe where the local hick car dealers pay very close attention to when tribal children reach legal age. Once the children are age 18, they receive over $100,000 in minor judgment funds. After the new vehicle, the illegal drugs, the stereo system, the big television and the fancy clothes, within six months most of the money is gone.

You are young. You might just have graduated from high school or are still in college. You have at least 60 years ahead of you provided God has blessed you with good physical and mental health, a smart brain and great looks. What will be your future? Will you finish your education? Understand that your education does not ever finish, even with a college degree. You keep reading and learning. Hopefully what you learned in school was how to learn. Question the acts of elected officials and criticize their decisions. This is the very essence of what the First Amendment and democracy are all about. What will your politicians do to your future? They will spend every last tax dollar you have on what they damn well please. And if you do not get involved and watch them, you will not like their actions.

A future that works requires participation in the political process. Despite its many flaws the political system in America works. However, it is not like a light switch that you just turn on and light magically comes out. Like the legal system, politics works because you make it work. You bust your ass and get involved and vote. The political system needs young people like you, who are honest to be elected to office and make decisions that will have profound effects on the lives of others.

We have a war on drugs because America's political leaders are a bunch of gutless liars. We had a war in the Balkans because politicians have decided that this is good policy. You can vote, and yes you can change bad laws that ruin the lives of thousands if not millions of people. This is your future. My office has drafted laws and walked them through the Utah legislature. It is hard work and vicious politics, but it can clearly be done.

You are free. Live, work hard, study, clean your house and yard, exercise, go for that bike ride, that walk in the woods; do it today. Go dancing, visit museums, go swimming. Whatever you do, do something and turn that electronic Valium off. But if you think that your future will be full of financial and emotional success and accomplishment by being a spectator in the game of life, think again. You can watch those people on television. They are participants. Again that is a choice. It is your future and your behavior. The average American watches six hours of television per day.

The future that will work is one where there is a global effort from all nations to peacefully explore the inner solar system. If we survive the next one hundred years, our technology will improve to the point of humans can consider trying to leave the solar system. Right now that is just not possible. With present technology, it takes approximately six months to visit Mars. Landing there with humans is a logistical nightmare. In the short run, it is far better to send robots rather than astronauts and cosmonauts. It is still too dangerous to send humans to Mars. By redirecting the inherent human energy away from the planet rather than at each other, we just might avoid burning the house down.

We are a very aggressive species. Finding proper outlets for that aggression is an important part of the social agenda of politicians who are truly interested in peace. The logical solution is to have rambunctious children play together outside of the earth's environment in outer space. Yes, it will be expensive. Peace is worth it. The future that will work for you and for every living creature on earth is one that respects God and Nature. Hopefully, that is what you learn when you are Hunting and Gathering. Whether it is in the Information Age or any other age, stay focused on that goal and your future will be very, very successful. I wish you good health and a long adventurous, wonderful life with much love and many friends.